IMAGES
of America

TUSCUMBIA

On the Cover: In 1902, men with vision thought it would be a great investment to operate an electric streetcar service between Florence, Sheffield, and Tuscumbia, Alabama. Streetcar service began with the arrival of the first streetcar from Sheffield on May, 10, 1904. Pictured here is a streetcar traveling north on Main Street as it begins to turn west on Fifth Street. Streetcars served the Tri-Cities Area until the operation was closed on February 3, 1933.

IMAGES
of America

TUSCUMBIA

John L. McWilliams

ARCADIA
PUBLISHING

ISBN 978-0-7385-8820-9

Published by Arcadia Publishing
Charleston, South Carolina

Printed in the United States of America

Library of Congress Control Number: 2011929595

For all general information, please contact Arcadia Publishing:
Telephone 843-853-2070
Fax 843-853-0044
E-mail sales@arcadiapublishing.com
For customer service and orders:
Toll-Free 1-888-313-2665

Visit us on the Internet at www.arcadiapublishing.com

Images of America: Tuscumbia *is dedicated to my parents,*
John Hubert McWilliams and Inez Walker McWilliams,
from whom I gained my interest in history.

Contents

Acknowledgments

The City of Tuscumbia has for many years tried to gather pictures of the city's history. Many citizens brought in pictures and gave them to the Tuscumbia Main Street Project. The Tuscumbia chapter of the Alabama Reunion Committee made an effort to gather and save as many pictures as could be found. These pictures are now part of the Tuscumbia Railroad Transportation Museum Collection.

Organizations such as the Muscle Shoals Railroad Club, Robbins Property Development Inc., Trenholm High School Reunion, Muscle Shoals Model Railroad Club, Tennessee Valley Authority, and Memphis & Charleston Railroad Historical Society, have either loaned or given pictures to the museum. Many individuals have brought pictures either on loan or as a gift to the museum. One family, the Jack Voorhies family, has placed many items on loan at the museum. My collection of pictures has been donated to the museum.

Unless otherwise noted, the pictures used in this book are a part of the Tuscumbia Railroad Transportation Museum collection.

A special thanks goes to Linda Cross and Brandon Romans, who suggested changes to the script and also proofread the book.

Introduction

Nestled in the foothills of Appalachia lies a small town with a unique history. When the white man arrived here about 1815, he found that the Native Americans had been living here for thousands of years. This land was fertile with plenty of fresh water from the area's springs. Nearby was the mighty Tennessee River connecting the area to many parts of what was to become the United States.

Gen. Andrew Jackson saw the need to connect New Orleans with Nashville with a road to assure that troops could be moved quickly if needed again at New Orleans. This road was the super highway of its day and passed through Tuscumbia. With the invention of the steamboat allowing for better trade up the Tennessee River to the foot of the great shoals of the Tennessee River, known as the Muscle Shoals, Tuscumbia was placed on the crossroads for the traveling public.

Tuscumbia was not built on the river but two miles up Spring Creek around a big spring. It was a beautiful place for a town but far away from the commerce of the river. The merchants began to search for a way to connect the young town to the river. There was a great place for a landing at the mouth of Spring Creek, but there was still the problem of transporting these goods to the downtown area. They decided to try something very new and somewhat unproven. They were going to build a railroad from the town to the river.

These men of vision drew incorporation papers in 1829. The Alabama legislature incorporated the Tuscumbia Railroad Company on January 30, 1830. This railroad was not only the first one in Alabama but also only about the fourth railroad incorporated in the United States. Tuscumbia was America's first frontier railroad town.

Many of these same men saw the possibility of bypassing the treacherous 43 miles of Muscle Shoals rapids by building a railroad from Tuscumbia to Decatur, Alabama. This new railroad was incorporated in 1832 as the Tuscumbia, Courtland & Decatur Railroad. The influence of these new industries had a big result: Tuscumbia doubled in size in just a few years and land prices increased. Tuscumbia was a booming town on the frontier.

Tuscumbia would play a major role in the Indian Removal Act. The first Native Americans affected by the act to pass through the area were a party of Creeks under Chief Chilley McIntosh. They had been forced to leave their homes in Georgia for Indian Territory out west. They arrived in Tuscumbia starving and short of proper clothing. They were welcomed in Tuscumbia as the citizens prepared food and provided clothing upon their arrival. They stayed in Tuscumbia about a week while they recovered enough to continue their journey. Chief McIntosh wrote a letter thanking the citizens for their help and generosity. He ended the letter with "as long as our Nation remains upon this earth, we will recollect Tuscumbia." This is the only known record of Native Americans acknowledging good treatment during their removal. Chickasaws, Cherokees, and Creeks would pass through Tuscumbia, and they all seemed to be treated well while here.

There was a dream in the South of connecting the Atlantic Ocean, preferably at Charleston, South Carolina, to the Mississippi River at Memphis, Tennessee. This dream took a big step with the birth of the Memphis & Charleston Railroad Company on January 7, 1850. This railroad quickly bought the Tennessee Valley Railroad (the old Tuscumbia, Courtland & Decatur Railroad Company and Tuscumbia Railroad Company) on June 4, 1851.

The railroad immediately began to replace the old wooden track system used by the Tuscumbia, Courtland & Decatur Railroad with a "T" rail system. Nine months later, trains began to operate from Tuscumbia to Decatur again. This was the first operating section of the Memphis & Charleston Railroad.

The railroad was completed on March 25, 1857, at a point a little west of Iuka, Mississippi. In a ceremony, a silver spike was driven connecting the railroad together. Once this was completed, a train carrying a barrel of water from the Atlantic Ocean headed to Memphis, Tennessee. A large "Marrying of the Waters" ceremony took place in Memphis, where the barrel of water was poured into the Mississippi River. Tuscumbia was now connected by rail to many points on the East Coast and the Mississippi River.

The railroad, along with its connection with the Tennessee River, placed Tuscumbia in the way of both armies during the Civil War. Many of the town's buildings, along with others in the area, were burned to the ground. To cause confusion, the union Army would burn all records and maps they could find. Tuscumbia would lose Tuscumbia Landing to federal flames and a large part of its commerce would be lost as well.

Tuscumbia was slow to recover from the Civil War. The growth of the railroad industry in the period from the 1880s through the 1920s brought rapid growth back to Tuscumbia. The main railroad yard for the Memphis & Charleston Railroad Company was moved from Huntsville, Alabama, to Tuscumbia. A new freight depot and passenger depot was built downtown.

The Memphis & Charleston Railroad Company sold out to the Southern Railway System in 1898. The new yard under construction north of town at the edge of Sheffield was then completed by the Southern Railway System. This was a large complex where a roundhouse and railroad shops became the number one employer in the area. New railroads, such as the Northern Alabama Railroad Company and Louisville & Nashville Railroad Company, began to serve both the new town of Sheffield and Tuscumbia.

The railroads began to move the main line from downtown Tuscumbia to the new city of Sheffield. They built a new depot on the main line on the western edge of town known as First Street Station or "New Station." Fifth Street Station was abandoned as a passenger depot. The tracks going through town were removed in 1948. Freight trains continued to serve Tuscumbia until the 1970s. The passenger depot became a community center and is a railroad and transportation museum today.

In the late 20th century, Tuscumbia became a town that time forgot. Today, the downtown contains some of the oldest commercial buildings in the state. Many of Tuscumbia's citizens played a major role in the history of the area, state, and the country.

This book is the story of a small town in America that had a major role in its development.

One

Big Spring and Spring Park

The big spring has been home for Native Americans for thousands of years. Thousands of gallons of fresh, clear, cold water flow from the spring daily. The Native Americans called the spring *Oka Kapassa* (cold water). Tuscumbia was first incorporated Ococoposo in 1820 after the Indian name. Ococoposo was changed to Big Spring in 1821. In 1822, the townsmen chose to change the name again. The choice of names were either in honor of Annie Dickson, the first white child born in town, or the Chickasaw chief living here when white men arrived. The name chosen by one vote was Tuscumbia in honor of Chief Tuscumba.

Tuscumbians chose to make the spring area into a park and fairgrounds. The grounds were used by Native Americans on their journey to Indian Territory during the period known as Indian Removal. Union and Confederate armies used the area during the Civil War.

The spring area was used for a fairgrounds and a recreational area until World War II. After the war, the fair moved away. The city decided to make the area a city park. Today, it is a beautiful park visited by thousands each year. This chapter covers the history of the park as it has been recorded in drawings and pictures.

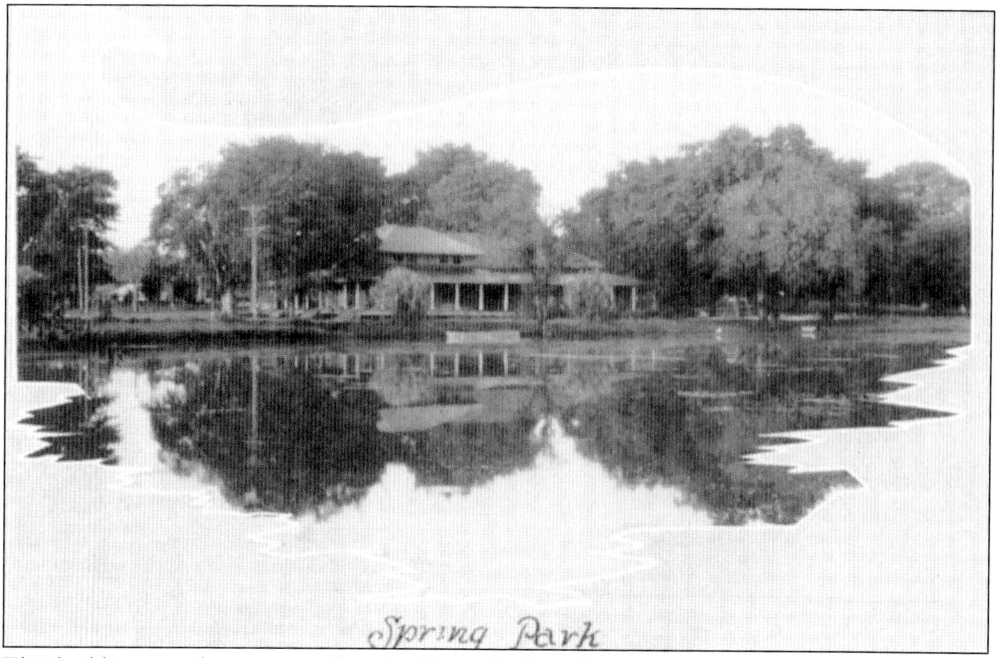

This building was the main pavilion for Spring Park and the Colbert County Fair around 1926. Contests were held for the best jams, food, clothing, and flowers. A flood around 1928 damaged the building beyond repair, and it was torn down. The two-story center pavilion in the park today was built in its place.

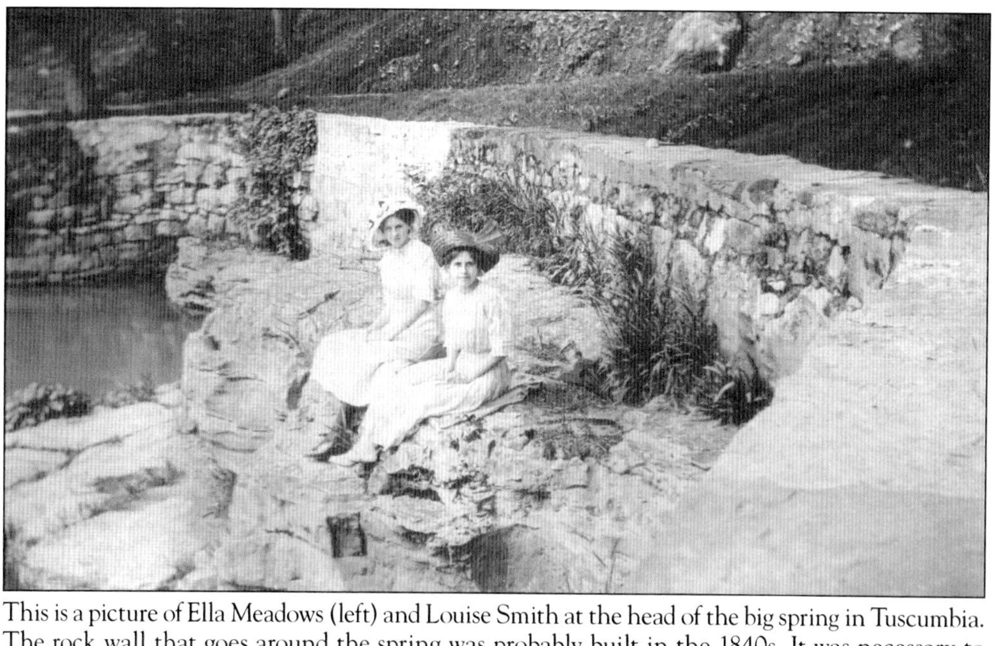

This is a picture of Ella Meadows (left) and Louise Smith at the head of the big spring in Tuscumbia. The rock wall that goes around the spring was probably built in the 1840s. It was necessary to stop the mud from washing down the hill from town into the mouth of the spring. This mud actually turned the flow of the spring and had to be stopped.

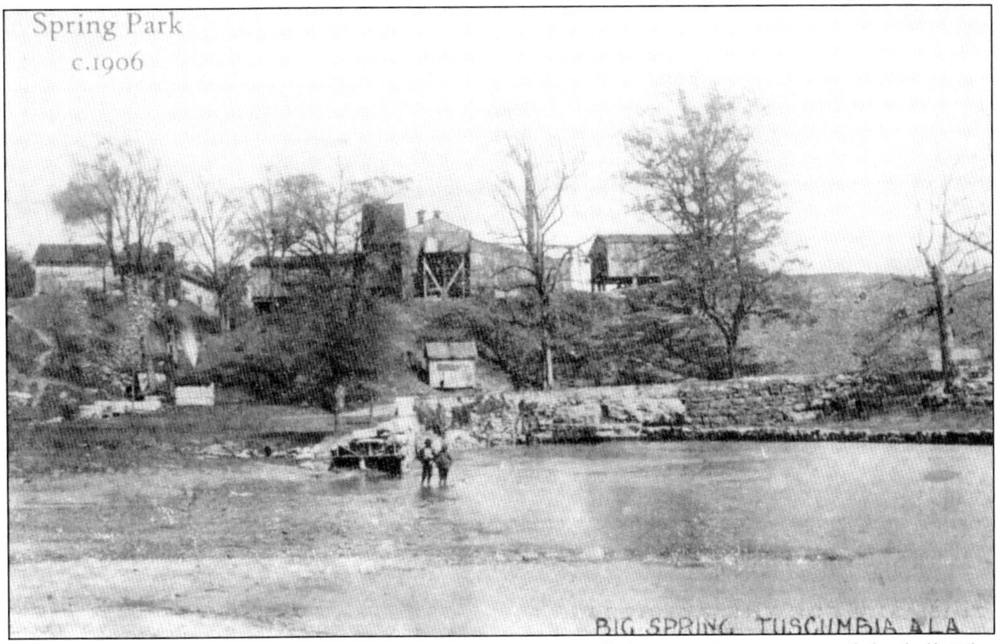

This is a good view of the spring with the cotton gin and the ice plant on top of the hill. The small buildings near the spring are water pump houses. The pumps supplied water for the ice plant and water to power steam engines operating the plants. The ice plant building on the left was torn down around 1900.

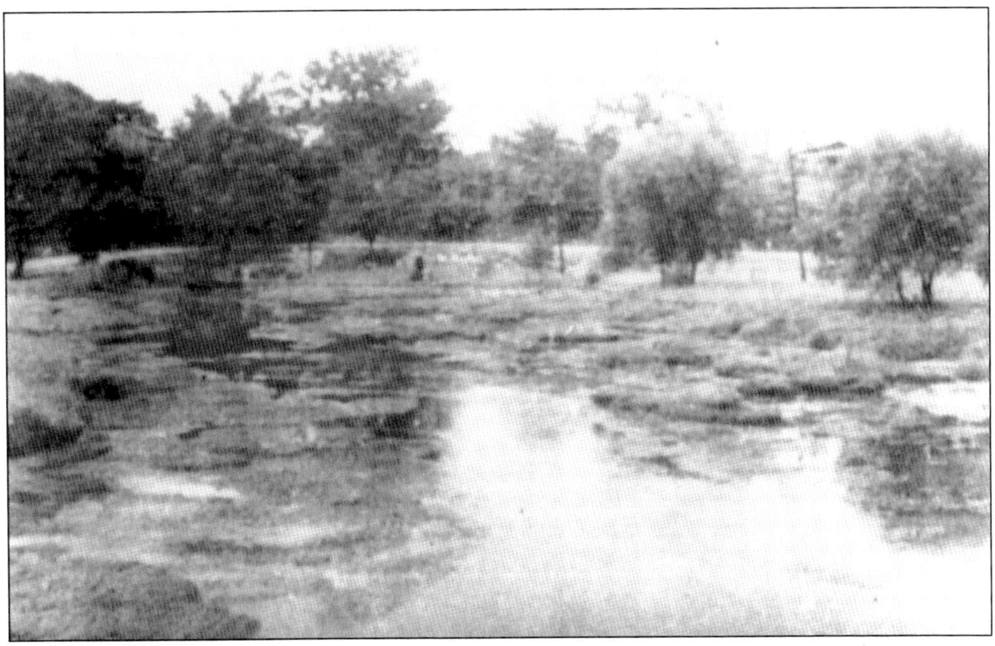

Aquatic growth has always been a major problem for Tuscumbians. Cleaning out the moss on a regular basis is one of the many tasks for those who have built dams across Spring Creek, like the Hindmans, who had a gristmill just downstream from the spring. Today, the growth is cleaned by cutting it and allowing it to float downstream.

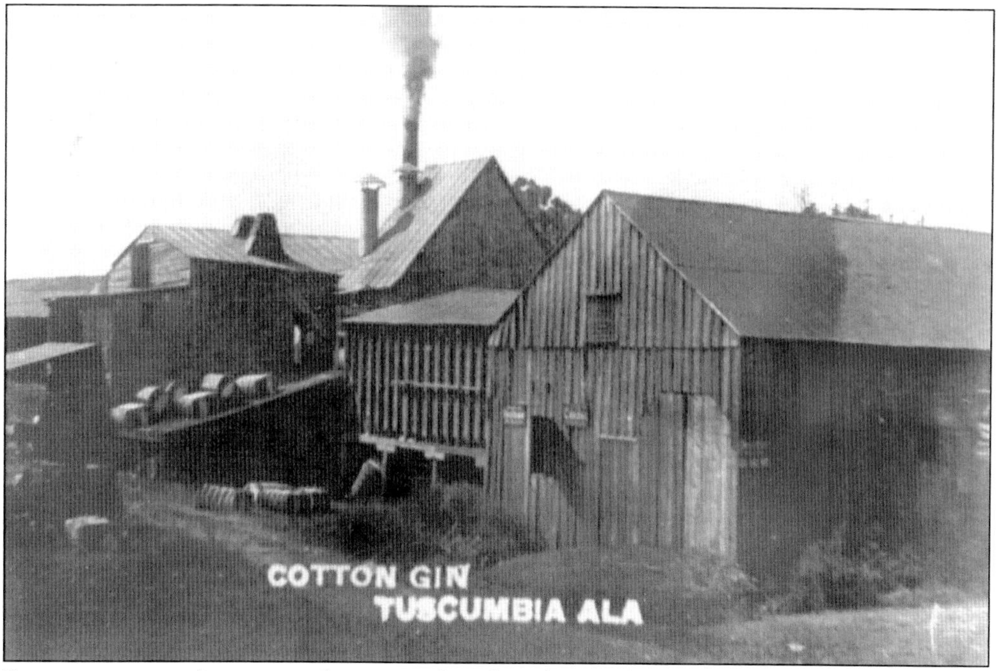

Since cotton was the main cash crop produced in the South, Tuscumbia, like many Southern towns, ginned its own cotton. These gins were served by wagons, railroads, and steamboats. Many merchants would grant credit to planters who would pay their debts by trading cotton. In Tuscumbia, the cotton gins were located on the hill at the head of the spring.

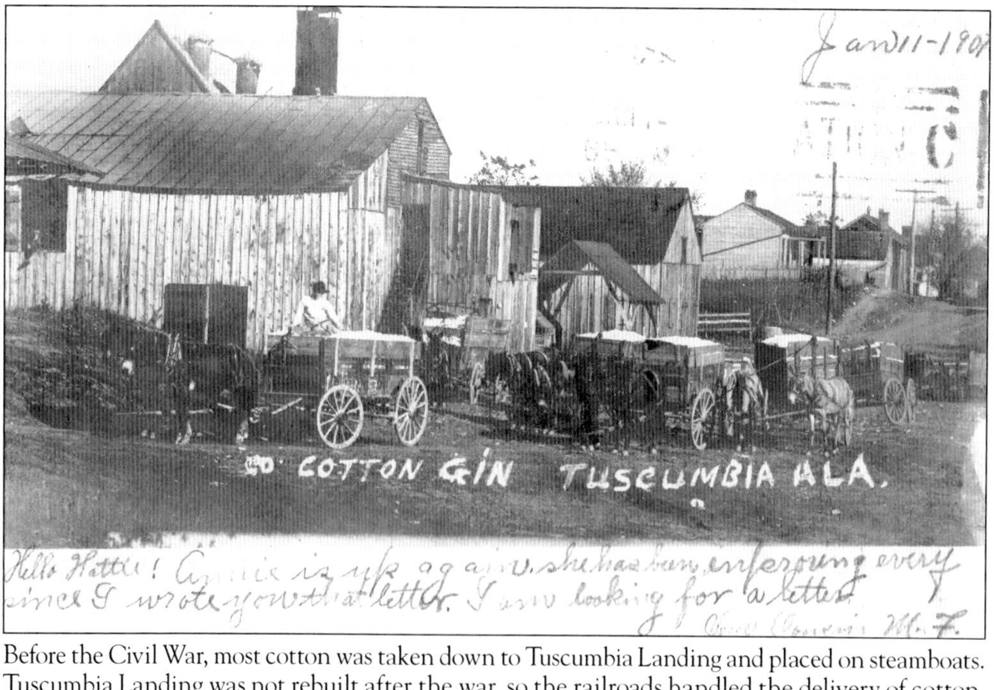

Before the Civil War, most cotton was taken down to Tuscumbia Landing and placed on steamboats. Tuscumbia Landing was not rebuilt after the war, so the railroads handled the delivery of cotton. This is a view of the cotton gin looking north up Dickson Street, which was part of Andrew Jackson's Military Road.

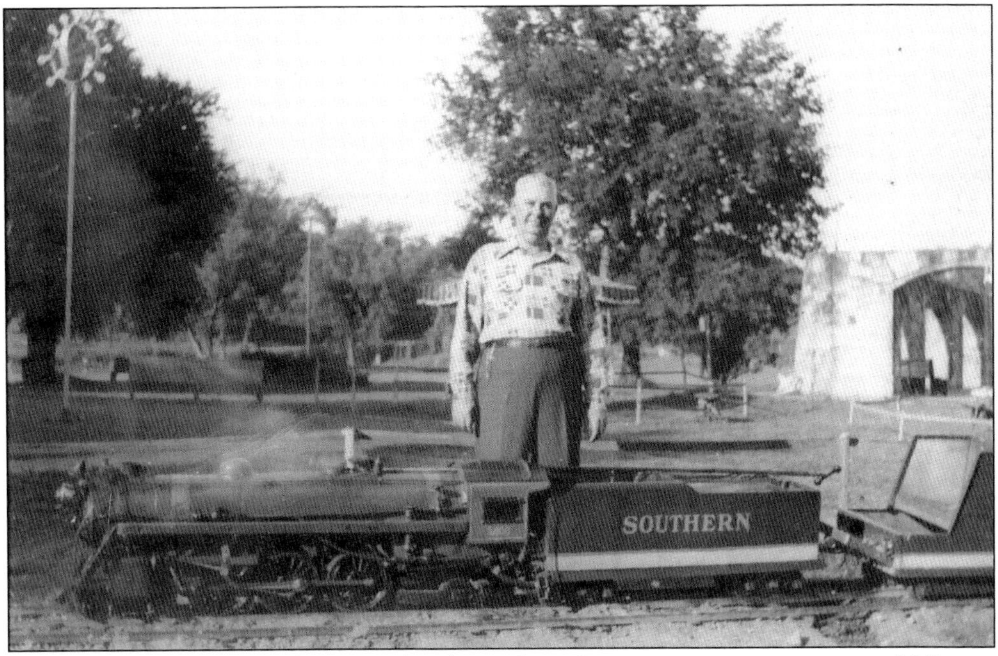

What would America's first frontier railroad town be without a train operating in its park? George F. Keys, a Southern Railway employee, built this narrow-gauge steam train for Spring Park around 1950. The engine is one gauge, and the cars are another. The structure in the background is the main stone pavilion.

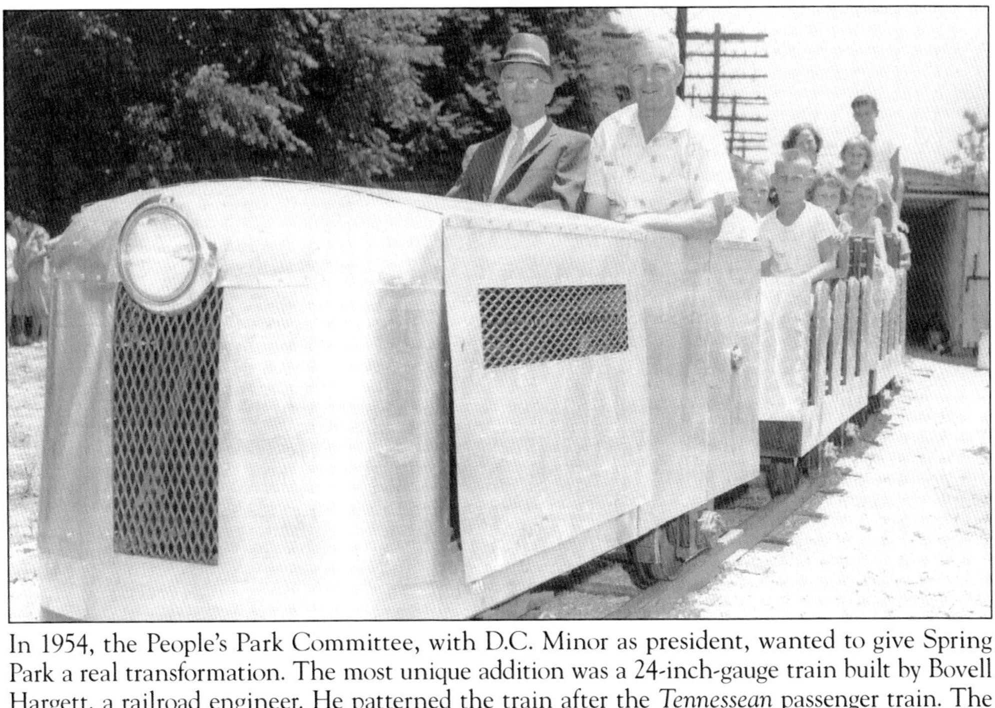

In 1954, the People's Park Committee, with D.C. Minor as president, wanted to give Spring Park a real transformation. The most unique addition was a 24-inch-gauge train built by Bovell Hargett, a railroad engineer. He patterned the train after the *Tennessean* passenger train. The inaugural run was on the Fourth of July in 1956; Mayor Henninger is pictured on the left, with Bovell Hargett as engineer.

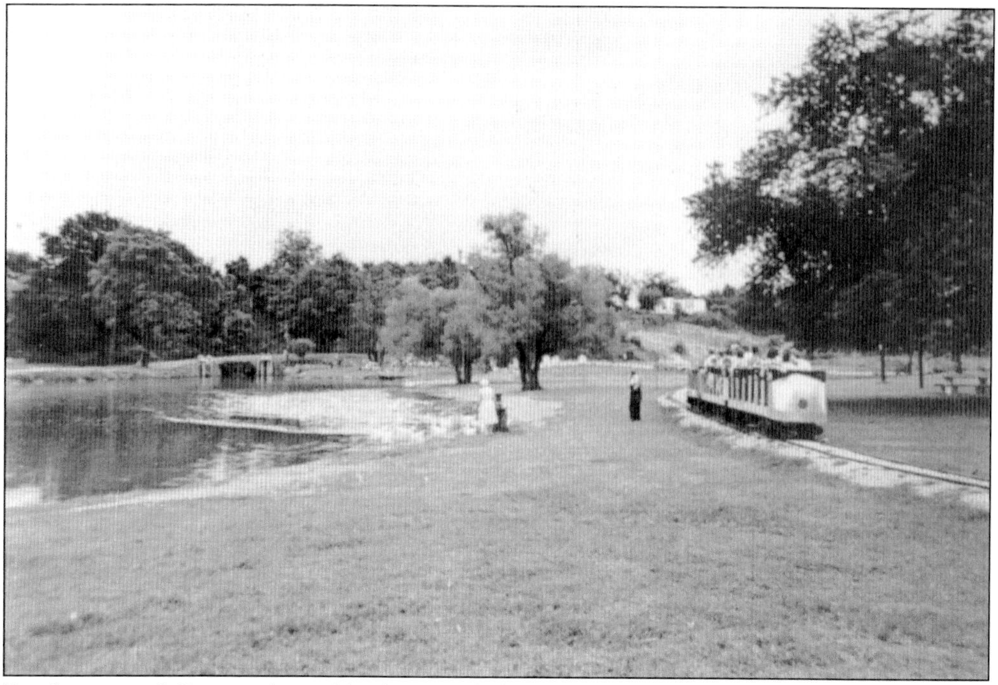

For the price of 10¢, people could ride around the track twice. The train was stored in a small building that was used not only as a station but also a tunnel. Many a young lady received her first kiss while passing through the tunnel. The train was a favorite for the people of Tuscumbia for approximately 20 years.

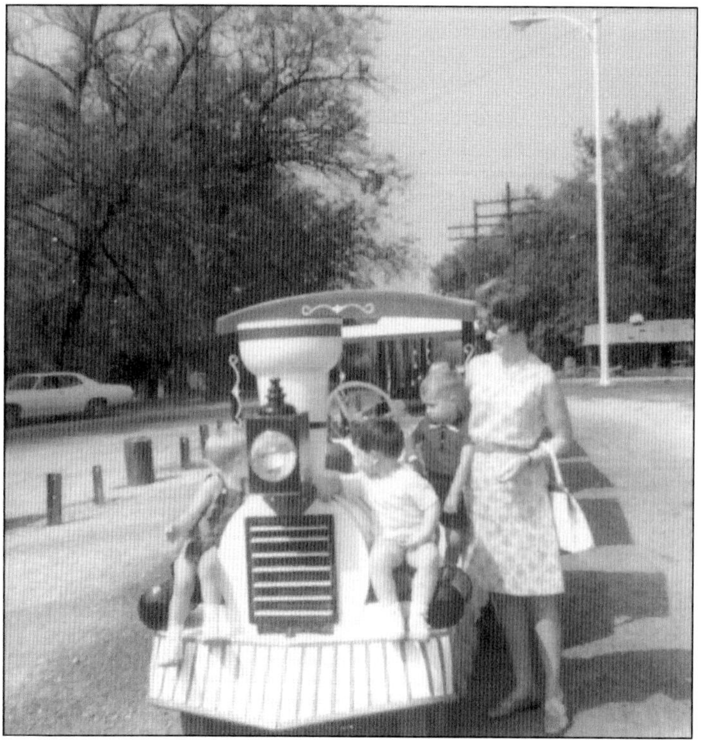

A storm in the 1960s downed trees in Spring Park, which destroyed part of the track. The city lacked funds to repair the track, so they paved the roadbed and purchased a rubber-tired train. Pictured here in 1968 are, from left to right, Billy Cox, Mark Sanderson, Danell Pace, and Marie Pace. (Courtesy of the Pace family.)

This drawing was made by a reporter for the *New York Illustrated News* during the Civil War. It was published in the *Saturday Evening News* on October 4, 1862. The rock wall around the spring was built in 1838. During rainy seasons, mud washed down from the town and stopped the flow of water from the spring. This wall was designed to control the mud flow.

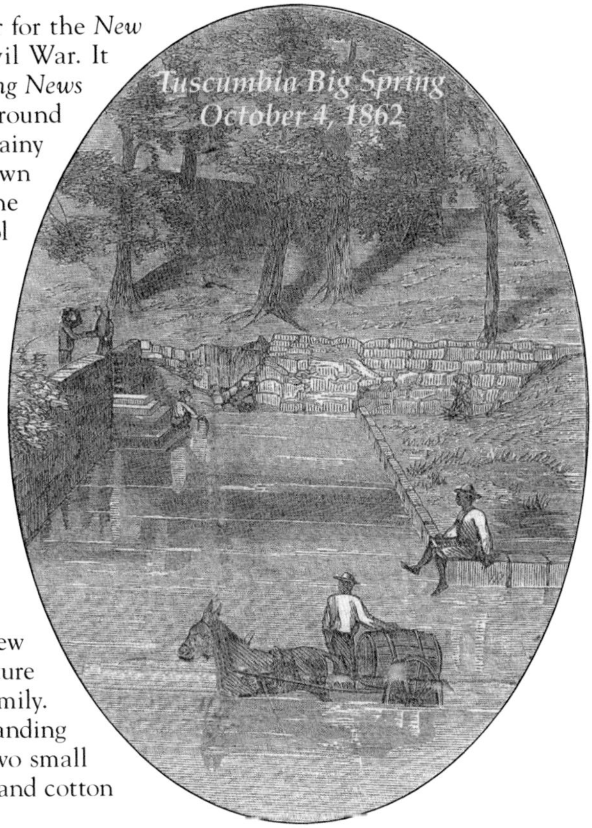

This photograph gives an excellent view of the rock wall. The family in the picture is thought to be the T.T. Rowland family. The rock ledge where the family is standing is part of the waterfall today. The two small buildings are to support the icehouse and cotton gin on top of the hill.

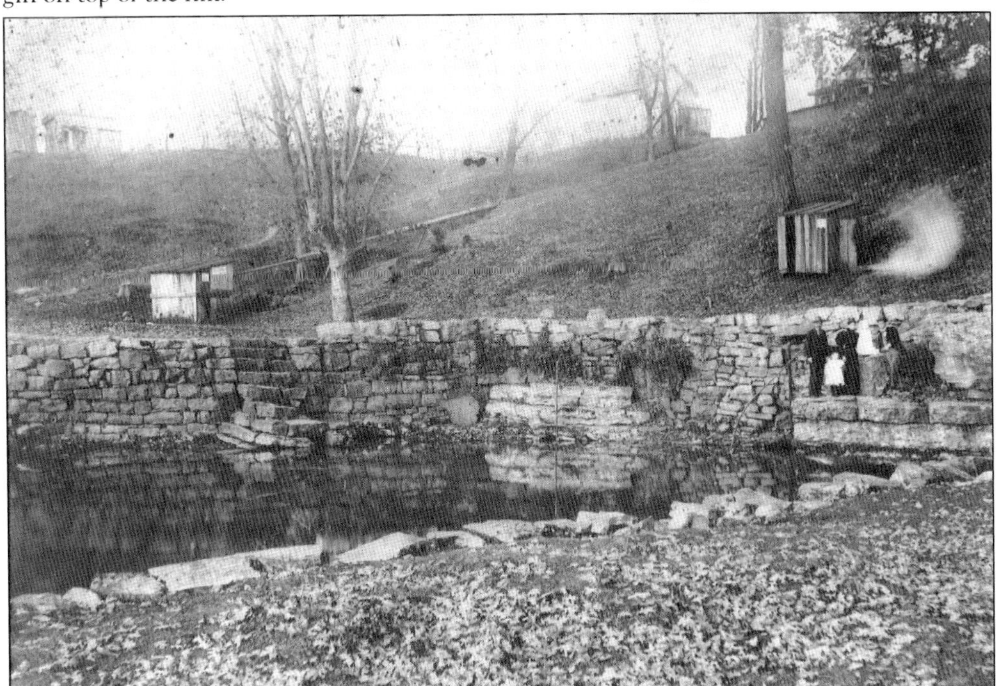

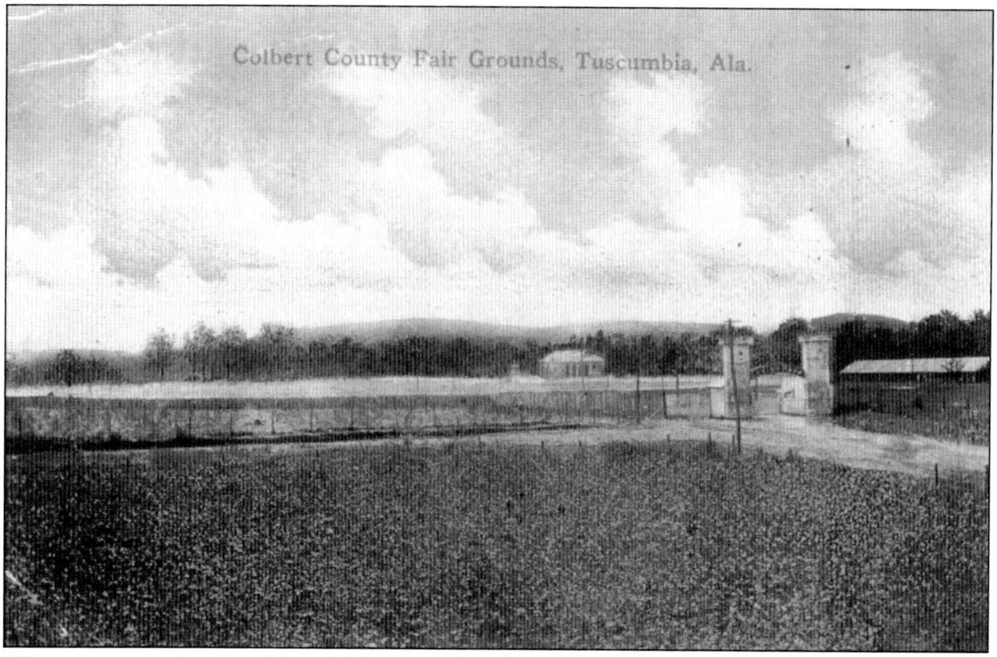

This is a postcard view of the old fairgrounds, which is where the Spring Creek Golf Course is today. The entrance castle gates are on South Main Street. The road leading north from the gates goes through the big spring. The fence to the left of the gates covers the baseball and football fields. The building in the background is the grandstand for the racetrack.

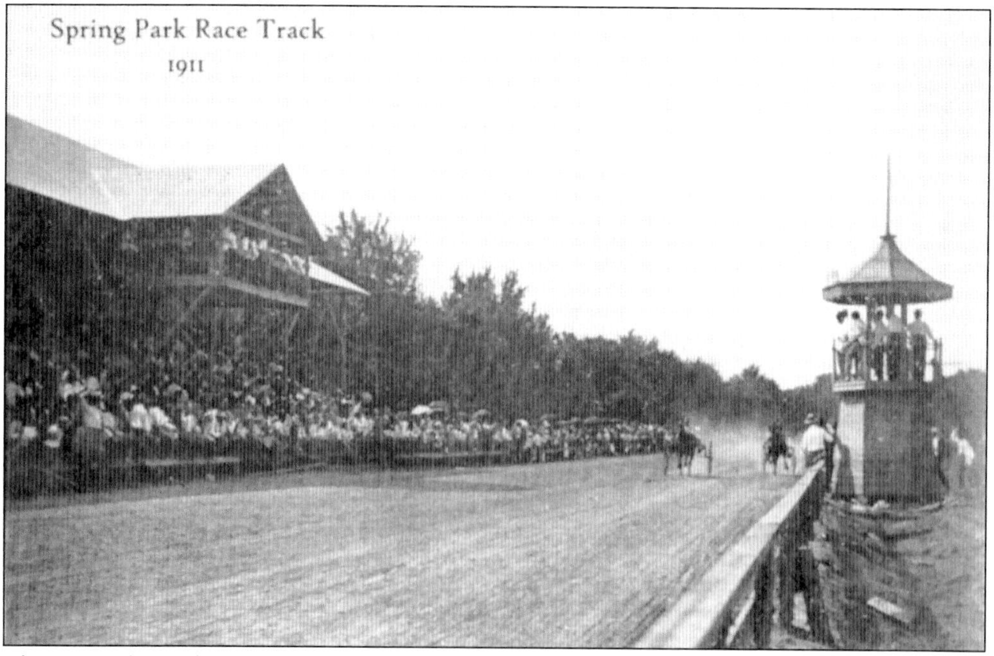

The racetrack was the center of activity at the fairgrounds. Horseracing, harness racing, and boxing matches were very popular events held regularly in front of the grandstands. The racetrack was located on Spring Creek Golf Course near fairway No. 3. Spring Creek is located just behind the grandstands.

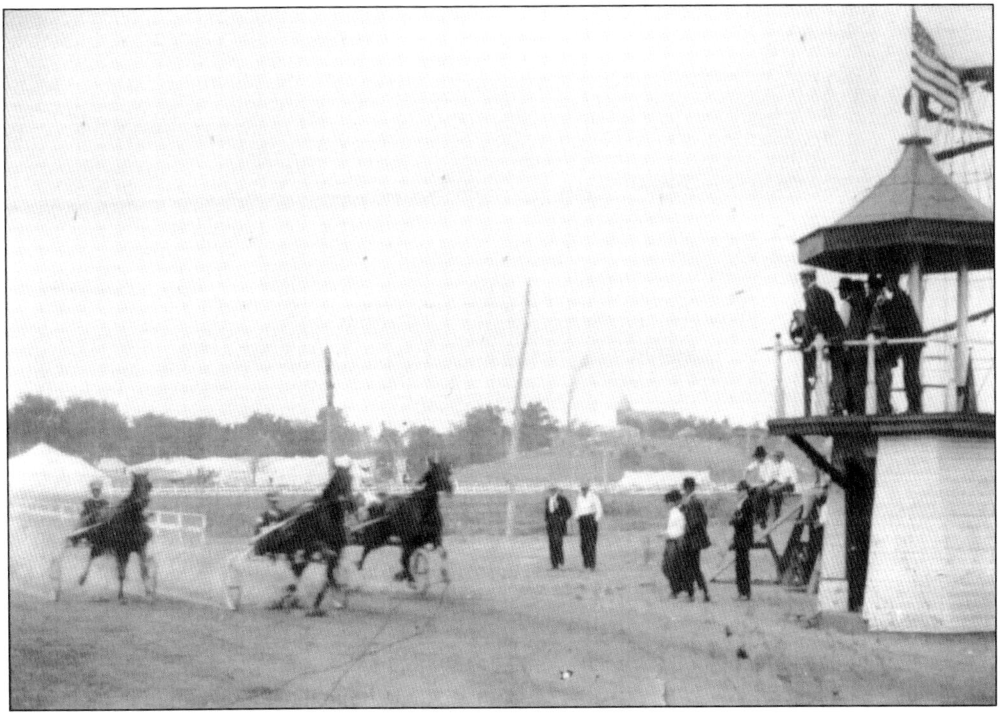

This photograph is an excellent example of horseracing at the Colbert County Fairgrounds. The smoke in the background is from the cotton gin on top of the hill above the spring. The steeple belongs to the Methodist church. The tents in the background are for displays at the Colbert County Fair.

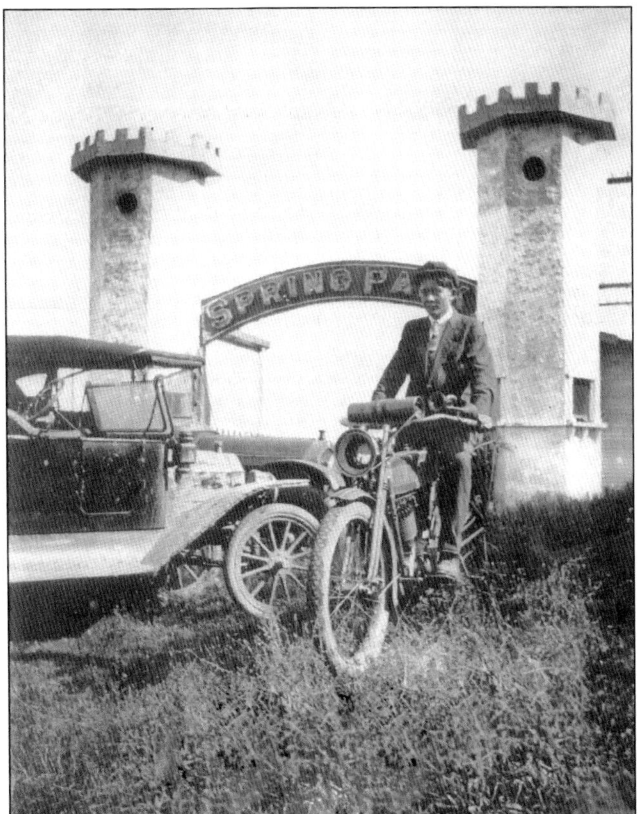

This 1920s photograph is an excellent view of the castle gates at the entrance to the fairgrounds on South Main Street. Pvt. A.J. Benton of the 17th Indiana Volunteers wrote during the Civil War, "The entrance to the fairground is by an eastern gate built in the form of an Italian castle with watchtowers overlooking the whole domain." (Courtesy of Virginia Cox.)

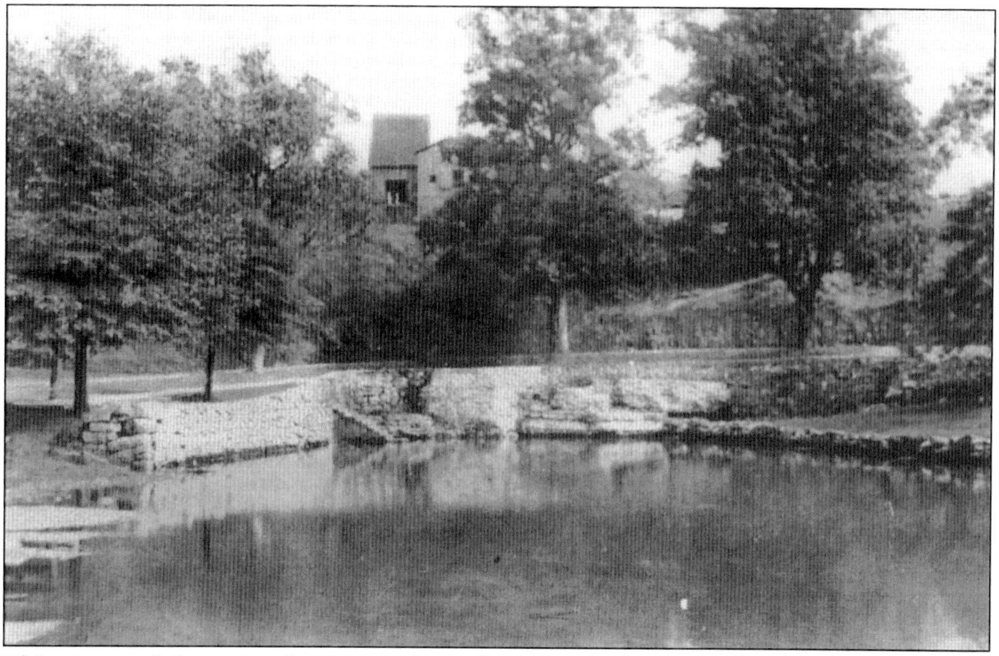

This picture of the spring shows a good set of steps going down into the water at the head of the spring. The original wall, which was built before the Civil War to help keep mud out of the spring, did not have steps. These particular steps were probably built at the same time as the dam during the 1920s by the Tuscumbia Amusement Company.

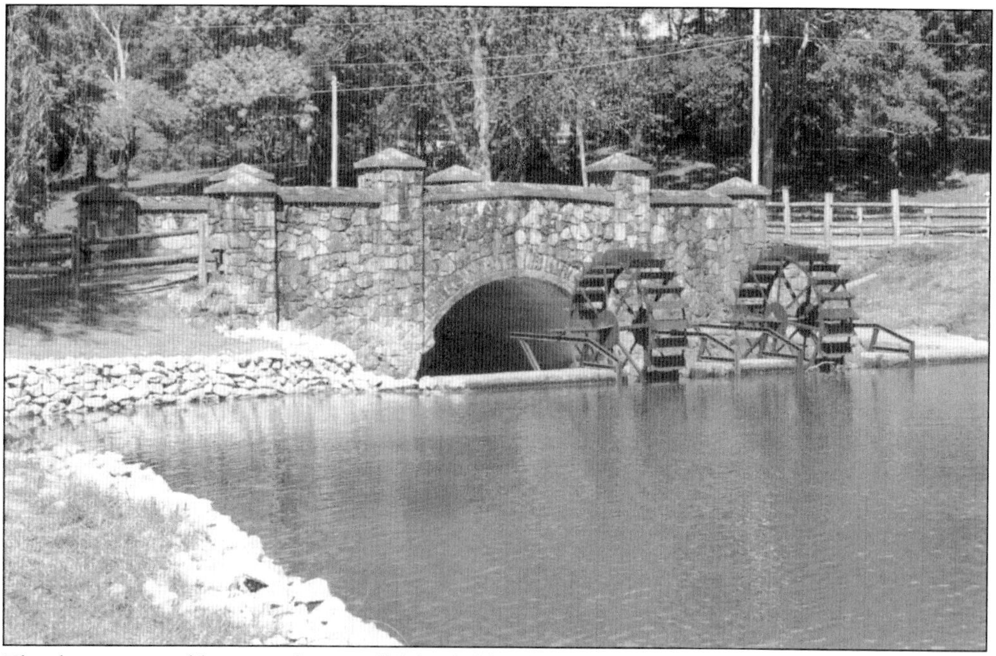

The dam, pictured here, made a small lake fed by the big springs. The stone bridge was built in the 1930s as a Works Progress Administration project. The base for the bridge kept washing out from rains, so men had to work extra shifts when it was not raining to get the foundation in. The metal water wheels are fairly new.

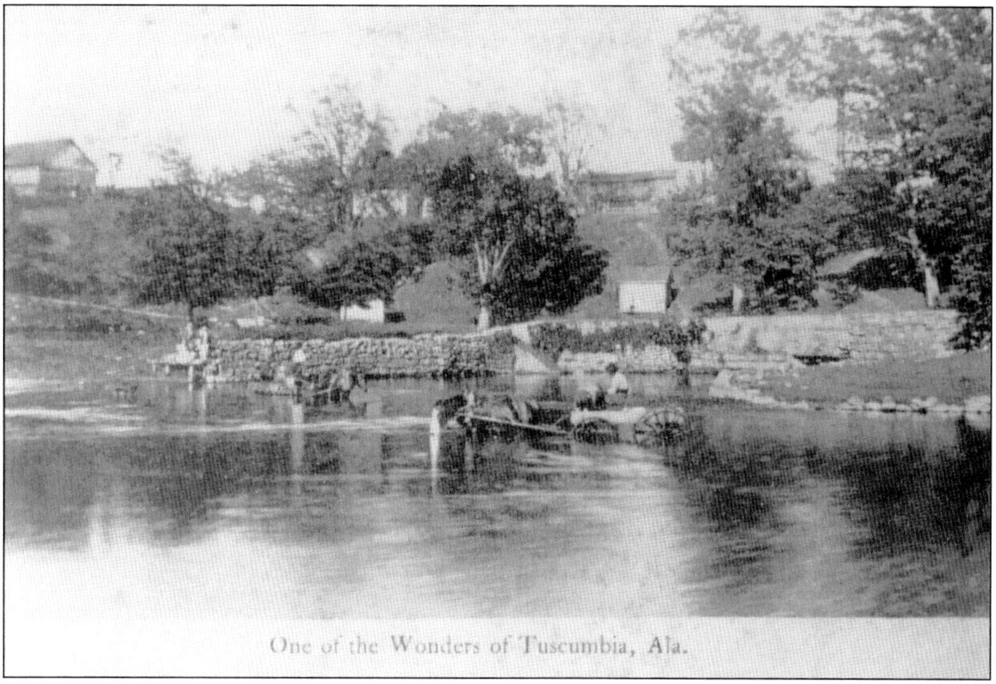

This picture shows a wagon going south from town through the spring on Main Street. The other wagon appears to be filling barrels with water. In the 1800s, water was delivered to the people in town by water wagons. The fire department also depended on water supplied to them by water wagons.

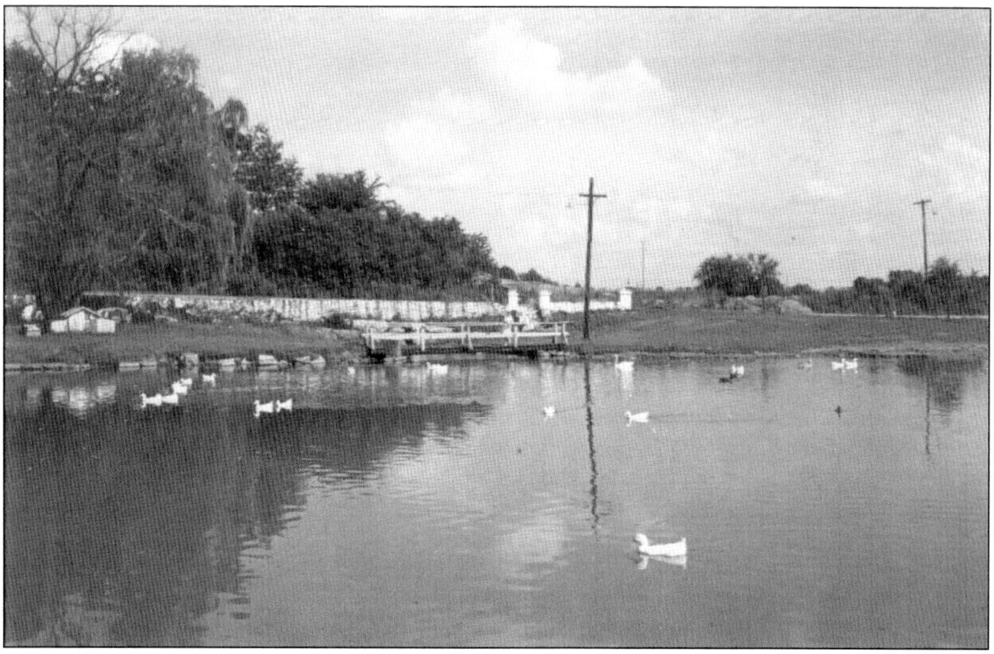

The Tuscumbia Spring is a double-headed spring. This picture shows the smaller spring with a bridge across it. The bridge was built using rails from the old train track from the 1950s. This bridge was removed during the park's renovation in 2001.

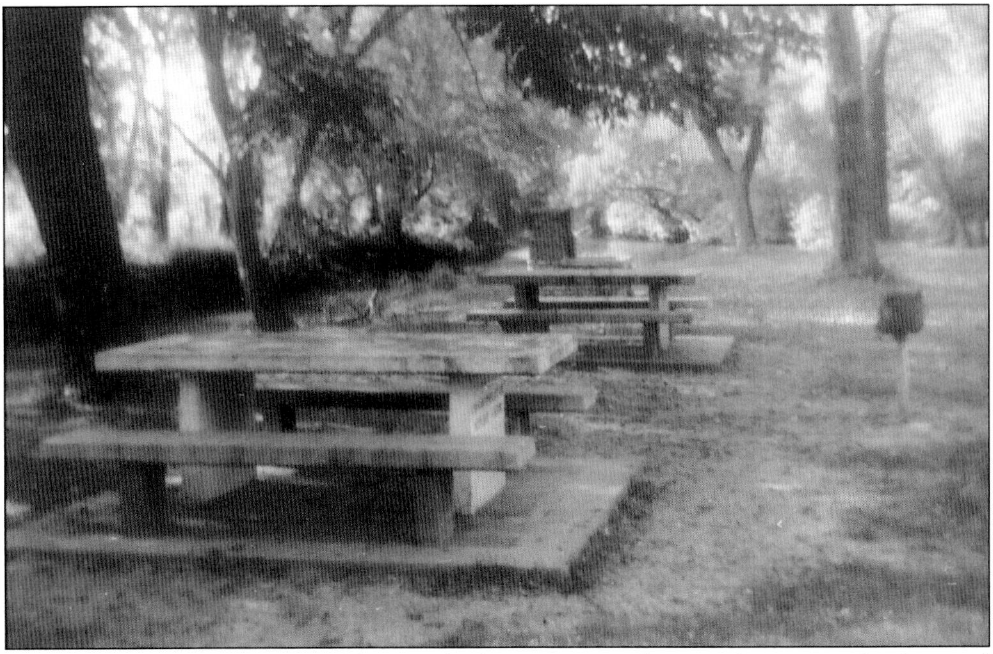

In the 1950s, several concrete tables were built in Spring Park. Many businesses, families, and organizations sponsored tables throughout the park. These two were located near the present location of the covered railroad bridge. These tables were removed when the present train was placed in the park in 2003. (Courtesy of Irvin Hargett.)

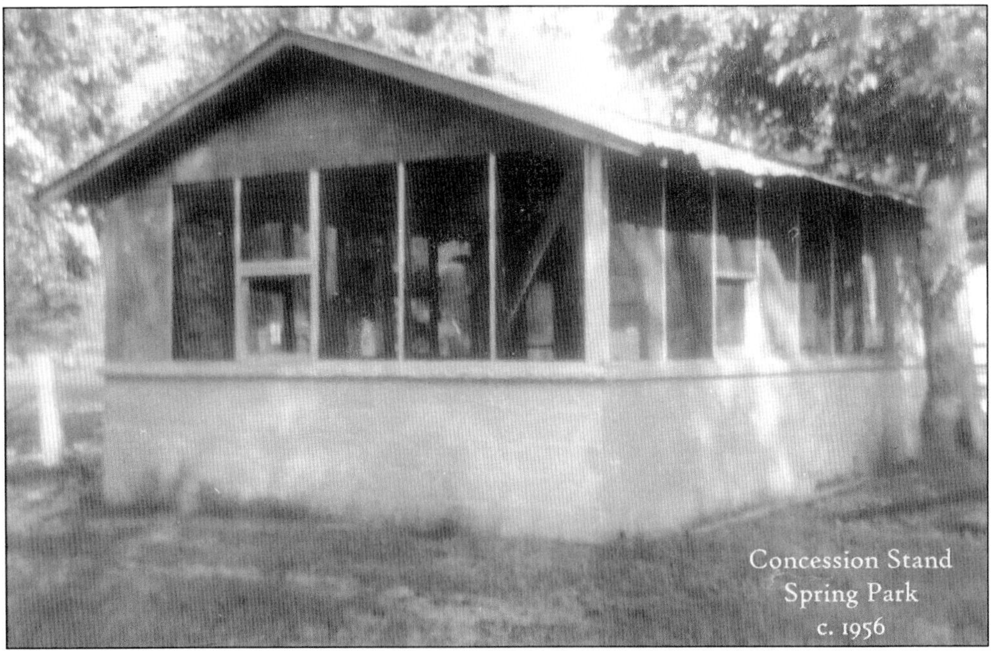

In the 1950s, the People's Park Commission, with D.C. Minor as president, began to transform Spring Park. The commission built a covered barbecue pit and concession stand. This is a picture of the concession stand. A new concession stand was built at this location in the 1970s. (Courtesy of Irvin Hargett.)

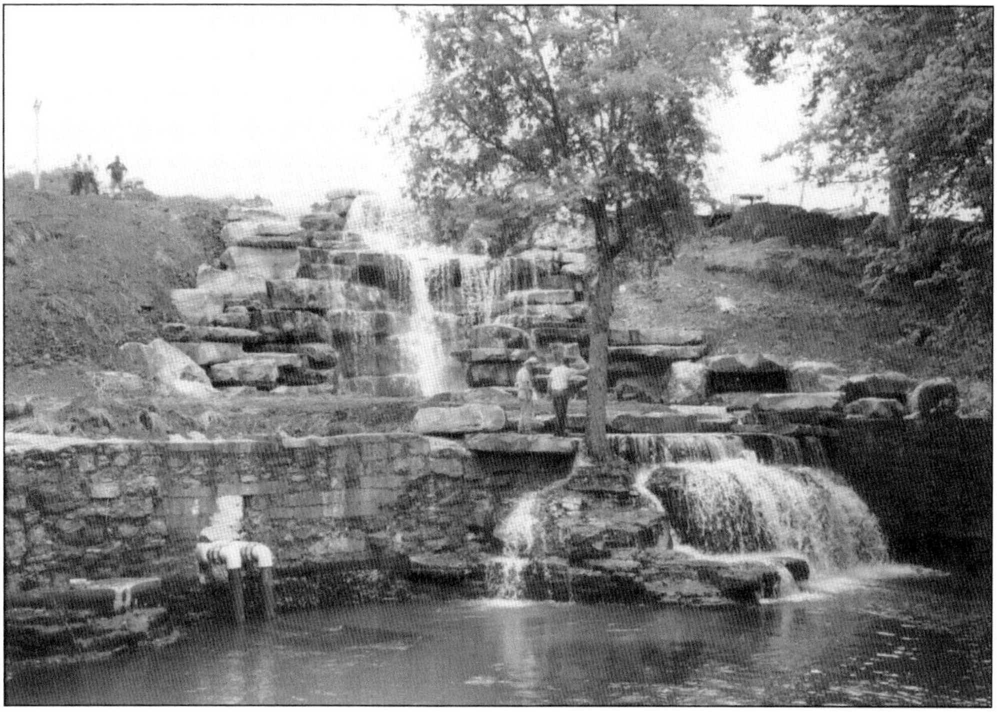

Spring Park was to undergo a major revitalization with the new century. Harvey and Joyce Ann Robbins offered to give the park a waterfall and animated fountain. Large sandstone rocks from all parts of Colbert County were used in the construction of the waterfall. Under the supervision of designer/overseer Audwin McGee, a crane was used to place each stone.

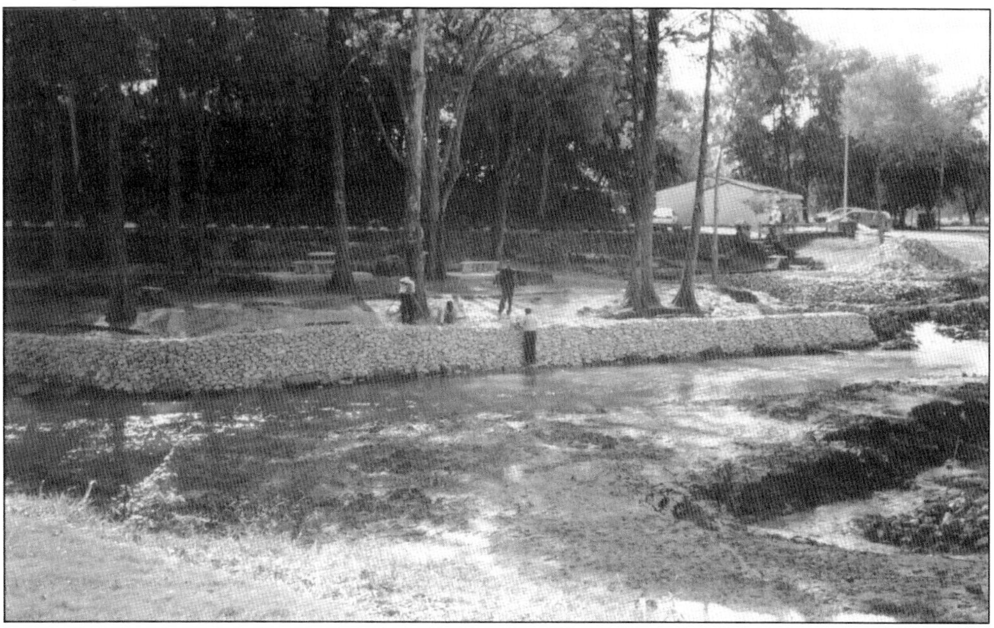

The spring was channeled around the construction area by digging a drainage ditch by the dam and stone bridge. The lowered water level allowed for the stacking of limestone rocks completely around the lake. Stone construction is seen here around the peninsula between the two springs.

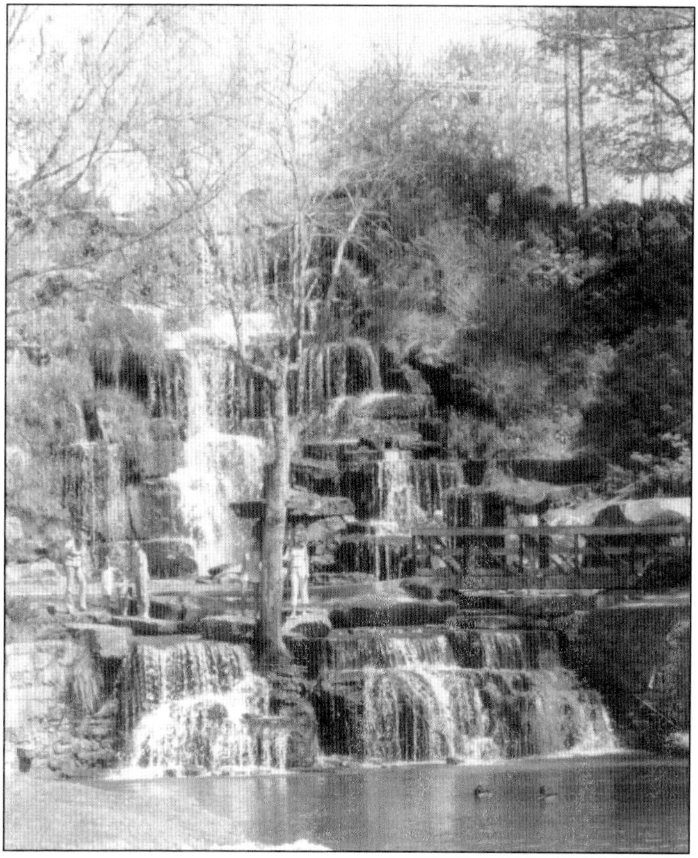

The largest stone used in the waterfall weighed 77,000 pounds. About 1,780 tons of sandstone were used in construction. Two pumps are used to pump water up from the spring to the top of the falls, where it flows across the waterfall, which is 80 feet long and 48 feet across.

The location for the fountain was to be in the center of Main Street where the street used to ford the stream. This location had a solid rock bottom allowing heavy equipment to prepare the foundation. This location would also allow the center pump to shoot water into the air high enough to be seen down Main Street.

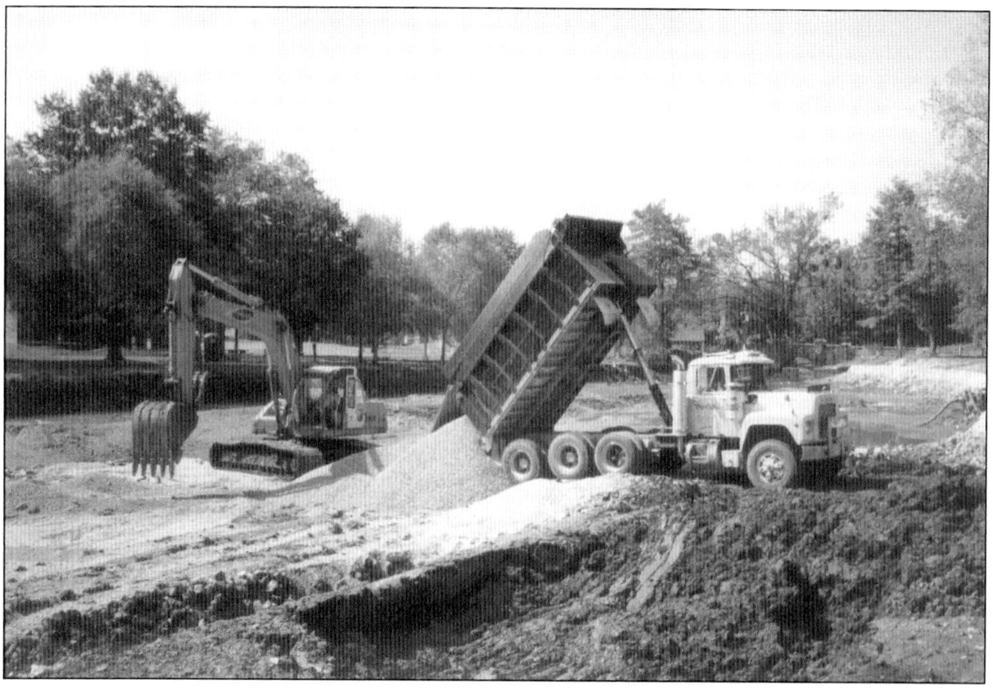

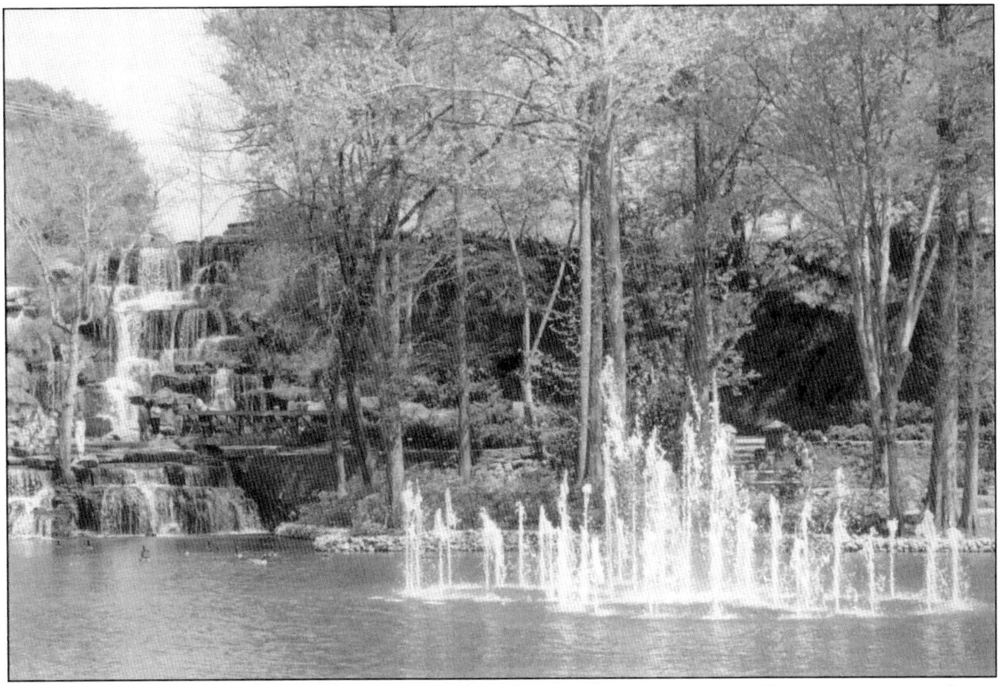

Fifty-one jets are choreographed to music as they shoot water into the air. The center jet can shoot water over 100 feet, while the 50 smaller jets shoot water approximately 50 feet. Approximately 150 lights are also choreographed to the music.

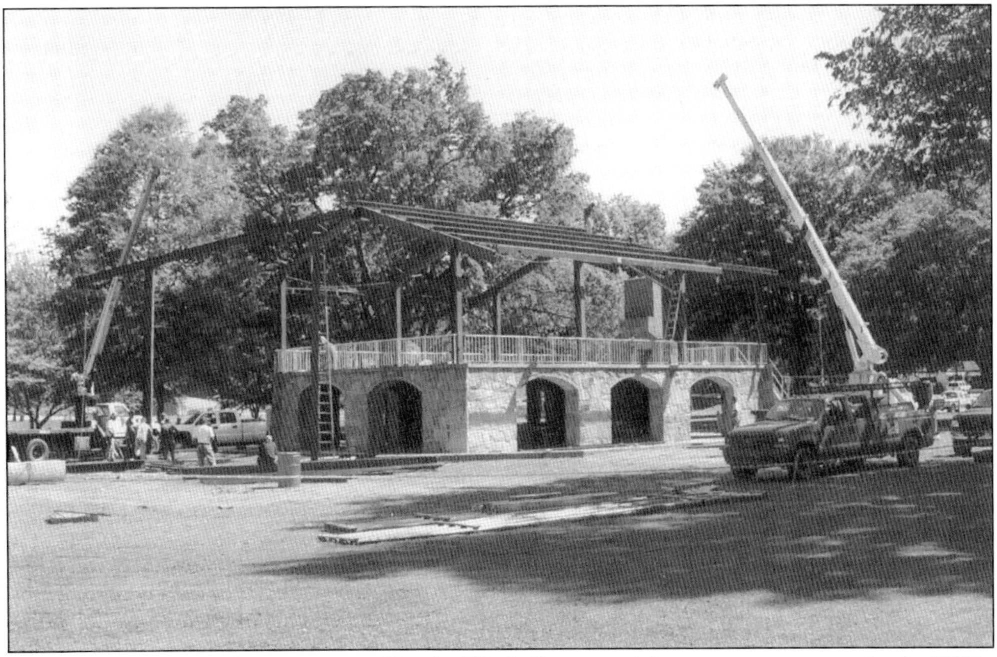

The park's center pavilion was started by the Works Progress Administration project in the 1930s, but only the four rock walls were completed. The concrete deck was placed on the walls in the 1950s. In 2002, the pavilion was enlarged by adding a stage. A metal top was built along with a stage on the west side.

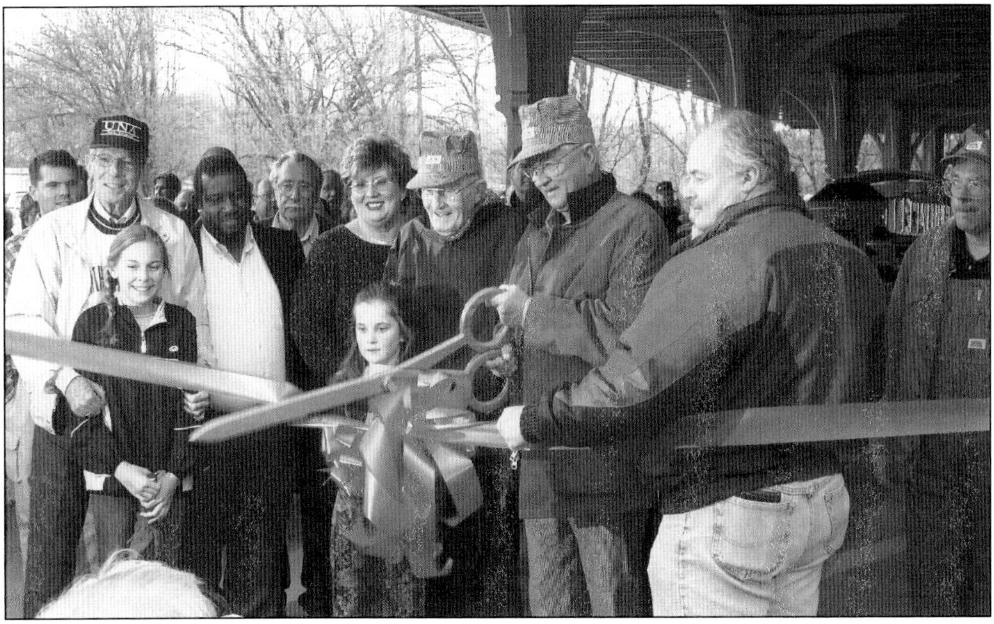

Tuscumbia received a great Christmas present in 2003 when Harvey and Joyce Robbins decided to give the park a train. Robbins Property Development, Inc., began construction on January 19, 2004. This photograph is of the ribbon cutting at the grand opening on April 3, 2004. Pictured from left to right are city councilmen Buddy Aldridge, Dennis Box, and Vicki Estes with coach Howard Chappell, Harvey Robbins, and Mayor Wade Gann.

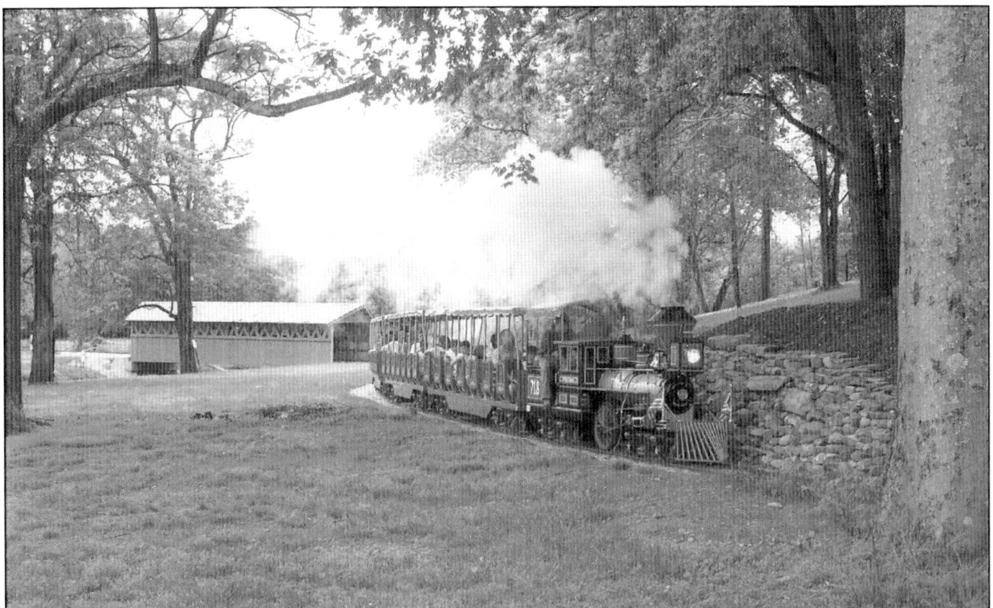

The narrow-gauge Chance Rides train has been a great hit for the park. The engine was given the name *Tuscumbia* and numbered in honor of the highly decorated World War II unit, the 718th Railroad Operating Battalion. The train is seen here pulling six cars. They have just crossed Spring Creek over a covered bridge. (Photograph courtesy of Linda B. Cross.)

Tuscumbia has a unique Native American history. When the United States developed a policy of Indian removal, Tuscumbians were against it. Generally, the Cherokee, Creek, and Chickasaws were treated well on their journey through Tuscumbia on their way west. In 2003, the Trail of Tears Motorcycle Ride chose Spring Park for its statue commemorating the removal. Branko Medenica was chosen as the designer and sculptor. The bronze statue was given the name *Sacred Tears*.

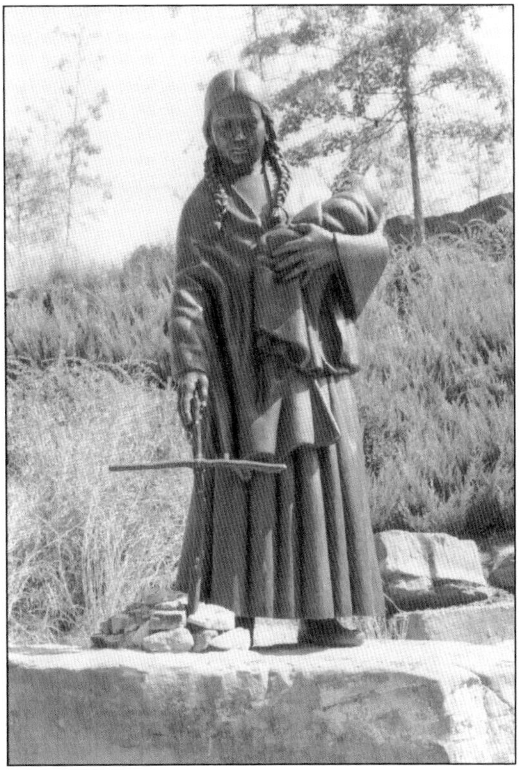

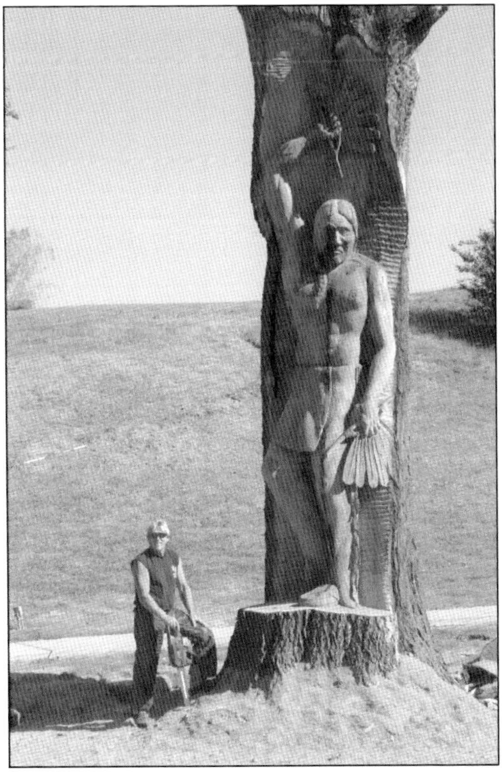

In 2004, a large oak tree in Spring Park next to the lake was struck by lightning and killed. It was suggested to Harvey Robbins that a Native American be carved into the tree. Brian Ruth, a master of the chainsaw, was commissioned to design and carve a Southeastern Native American tribute into the tree stump. In the fall of 2005, the artist completed the sculpture in two weeks.

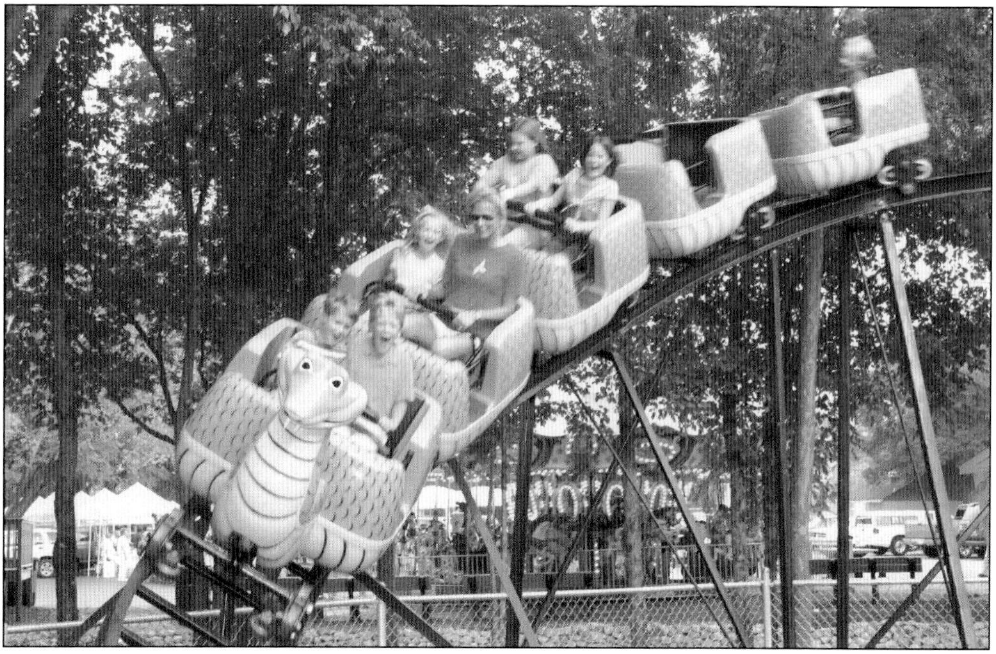

The children of Tuscumbia received a great surprise in the summer of 2005 when the Tuscumbia Railway Company, Inc., was given a carousel and roller coaster to be used in Spring Park. This roller coaster was built by Miler Coaster Company as the Python Pit. This ride has become a favorite for many.

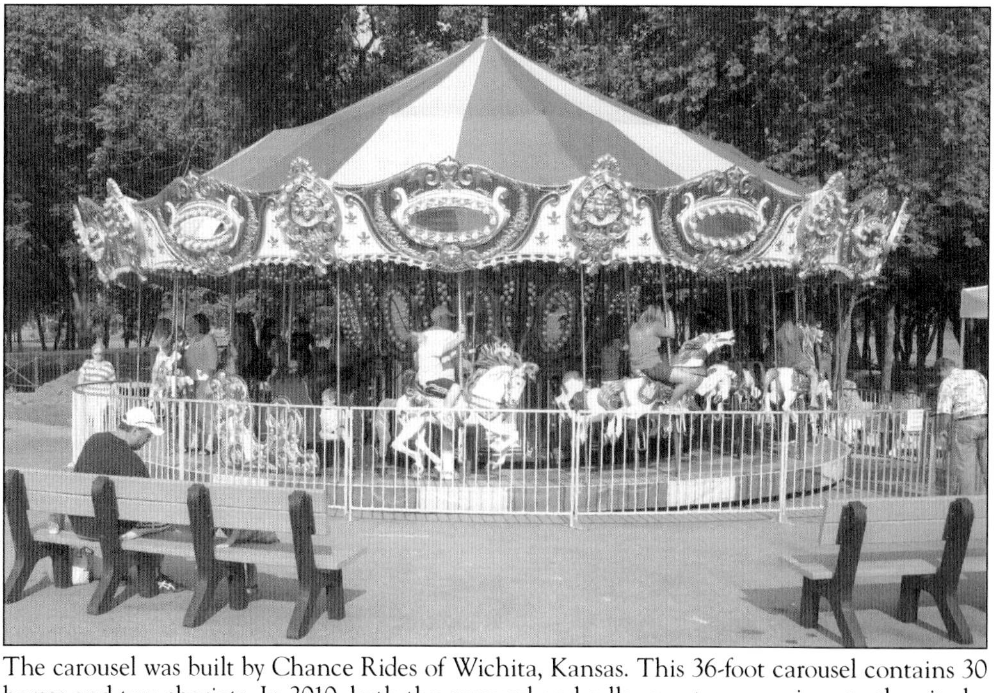

The carousel was built by Chance Rides of Wichita, Kansas. This 36-foot carousel contains 30 horses and two chariots. In 2010, both the carousel and roller coaster were given to the city by the Tuscumbia Railway Company, Inc. Today, all the rides are operated by the Tuscumbia Park and Recreation Department.

Two

America's First Frontier Railroad Town

Tuscumbia became America's first frontier railroad town in 1830 with the incorporation of the Tuscumbia Railroad Company by the state legislature. Not only was the railroad the first in Alabama but possibly the fourth incorporated in the United States. Businessmen of the area saw a future in building a railroad around the 43 miles of rapids in the Tennessee River between Tuscumbia and Decatur, Alabama, known as the Muscle Shoals. The Tuscumbia, Courtland & Decatur Railroad was incorporated in 1832 and connected Tuscumbia with Decatur, Alabama. These railroads became the heart of the Memphis & Charleston Railroad in 1851 and part of the Southern Railway System in 1898.

Tuscumbia became a transportation center. The US Postal Service soon followed the railroad routes. In 1843, almost 50 stagecoaches a week entered or left Tuscumbia to meet the mail delivered by rail to Tuscumbia. The telegraph also followed the railroads, making Tuscumbia a telegraph center.

The railroads outgrew the yard in Tuscumbia. In the late 1800s, the Memphis & Charleston Railroad Company expanded its yard north of town between Tuscumbia and the new town of Sheffield. Today, the Norfolk Southern Railroad has a hump yard just south of the city of Muscle Shoals.

This chapter covers the rich history of railroading in Tuscumbia and the area known today as the Shoals.

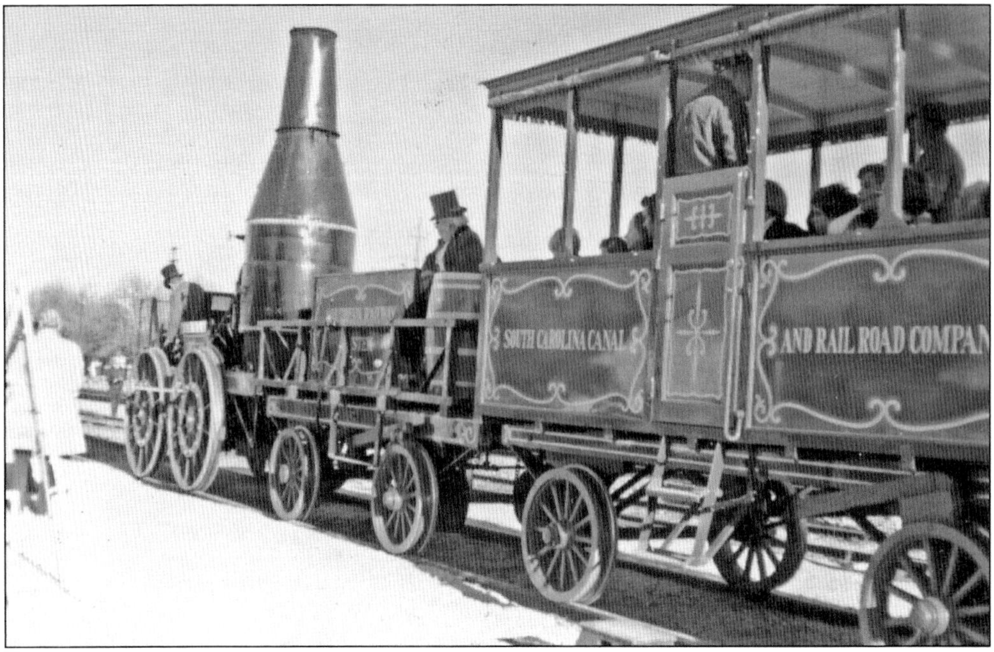

The first successful steam passenger train in the United States was the *Best Friend of Charleston* of the South Carolina Canal & Railroad Company. This replica, owned by the Southern Railways System, was giving passengers a ride in the old Tuscumbia Yard just west of the depot in 1982.

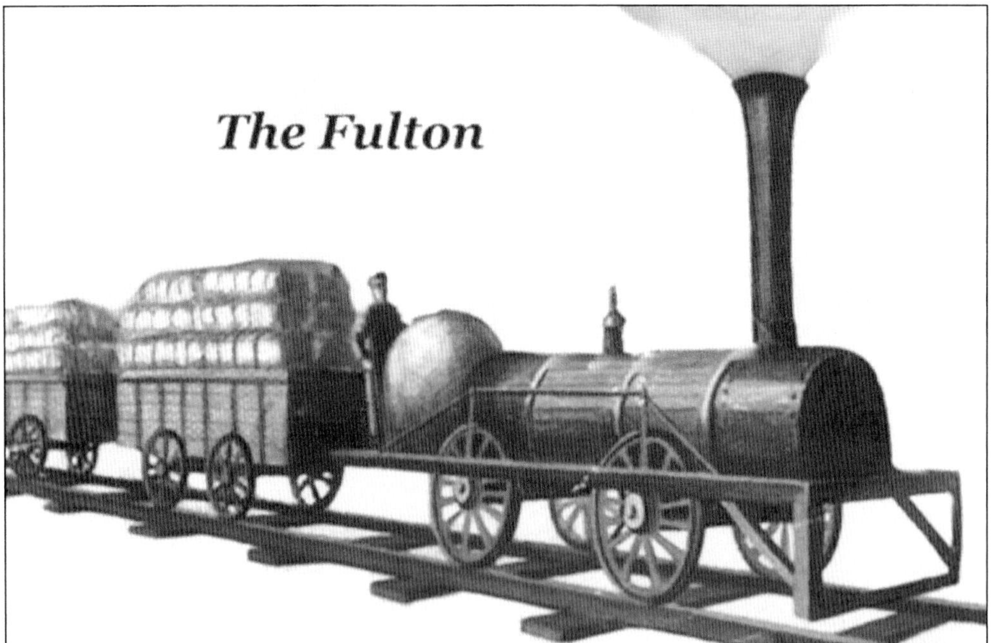

The first steam locomotive purchased by the Tuscumbia, Courtland & Decatur Railroad came from England and was named *Fulton*. The *Fulton* was a standard gauge engine of 4 feet, 8.5 inches. This rendering by Patricia Haskins McWilliams was based on an etching found in the *Leighton News*.

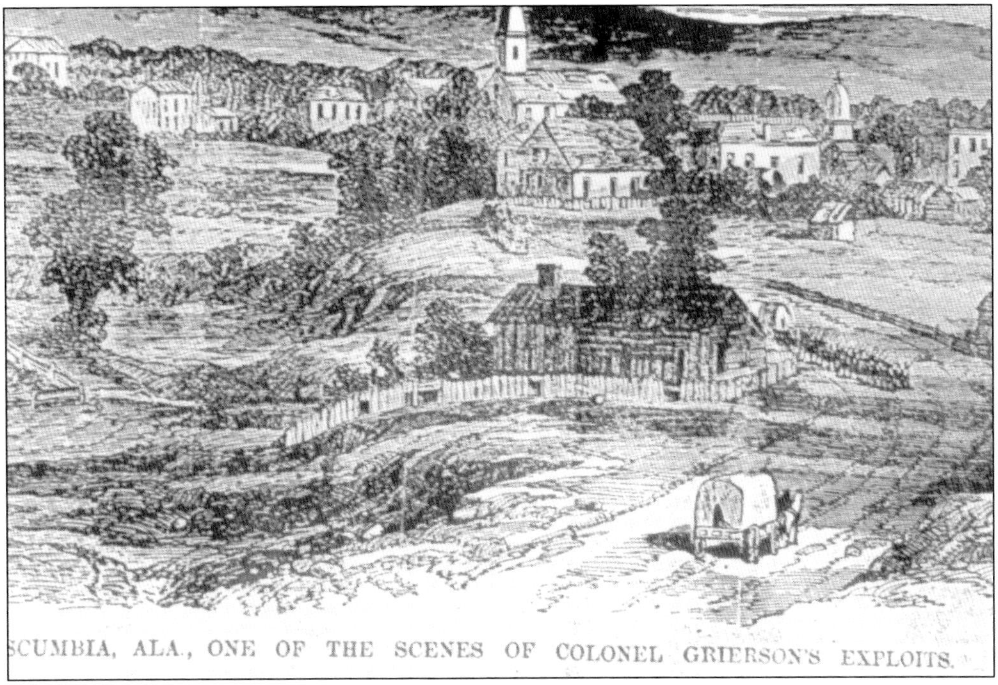

Tuscumbia quickly grew once the railroads began operation. The town doubled in size in the early 1830s. By the time the Civil War started, Tuscumbia was one of the larger towns in Alabama. This is a drawing of Tuscumbia made by a Union correspondent during one of the Yankee occupations of Tuscumbia. The large structure with roof damage in the center is thought to be the railroad shops.

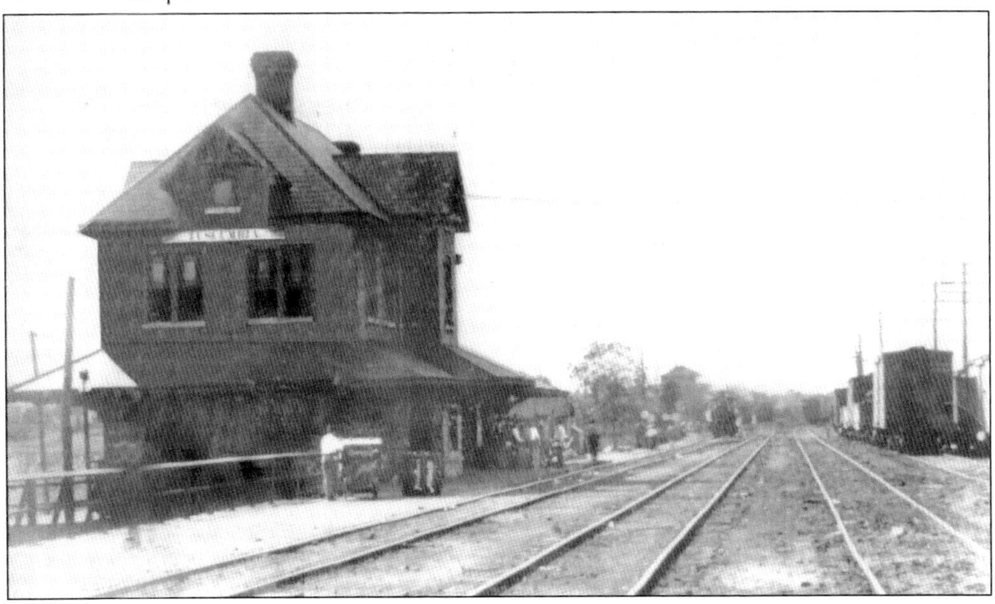

This photograph, taken in 1906, is the Fifth Street Depot and rail yard. Men are standing just outside the waiting room as the passenger train comes into the station from Memphis, Tennessee. The two-story section of the depot contained offices for the railroad officials. The men in this depot were responsible for operations of trains between Memphis and Chattanooga, Tennessee.

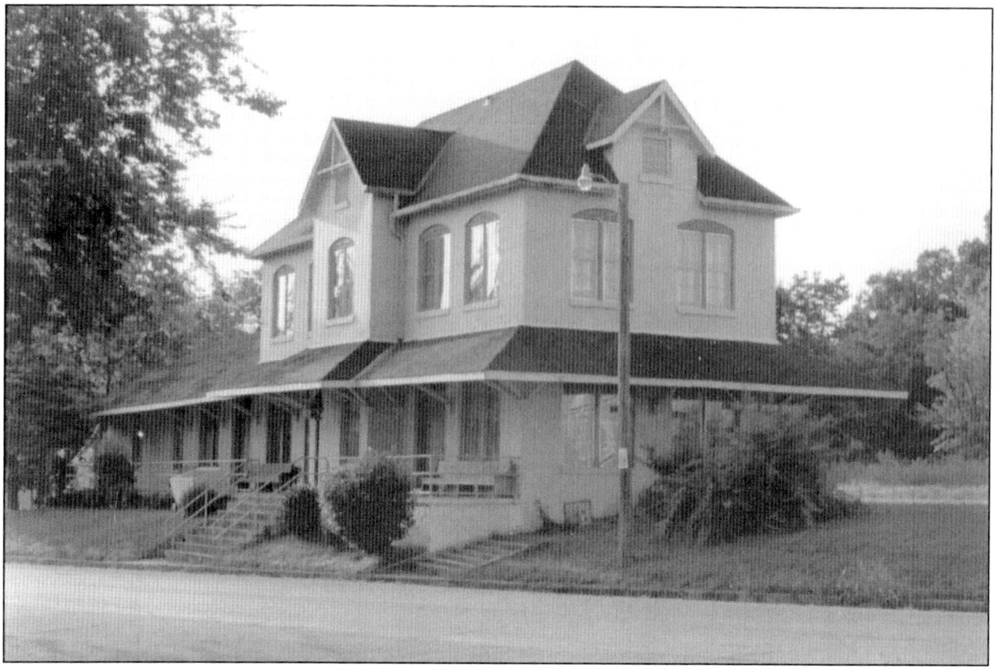

The Memphis & Charleston Railroad began to expand and moved its offices and rail yard from Huntsville, Alabama, to Tuscumbia after the Civil War. This movement required a new passenger station and freight station to be built in Tuscumbia. These were constructed in 1888. This is the front of the Fifth Street Depot, as seen from Fifth Street around 1970.

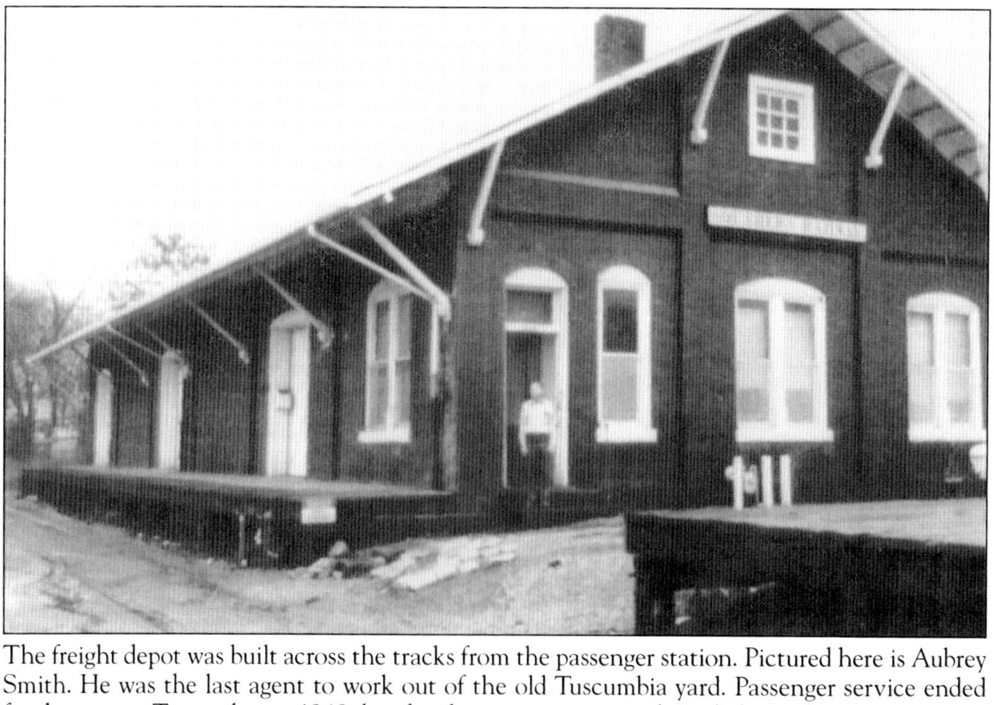

The freight depot was built across the tracks from the passenger station. Pictured here is Aubrey Smith. He was the last agent to work out of the old Tuscumbia yard. Passenger service ended for downtown Tuscumbia in 1948, but freight service continued until about 1980. (Courtesy of Aubrey Smith.)

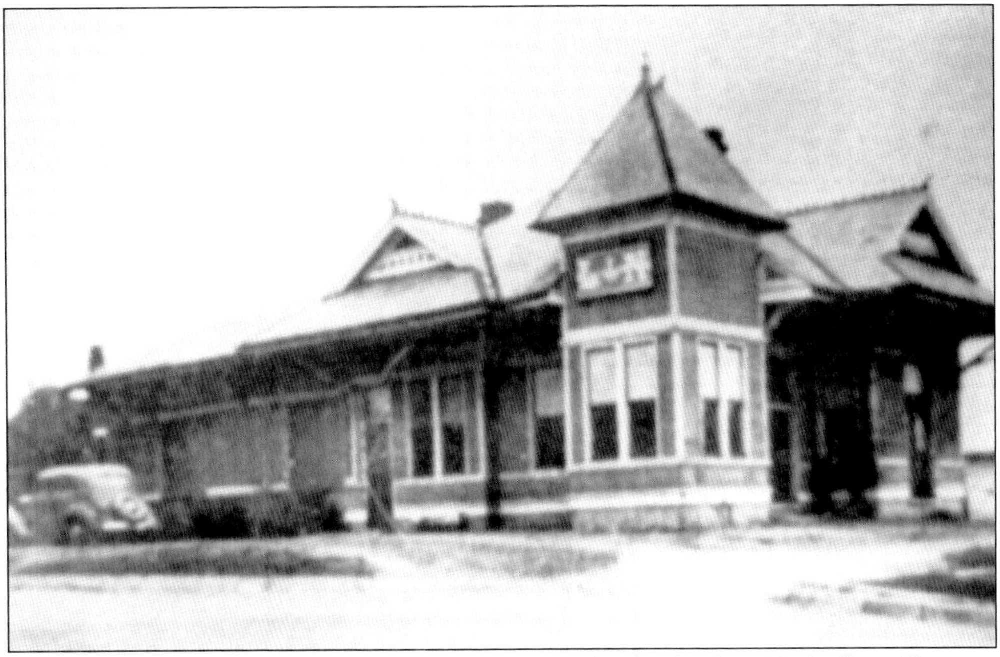

The Louisville & Nashville Railroad Company acquired rail rights from Nashville to Florence, Sheffield, and Tuscumbia. They built a station on the east side of Water Street, just a block south of the Colbert County Courthouse, with its main line in the center of Water Street. The railroad discontinued service, and the depot was torn down around 1955.

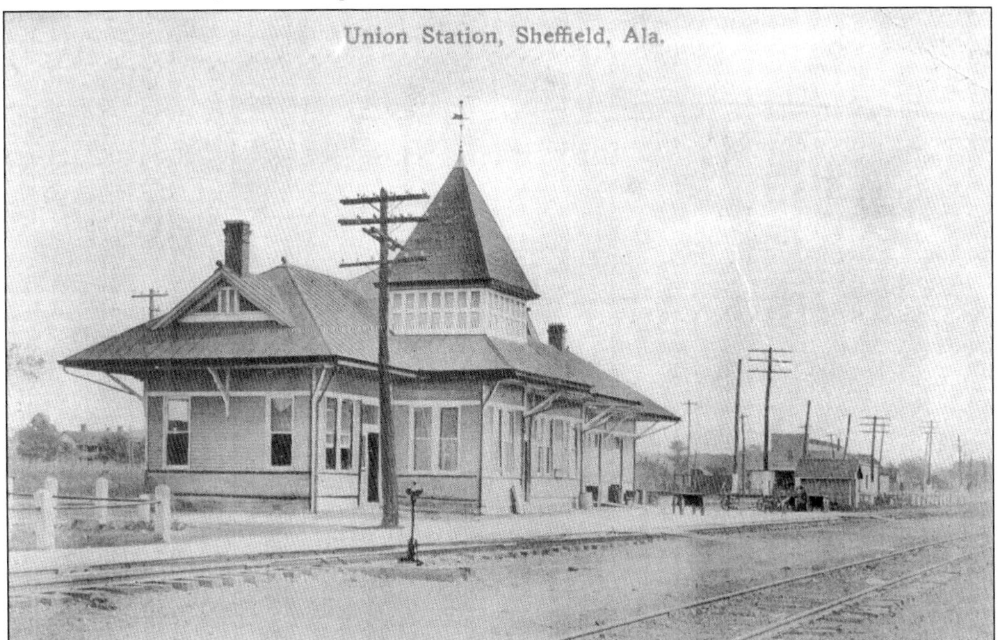

Sheffield became a major intersection of railroads. The Memphis & Charleston Railroad, Louisville & Nashville Railroad, Sheffield & Tuscumbia Street Railroad Company, and Northern Alabama Railroad needed a passenger depot. Union Station, pictured here, was built on First Street on the north side of the tracks, just west of Atlantic Avenue.

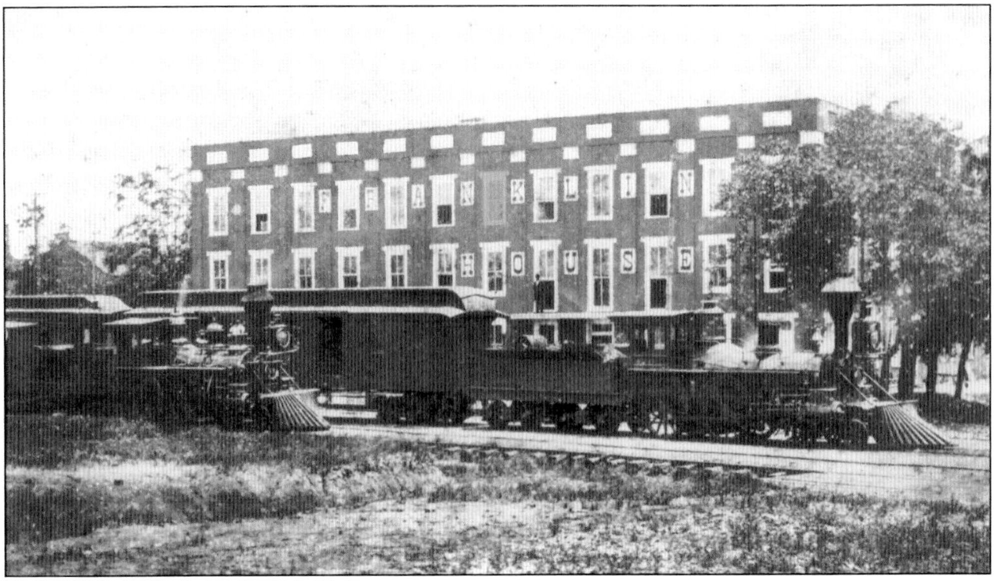

Early railroads in the area used hotels as their stations. The Franklin House was built by Robert Ransom in 1832 to be near the Tuscumbia Railroad Company and Tuscumbia, Courtland & Decatur Railroad Company. When the Memphis & Charleston Railroad Company purchased these railroads, the Franklin House became its station. Pictured are two trains headed west in front of the Franklin House.

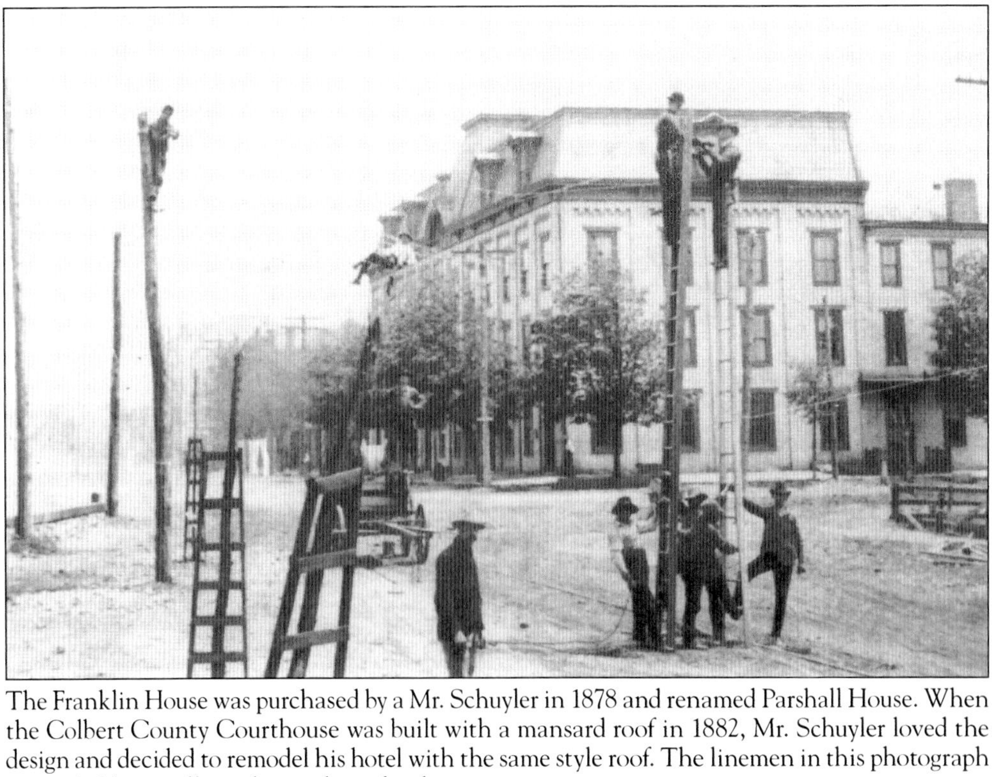

The Franklin House was purchased by a Mr. Schuyler in 1878 and renamed Parshall House. When the Colbert County Courthouse was built with a mansard roof in 1882, Mr. Schuyler loved the design and decided to remodel his hotel with the same style roof. The linemen in this photograph are probably installing electric lines for the streetcars.

The Parshall House was the center of Tuscumbia's night life for decades. The hotel had an icchouse, barbershop, bootblack's room, bathing room, livery, and a porter's lodge. The basement was used as a saloon and gambling center. An attached large dining room was used for many social events. The Parshall House burned on October 11, 1915.

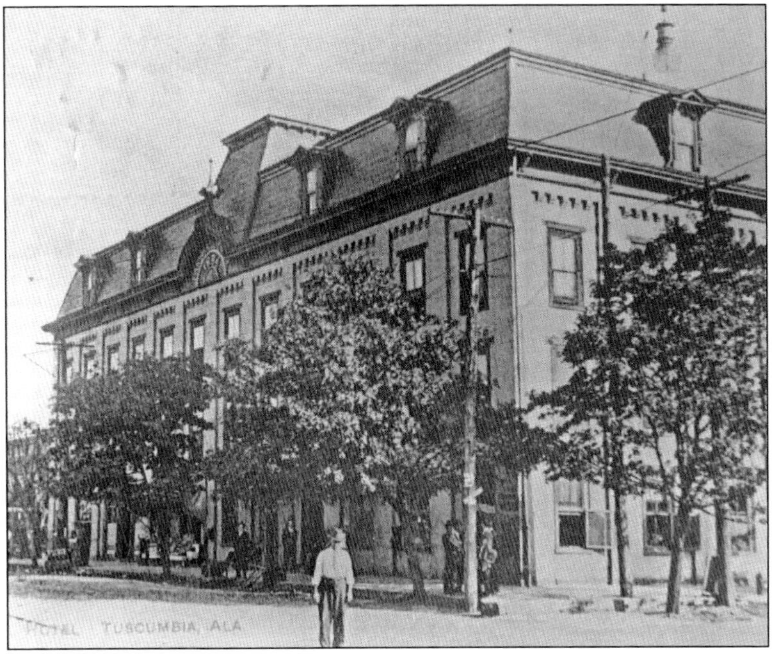

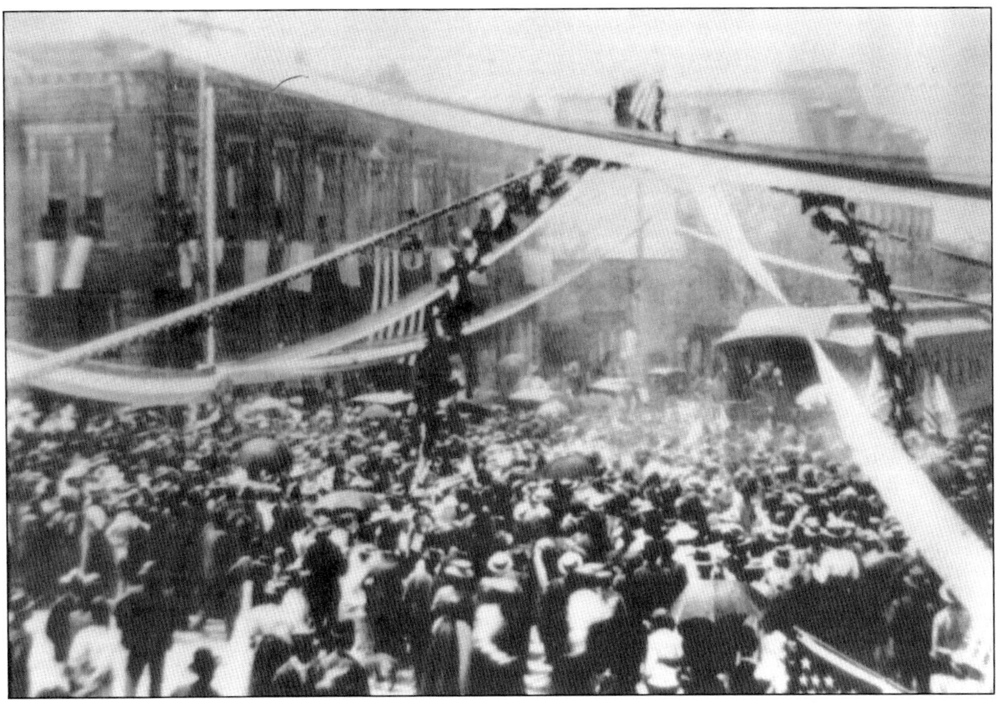

On May 1, 1901, Pres. William McKinley received a royal welcome to Tuscumbia. His seven-car train stopped on Fifth Street, with the rear car resting under a beautiful magnificent arch with flags and bunting displayed in profusion. The president received a rousing cheer when he appeared on the rear platform. Once the festivities were over, the train continued on its tour of the country.

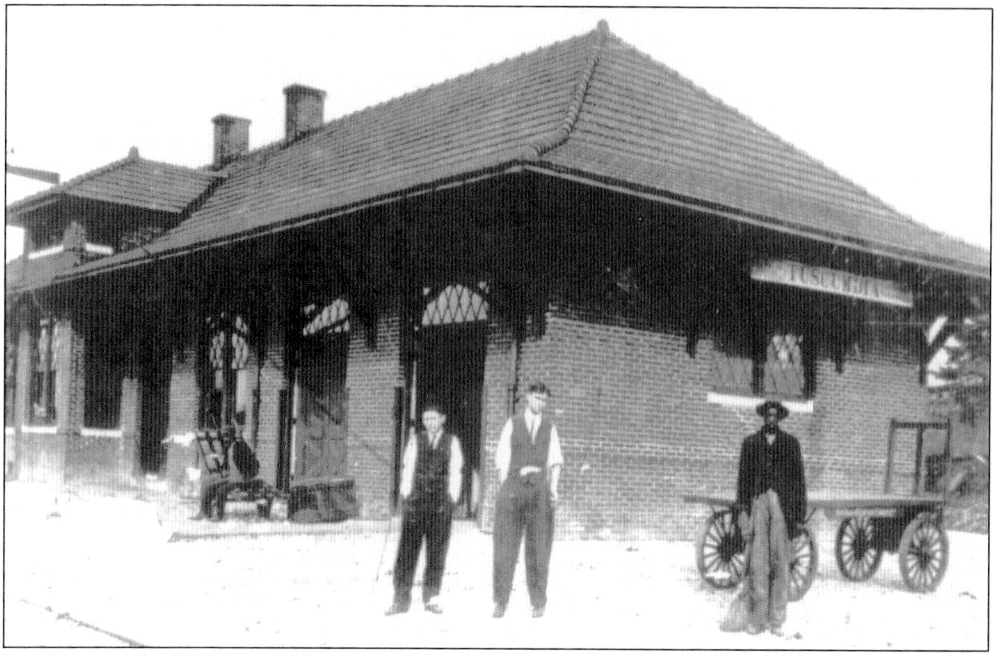

Southern Railway had a problem serving both Tuscumbia and Sheffield on the same main line. The decision was made to stop serving Tuscumbia at Fifth Street Depot and replace it with another station at the intersection of West First Street with the main line. This station became known by two names, First Street Station or New Station.

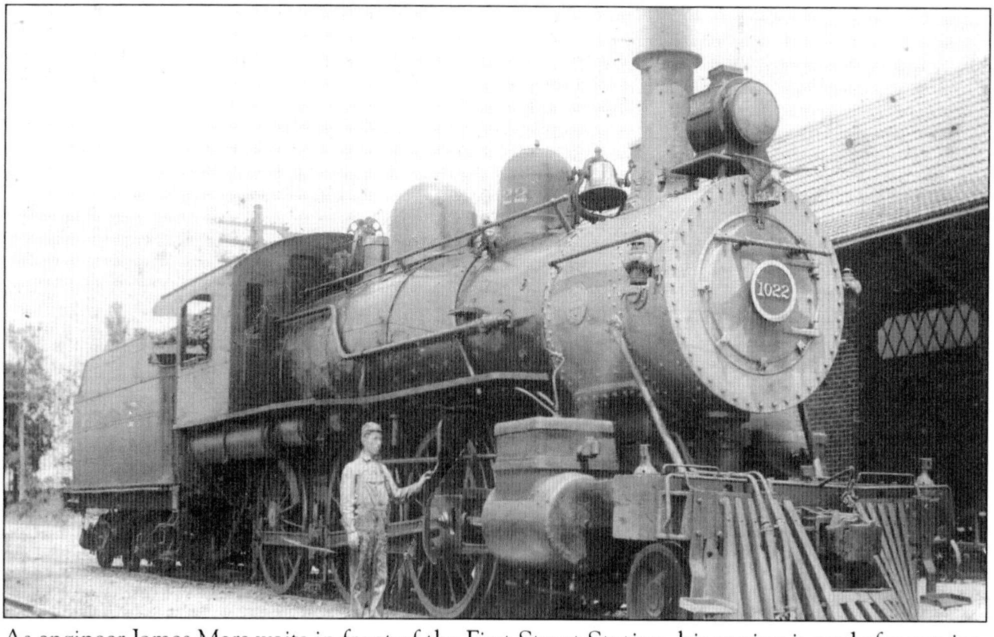

As engineer James Mars waits in front of the First Street Station, his engine is ready for service. When Southern Railway stopped service at the Fifth Street Station, Tuscumbia sued, claiming unfair treatment. Tuscumbia won. Southern Railway was forced to use both stations. The *Tennessean* stopped at First Street, while Nos. 35 and 36 used Fifth Street Station. The North Alabama Railway also stopped at Fifth Street Station.

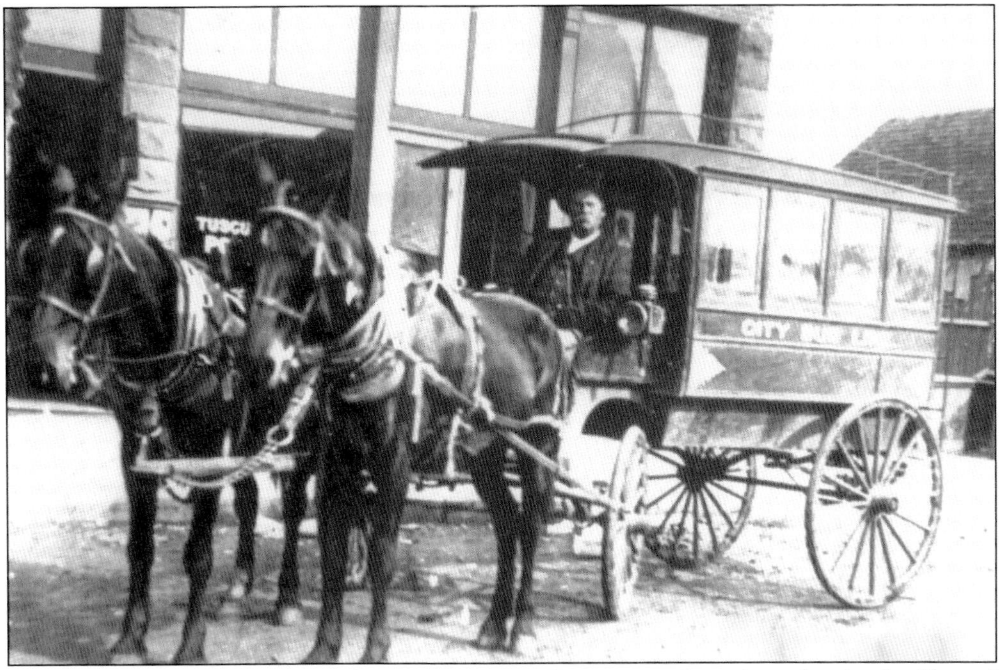

Tuscumbia refused to build a road to New Station. The streetcar line also refused to build a rail line to the station, arguing that it was cheaper for them for everyone to get off the train at Union Station in Sheffield and take the streetcar back to Tuscumbia. William F. McKinney saw a need and started the first cab company, meeting the trains at New Station. (Photograph courtesy of Jonathan Robert McKinney.)

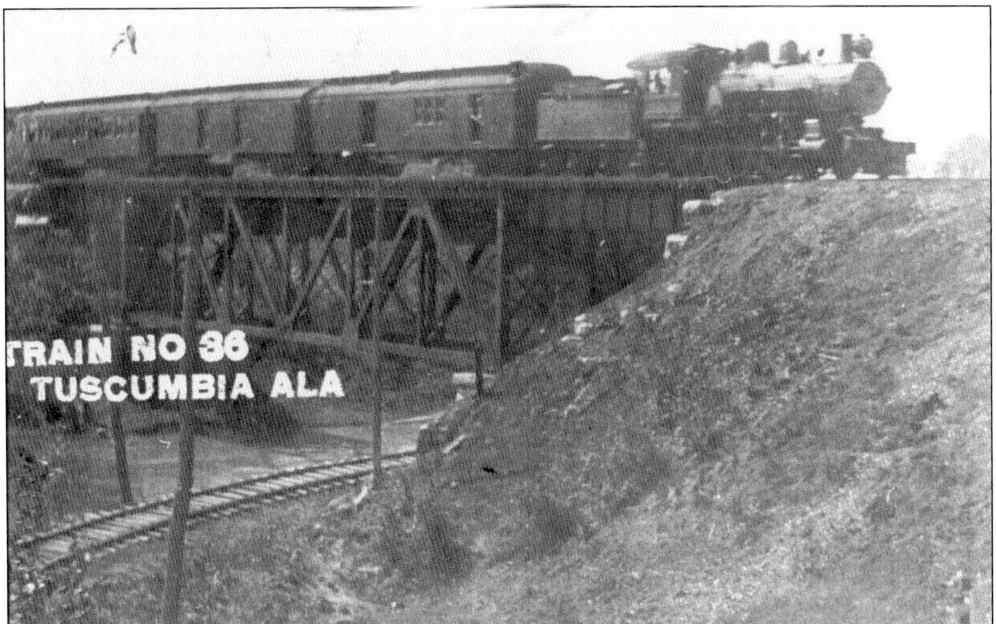

The numbering system for Southern Railway had all eastbound trains with even numbers and all westbound trains with odd numbers. Train No. 36 is seen crossing Spring Creek heading into Fifth Street Station. The tracks under the bridge running next to the creek are streetcar tracks.

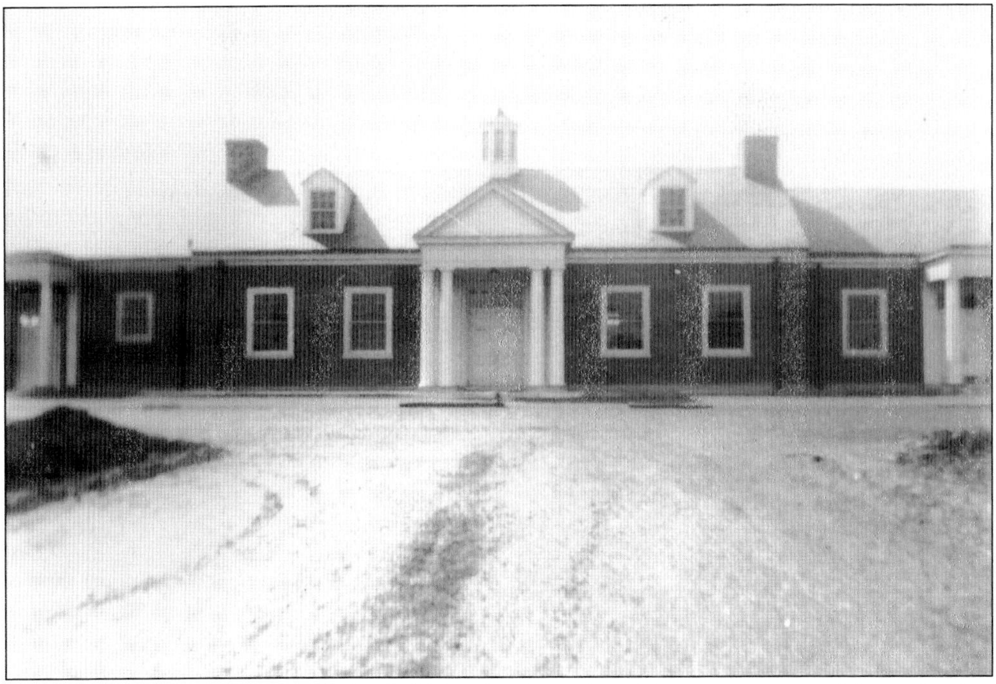

After World War II, the city of Sheffield fought the railroad for a new station. Union Station downtown had been constructed in 1899 and was not suitable for Sheffield's needs. The Southern Railway decided to build a new passenger station near old Loyall Yard between Tuscumbia and Sheffield. It was to serve the whole Shoals Area.

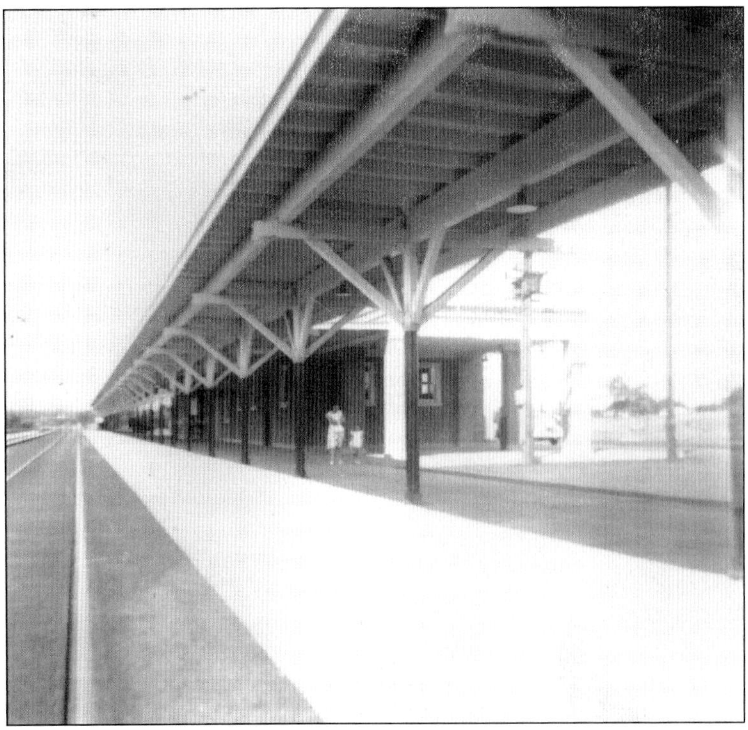

Work on the new station began in April 1947. The new station would replace Tuscumbia's Fifth and First Street Stations and also Union Station in Sheffield. Brice Construction Company completed the building in June 1948. At 1:00 p.m. on June 13, 1948, the last passenger train pulled into Tuscumbia. America's first frontier railroad no longer had rail passenger service.

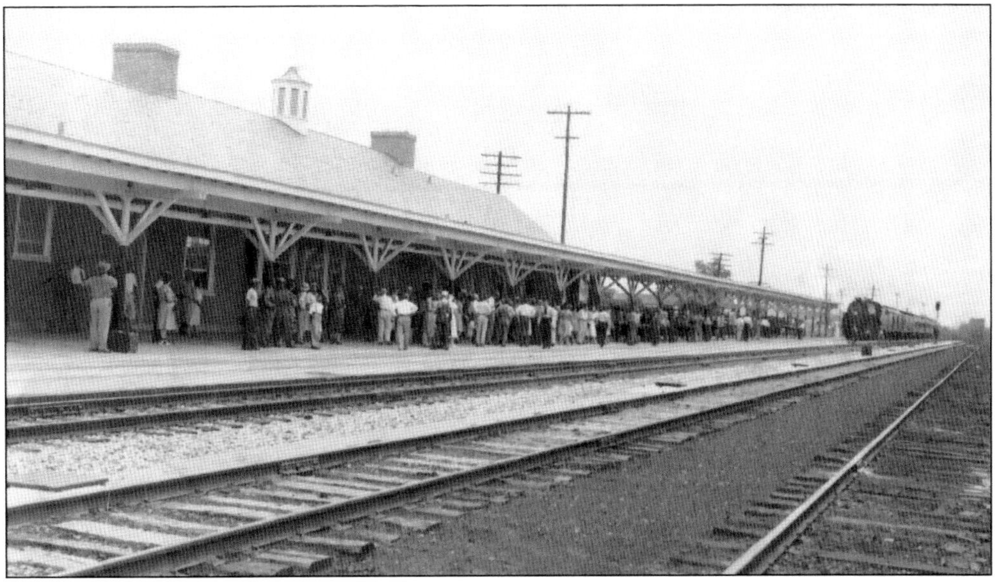

On June 15, 1948, train No. 36 with engine No. 6491 bypassed Tuscumbia and pulled into the new Muscle Shoals Station. The same crew that had left Tuscumbia's Fifth Street Station the day before was the first into the new station, conductor John Abbott, baggageman M.G. Lowery, flagman O.O. Osburn, fireman Percy Ricks, porter Will Martin, and engineer F.M. Fitzgerald.

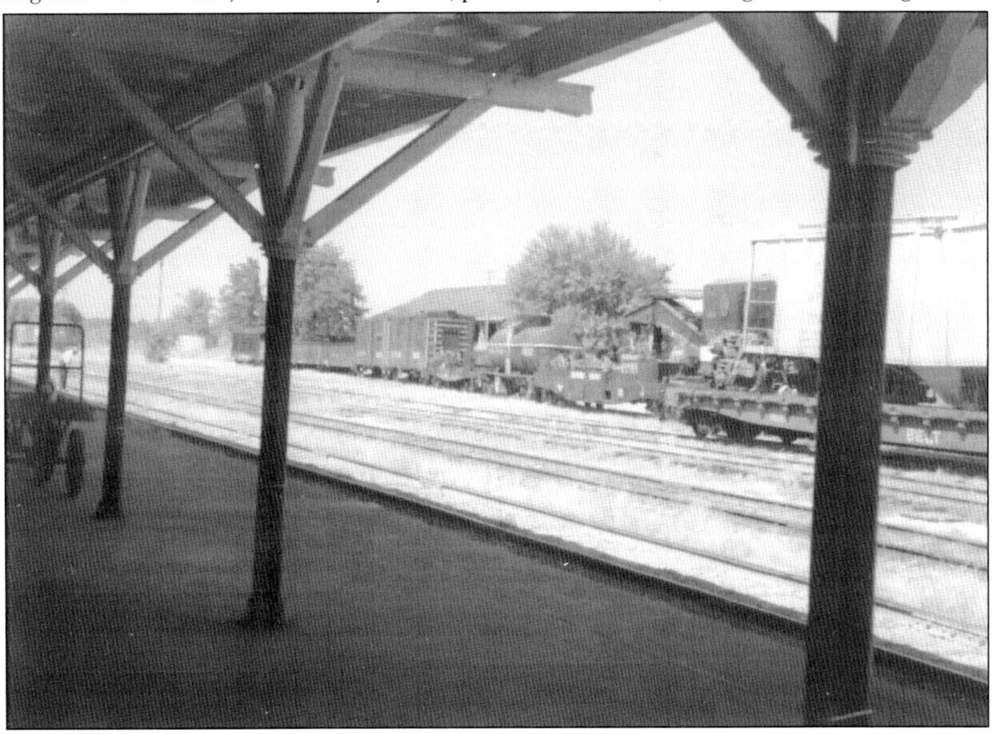

This is a view of old Loyall Yard from Muscle Shoals Station. Remnants of the old shops can be seen in the background. The old roundhouse was on the far side of the trees. The photograph shows the storage tracks used to store the derrick. The covered hopper car on the flatcar shows that the derrick had been used recently.

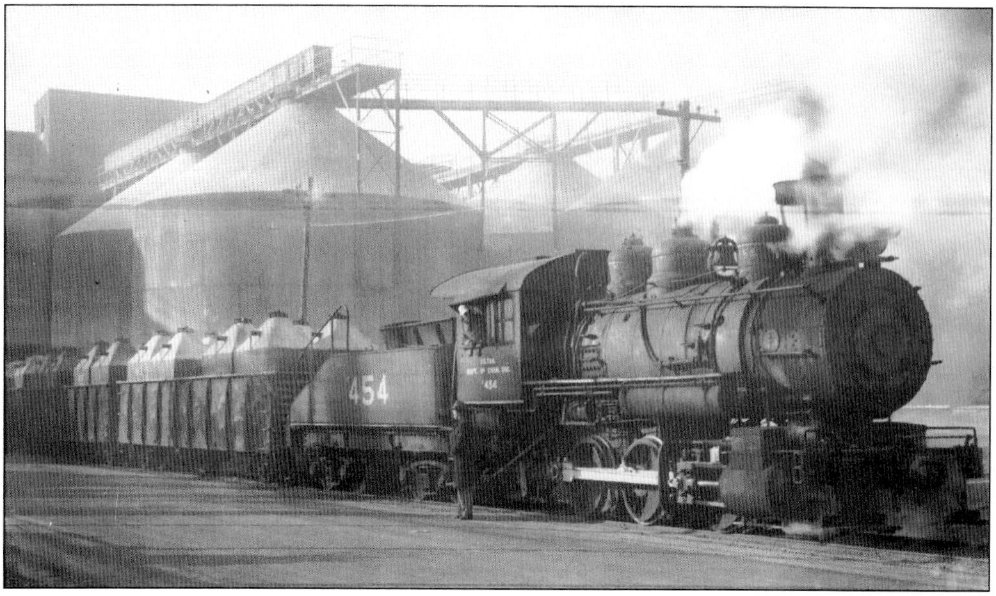

Steam locomotives moved all types of freight for decades. The introduction of diesel-electric locomotives changed things quickly. Pictured here is the last run for Tennessee Valley Authority steam power. Standing on the ground is Roy Marks, and in the locomotive is either Oakley Butler or Panama Bettingfield.

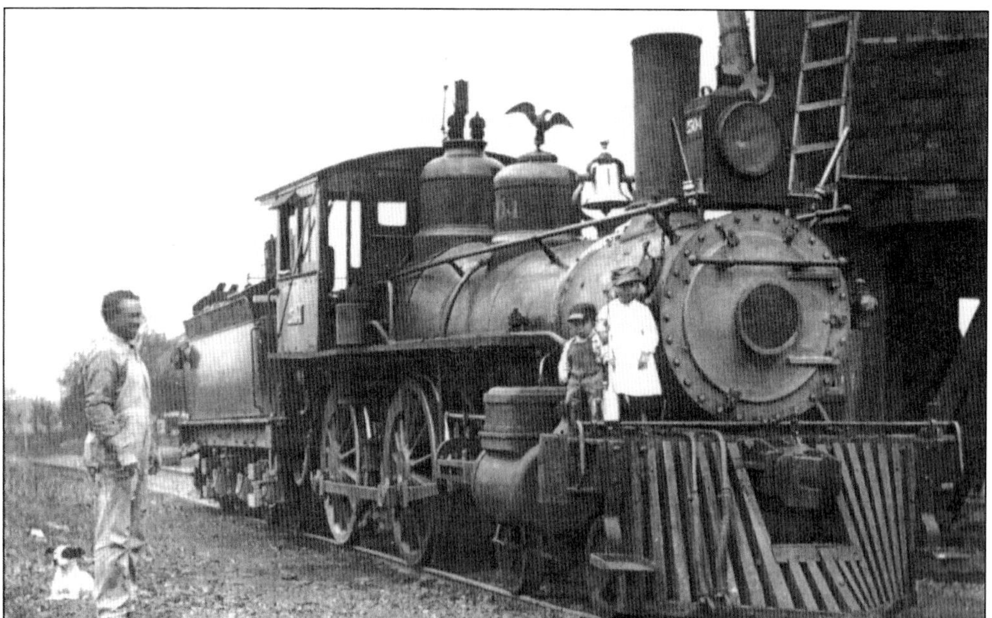

This 4-4-0 locomotive was used on the Riverton Branch. This short line ran from the Southern Railway System main line at Margerum, Alabama, to Riverton, Alabama, and back twice daily. Pictured are the engineer J.W. Edwards and his children J.W. Edwards Jr. and Lena Edwards.

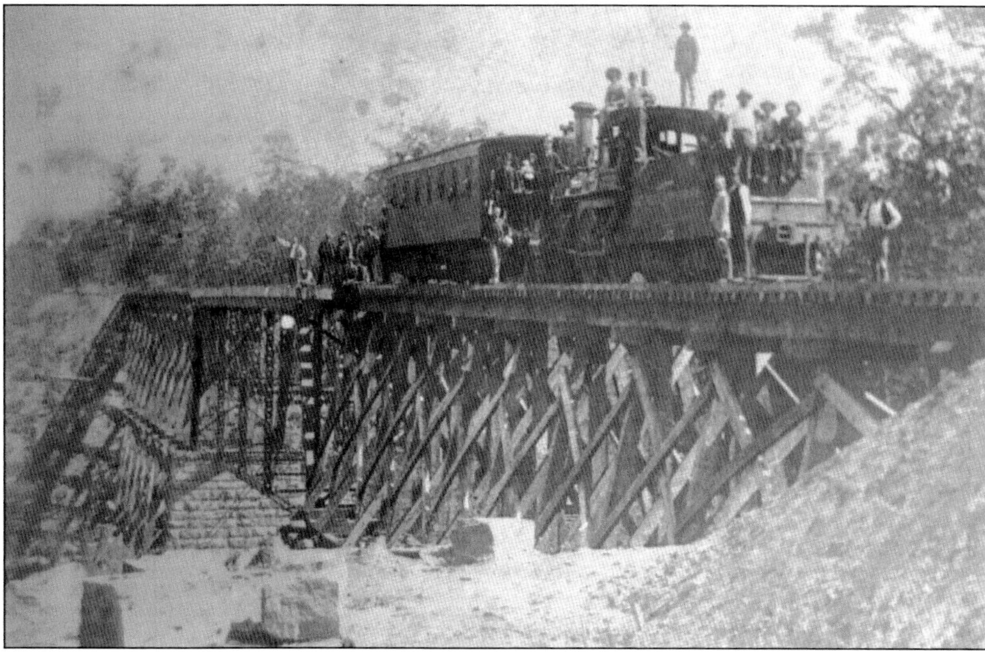

The Northern Alabama Railroad was built in the late 1800s and ran from Sheffield to Birmingham, Alabama, with stops in Tuscumbia. This is a picture of the proud crew after completion of this trestle at Bear Creek, Alabama. The Southern Railway System purchased the Northern Alabama; it is part of the Norfolk Southern Railway Company today.

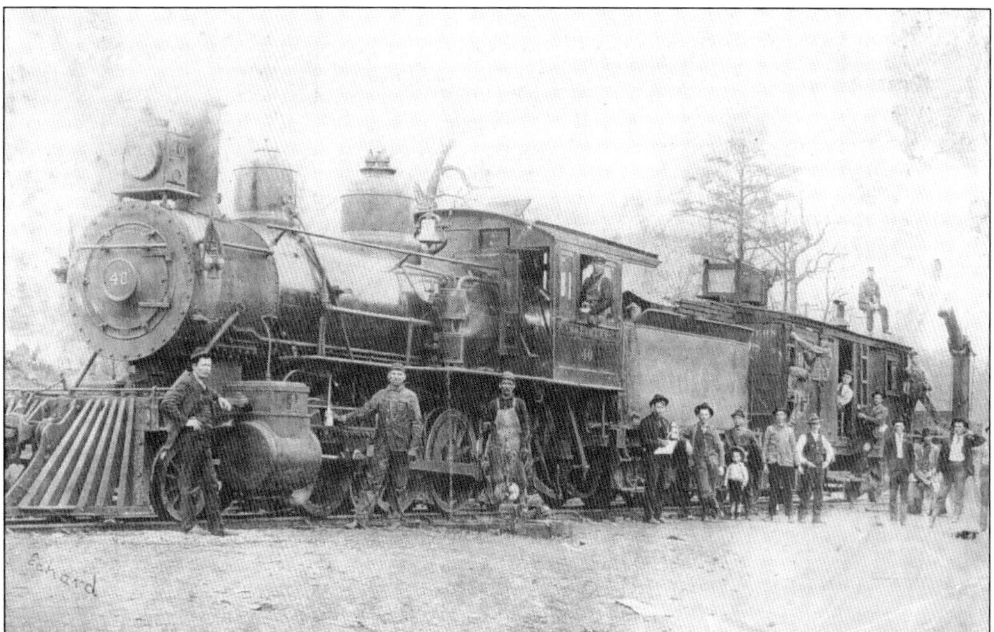

This is the train most loved by railroad employees, the pay train. In the early days of the Southern Railway System, this pay train would be met by Southern Railway employees dressed in their Sunday best. The pay train was regularly powered by engine No. 40. Notice the guards on top of the pay car.

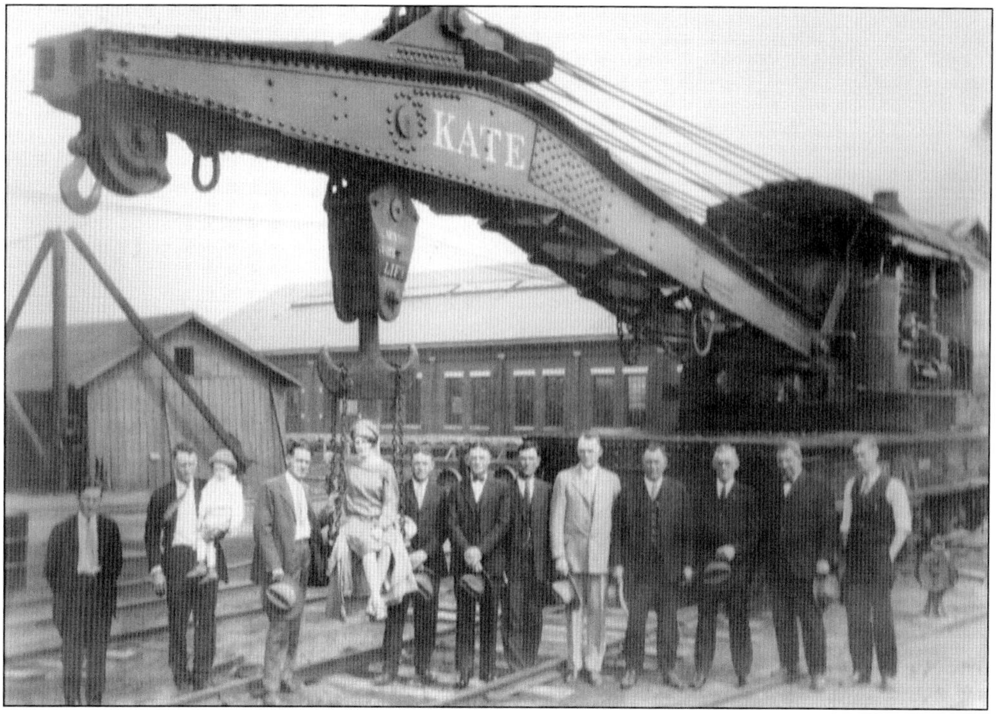

This is a 1927 photograph of Southern Railway's steam derrick. This "Big Hook" was named *Kate* in honor of Kate Beck, who is sitting on the hook. Pictured are, from left to right, Tommy Allen, Drew Fischer with son Lewis Fischer, Tom Beck, Jim Beck, Harvey Phillips, Joe Hewitt, Arthur Dillahunty, Tom Gary, C.F. Allen, Fred Wietzell, and Earnest Williams.

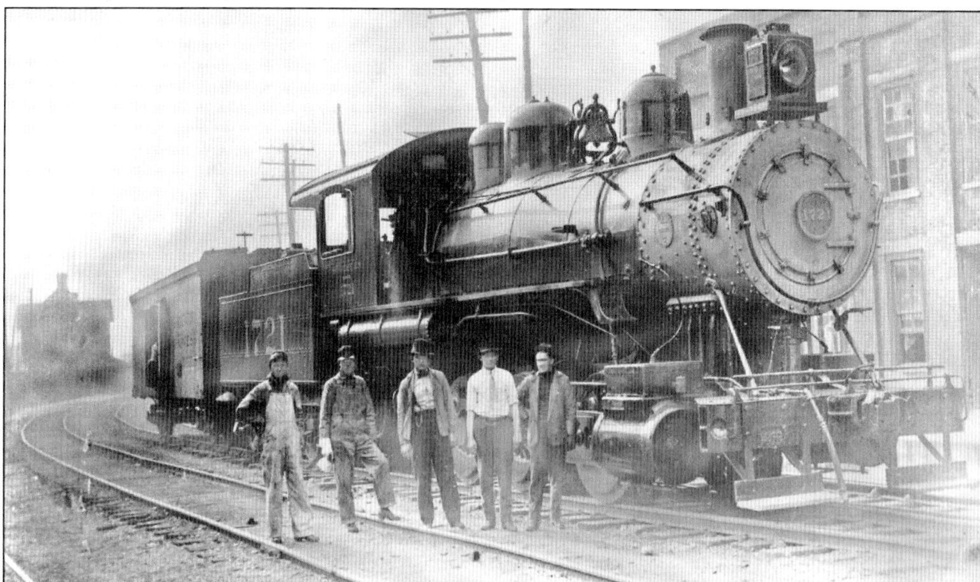

Switch engine No. 1721 is on the eastern end of Tuscumbia yard on Fifth Street. Commerical Row consists of the buildings to the right, and the Fifth Street Depot is in the left background. The crew is composed of, from left to right, engineer Ed Hamlet, fireman Arthur Jackson, foreman Will Mitchell, switchman J.D. Shelley, and switchman Noah Underwood.

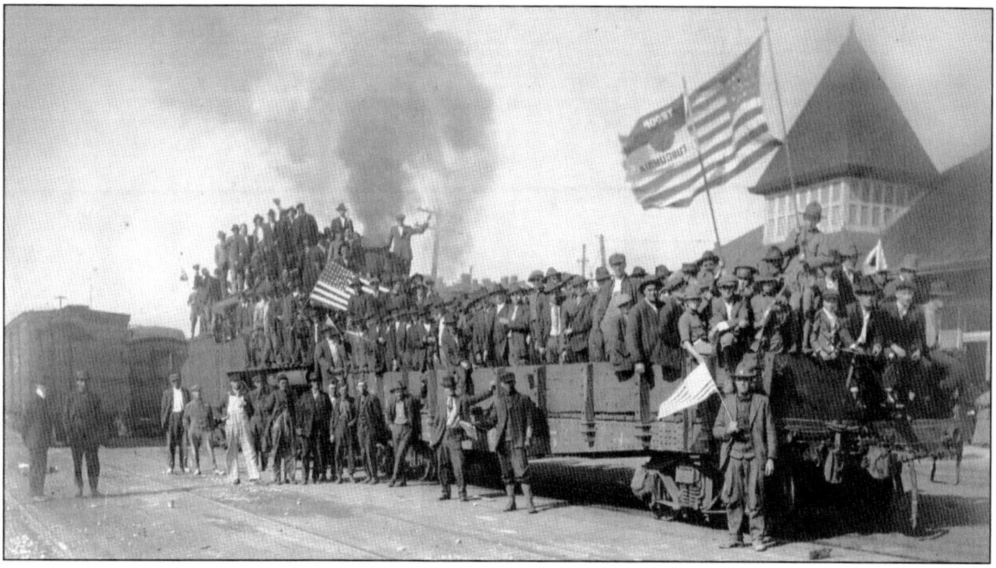

This photograph was taken in front of Union Station in Sheffield. The date and event are unknown. Judging by the stars on the flags, it was probably the late 1800s. This military unit is flying the Troop Tuscumbia flag. They may be soldiers from the Spanish-American War.

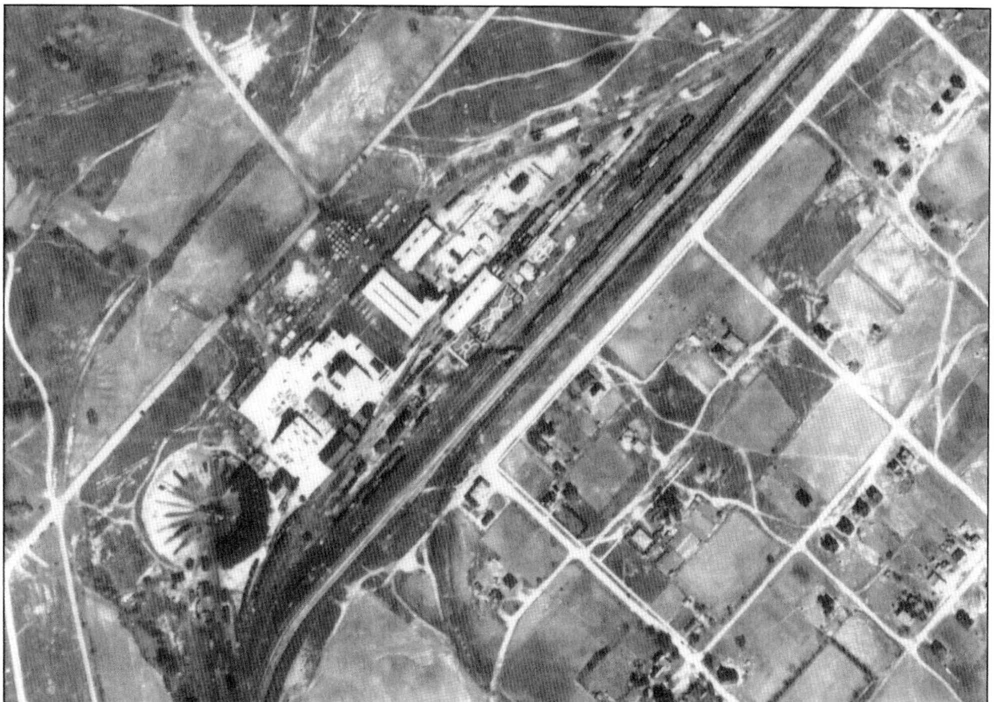

The Tuscumbia rail yard was quickly outgrown. The railroad looked at two spots for expansion. One was on the outskirts of Tuscumbia near Oakwood Cemetery. The other was just off the old Tuscumbia Railroad Company roadbed between Sheffield and Tuscumbia. The second was chosen. This is an aerial view of the complex in 1935. The major road running northeast and southwest is Shop Pike.

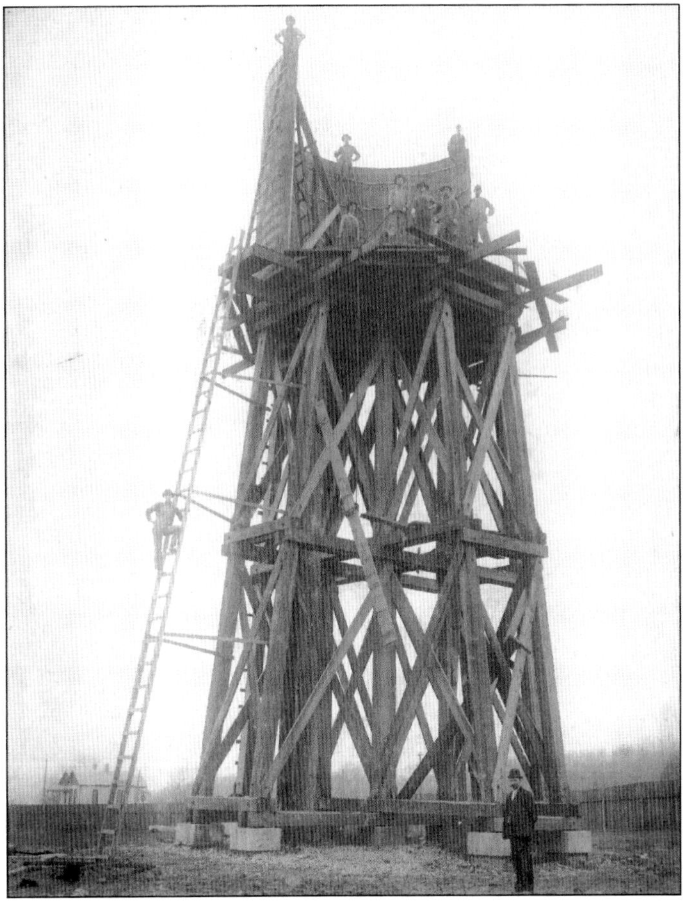

The expansion of the yard required more water for the steam engines. This photograph shows the construction of one of the water tanks. One of the tanks was located near the roundhouse, while another was at the east end of Loyall Yard.

The addition of the Loyall Yard and shops made Southern Railway a major employer. In 1913, the railroad hired some new apprentices. They included Ike Ikard, David Staples, Bill DeVaney, J. Douthit, Charles Manush, Bernard Rogenbuck, and Arthur Bradley.

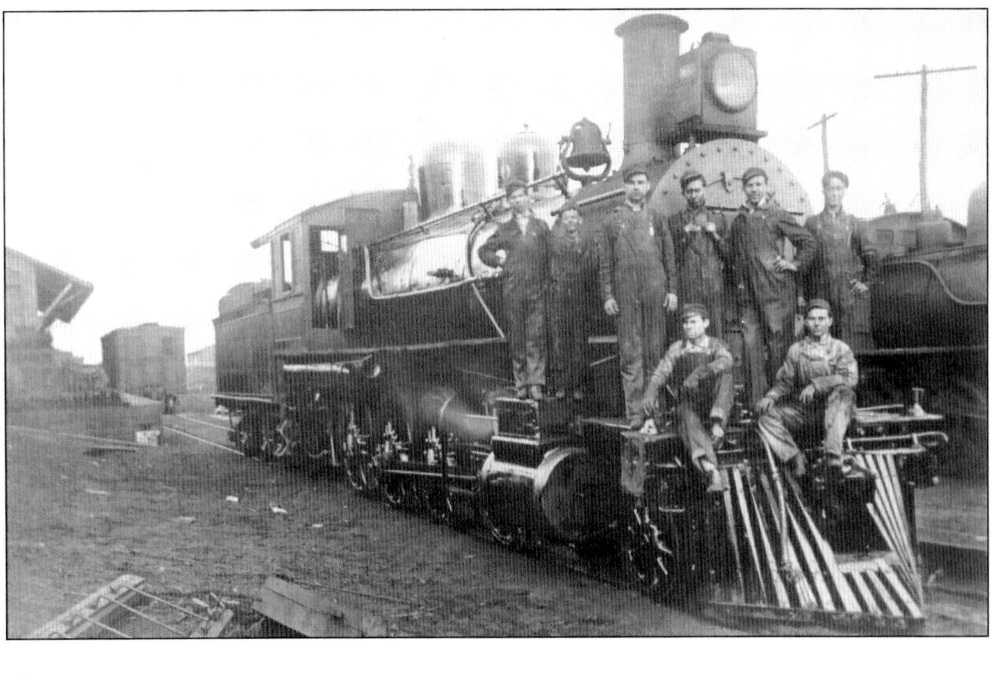

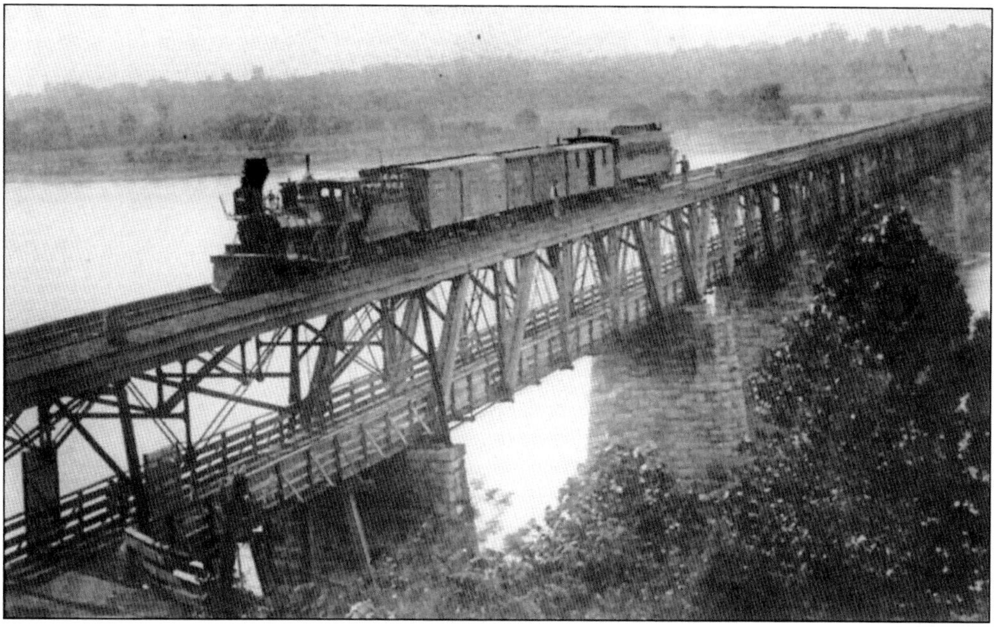

Written into the charter of the Memphis & Charleston Railroad Company by the state of Alabama was the requirement to build a branch line to Florence, Alabama. This required a bridge to be constructed across the Tennessee River. The bridge was completed just before the outbreak of the Civil War, only to be burned during the war. This is a Memphis & Charleston Railroad train crossing the river in the direction of Tuscumbia.

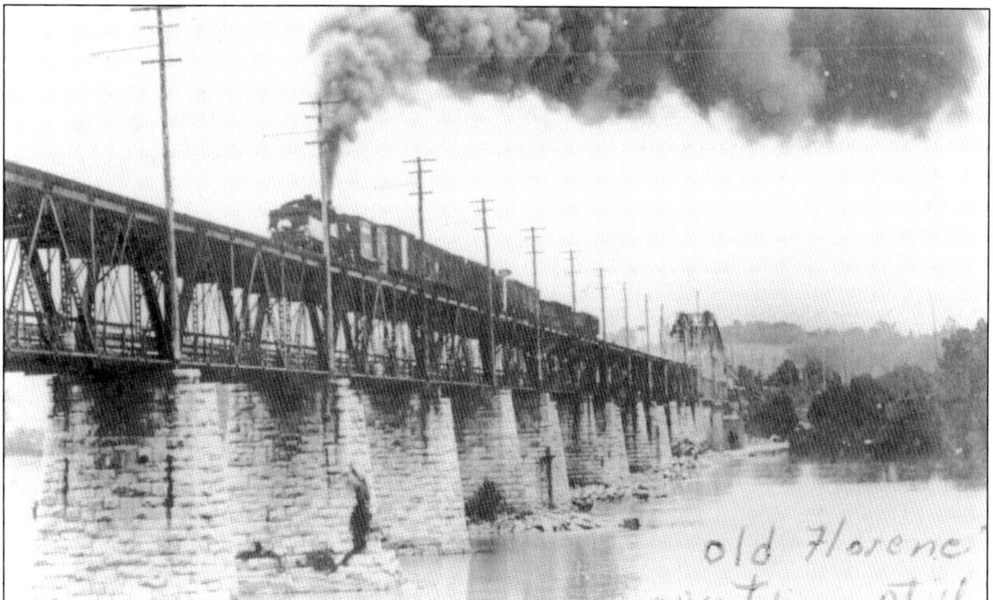

In 1870, the Memphis & Charleston Railroad rebuilt the Florence Bridge. The wooden structure was designed to carry 20,000 pounds. On May 6, 1892, a heavy freight train left Tuscumbia and completed some switching in Sheffield. On its way to Florence, five cars with the engine and tender fell into the river when the bridge collapsed. In 1893, the bridge was replaced with this steel structure.

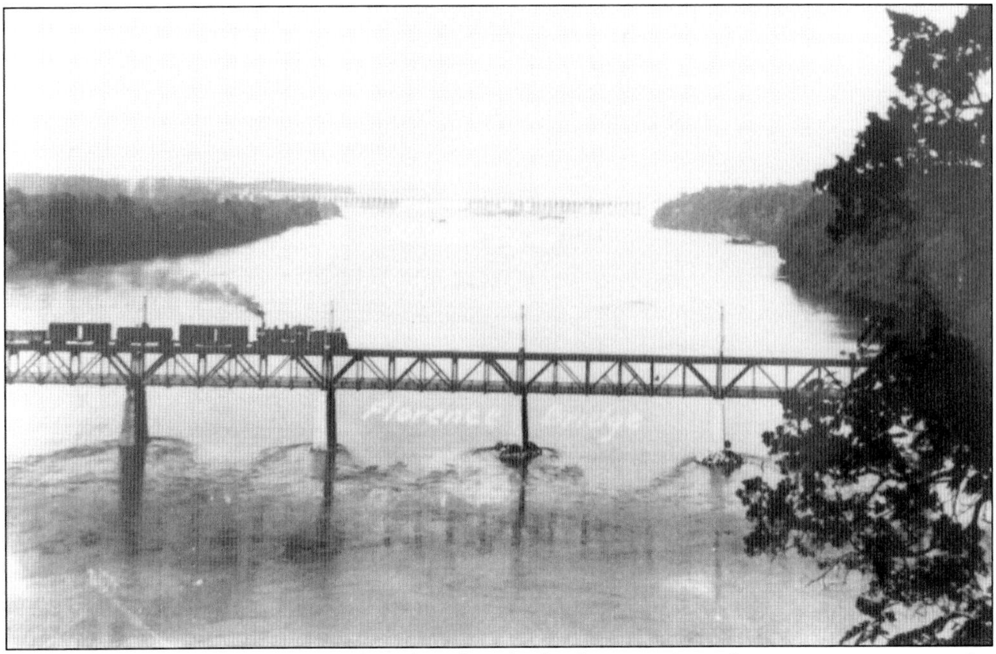

The Florence Bridge, as local people referred to the bridge, was the only structure spanning the Tennessee River in the Shoals for years. The Memphis & Charleston Railroad (Southern Railway System), Louisville & Nashville Railroad, and the streetcars crossed the river on the top portion of the bridge. The lower passageway was designed for wagons or automobiles. Wilson Dam is in the background and became the second river crossing.

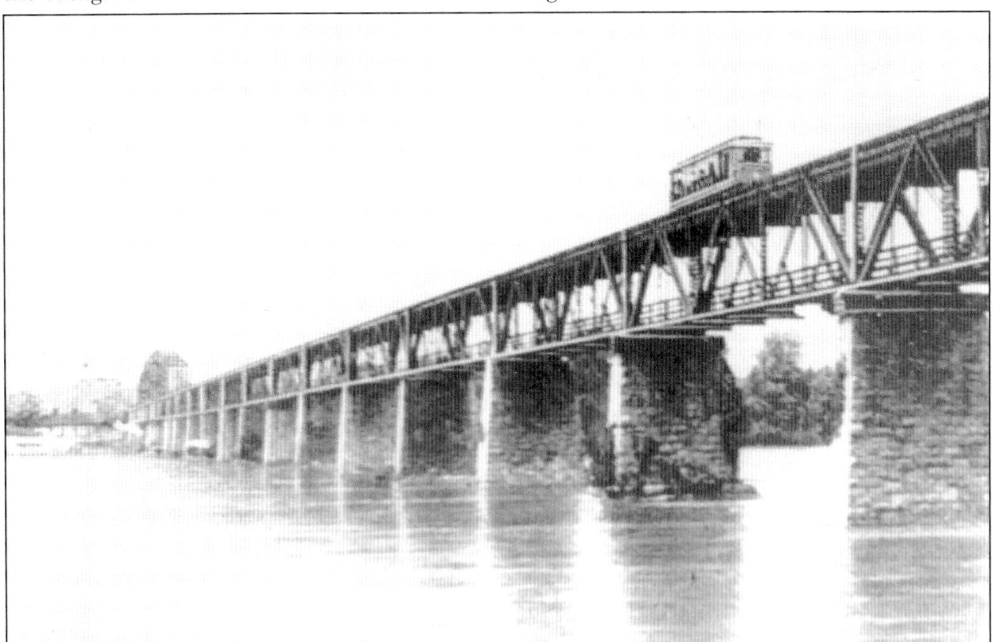

This streetcar is crossing the Florence Bridge between Sheffield/Tuscumbia and Florence. The streetcar was an open side car with nothing to protect the passengers from falling into the river below. Traveling in the car could be an experience, especially if there was a storm.

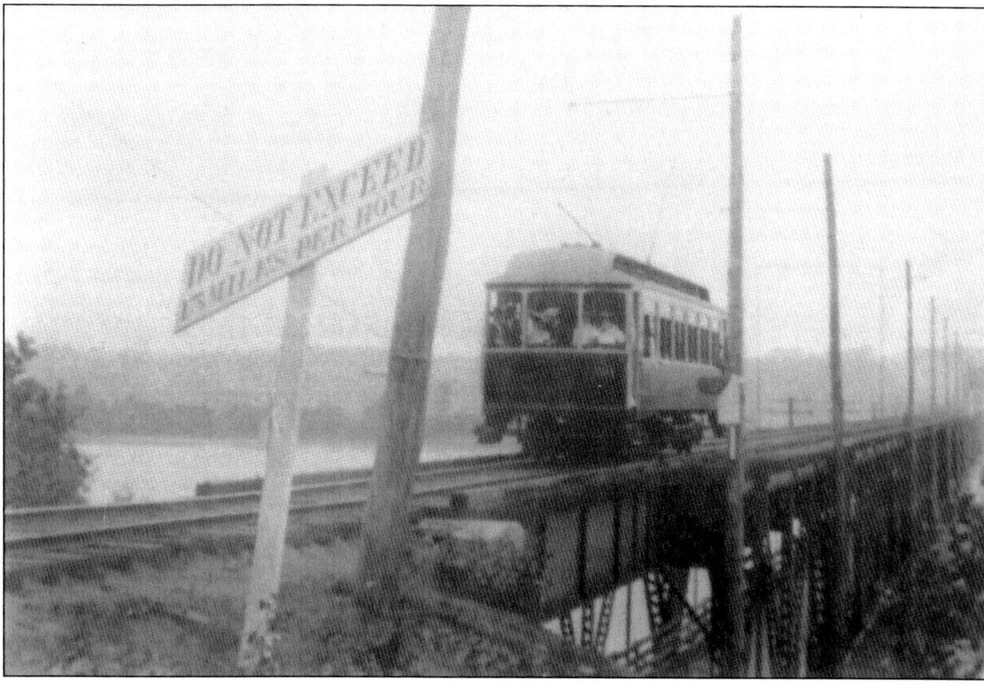

Most people who crossed the river by streetcar preferred to ride in this completely enclosed car. The overhead electric power grid can be seen in this picture; the support poles are on the right. With Florence in the background, the car is approaching the south side of the bridge.

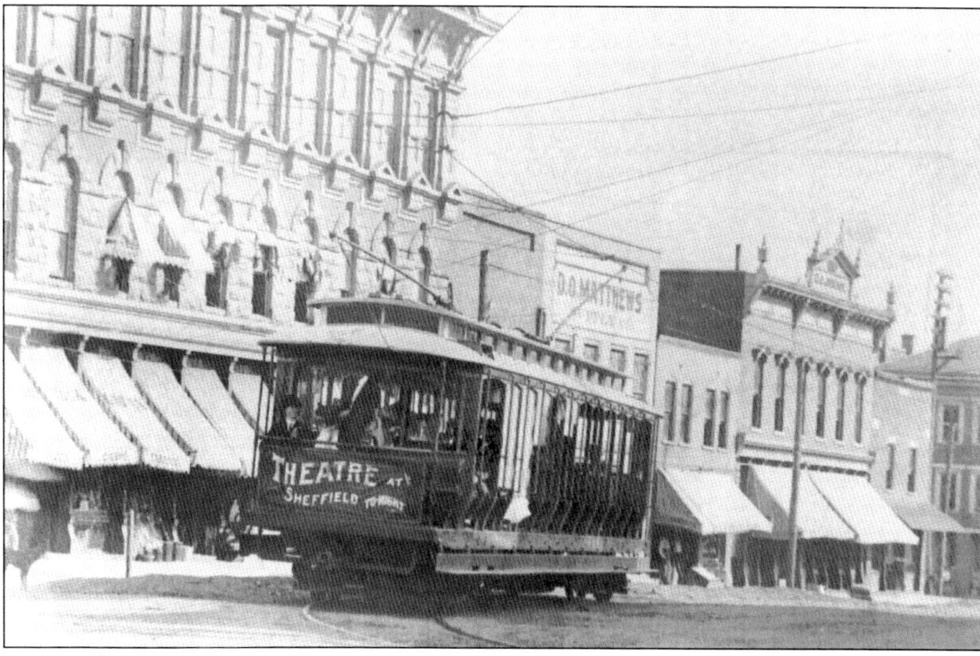

In 1902, the planning of an electric streetcar system connecting Florence, Sheffield, and Tuscumbia began. The Sheffield Railway Corporation was formed in 1903 to construct, maintain, and operate the streetcar system by George Parsons of Maine, Henry Parsons of New York, and J.W. Worthington of Sheffield.

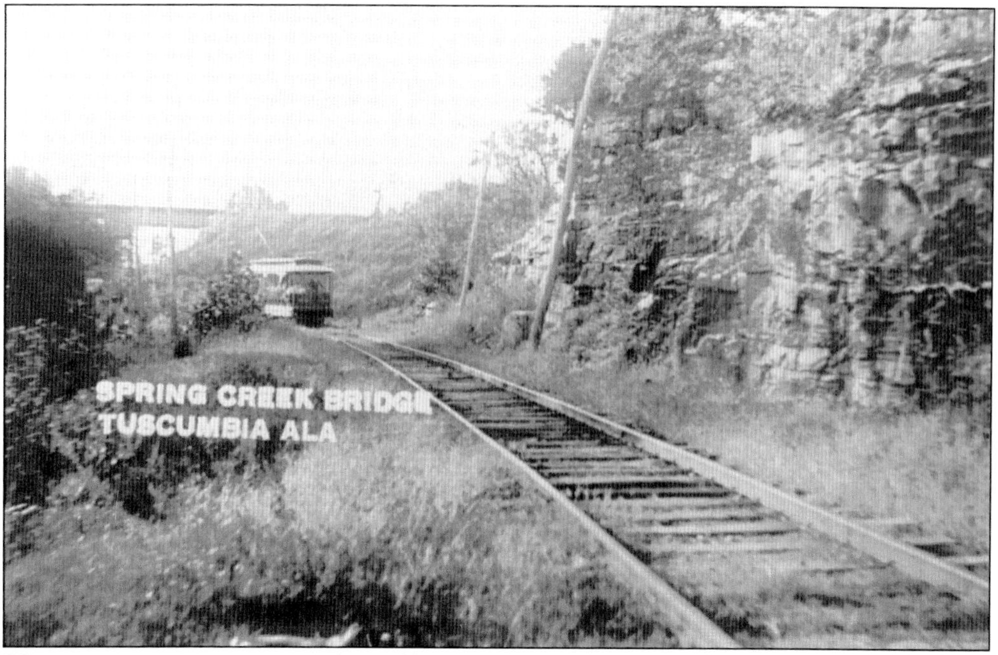

The streetcar system was most welcomed by workers who traveled to their jobs daily at the furnaces in Sheffield and Southern Railway System shops. The streetcar in this picture has just left the Southern Railway shops and is passing under the railroad trestle spanning Spring Creek. The next stop is Tuscumbia.

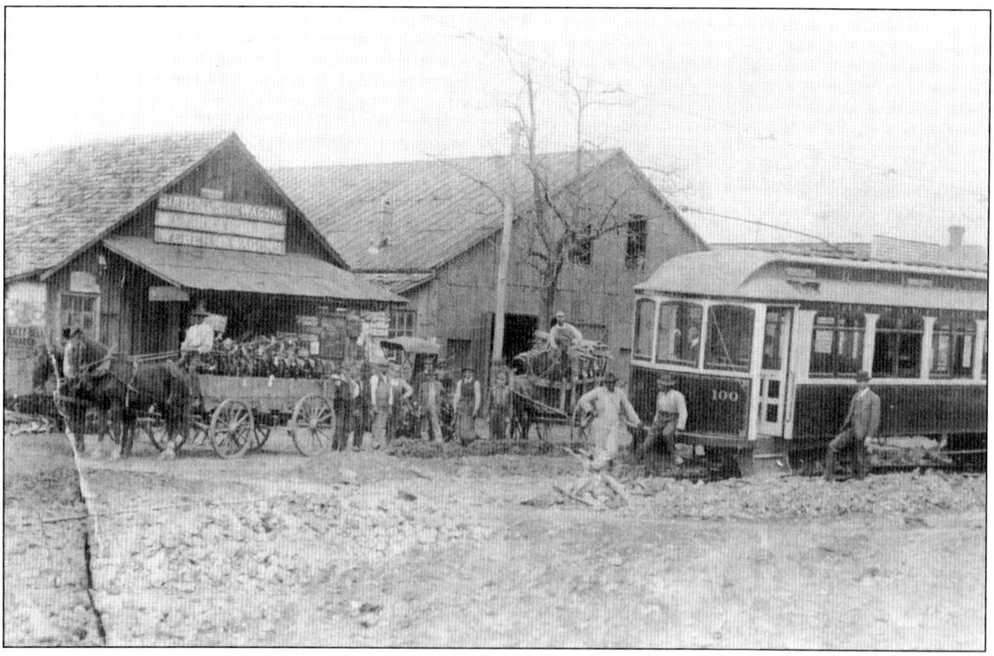

The initial trips were welcomed by large crowds along the streets, creating a festive atmosphere. This car is stopped on Water Street near the corner of Sixth Street. Barton Agricultural Works, operated by T.T. Rowland, is in the background. John T. Chidester had his stage line here but moved his business to Arkansas, where it became part of the Overland Stage Company.

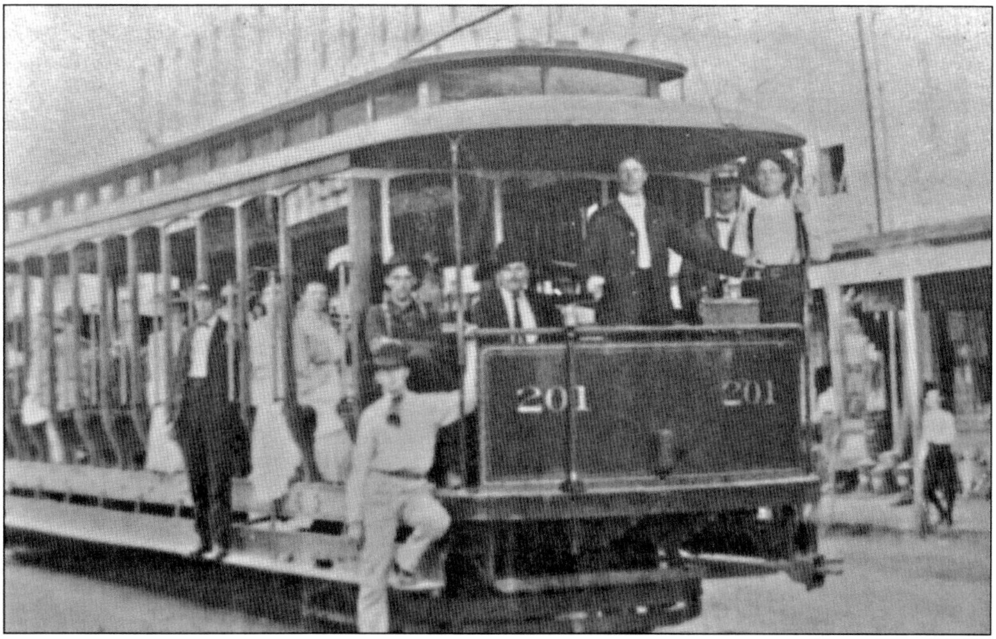

This streetcar is traveling south on Main Street with the Kirk Isbell and Bickley Buildings in the background. The streetcars made a loop around the city block between Main and Water Streets and Fifth and Sixth Streets. The streetcars operated for 28 years. At midnight on February 3, 1933, Alabama Power Company, which had purchased the line from Sheffield Railway Company, ceased operations.

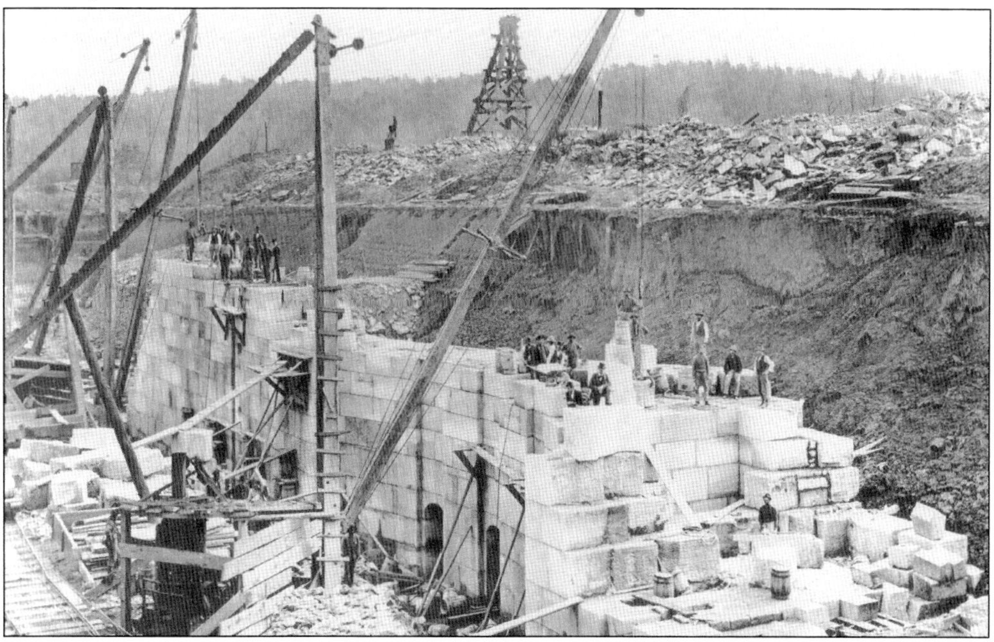

The largest problems for river traffic reaching Tuscumbia Landing and Florence Landing were Bee Tree Shoals and the larger Colbert Shoals near the Riverton and Waterloo area. These could stop river traffic during times of low water. In 1893, construction of a canal with lift spans was started to allow boats to cross over Colbert Shoals in low water.

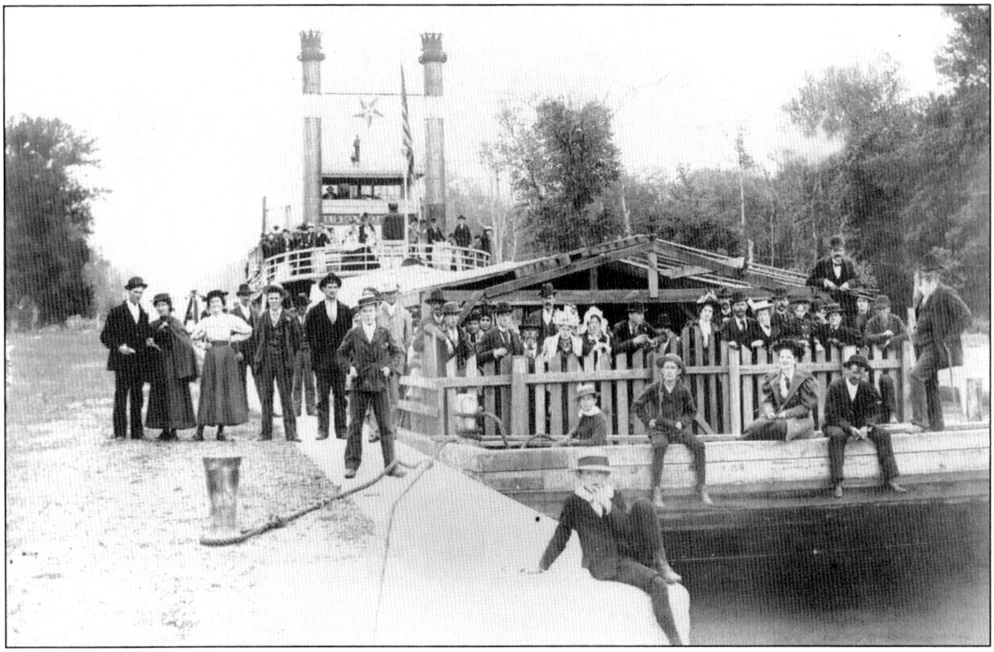

This canal at Riverton was finished in 1911. The first boat went through with great fanfare, and the Tennessee River was open to the Tri-Cities. The canal was used until Wheeler Dam was built. The construction of Wheeler Dam, part of the Tennessee Valley Project, not only flooded the canal but also the town of Riverton.

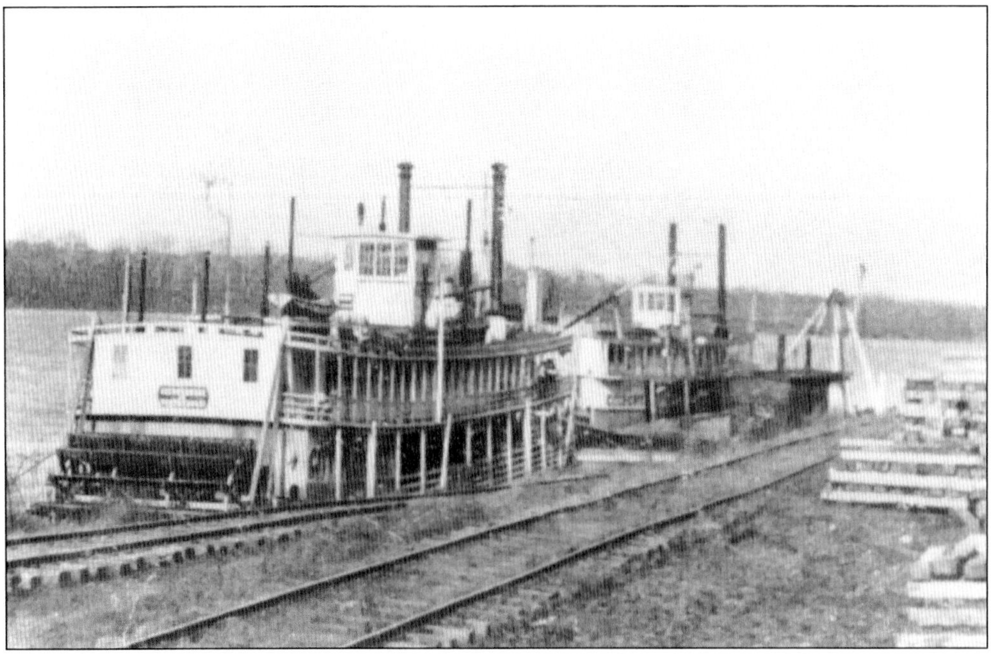

Tuscumbia Landing, located at the mouth of Spring Creek, only operated for about 30 years before being destroyed by Federal troops during the Civil War. The landing was never rebuilt. A new landing, pictured here, was built upstream near where Riverfront Park in Sheffield is located today.

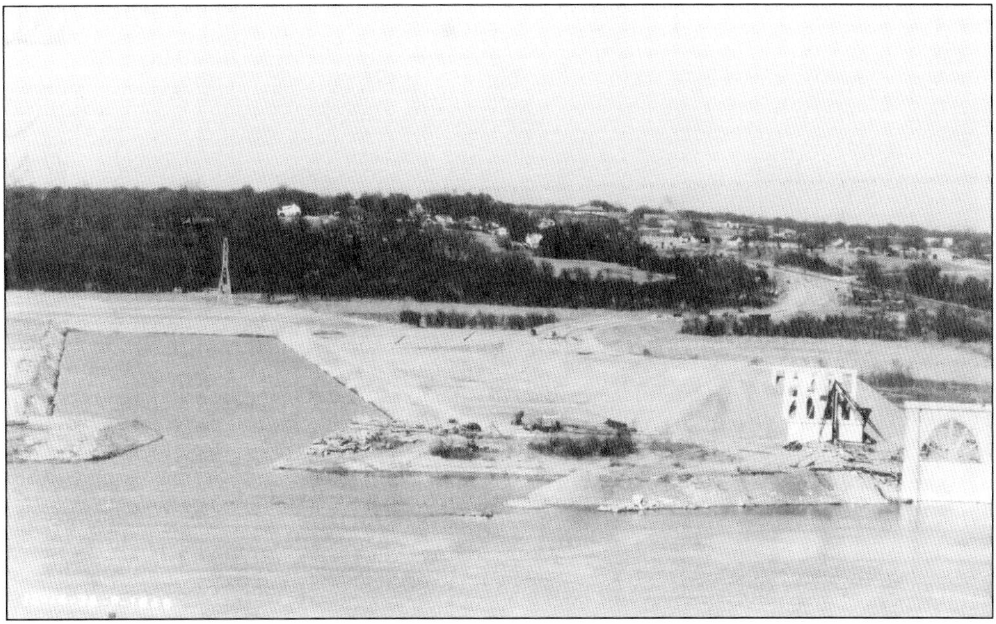

The Shoals Area grew, and the railroad bridge was unable to handle the automobile and truck traffic. The construction of a new bridge across the Tennessee River began in 1938. Soil removal to build the highway ramp created a harbor just west of the bridge. The beginnings of O'Neal harbor are visible in this picture.

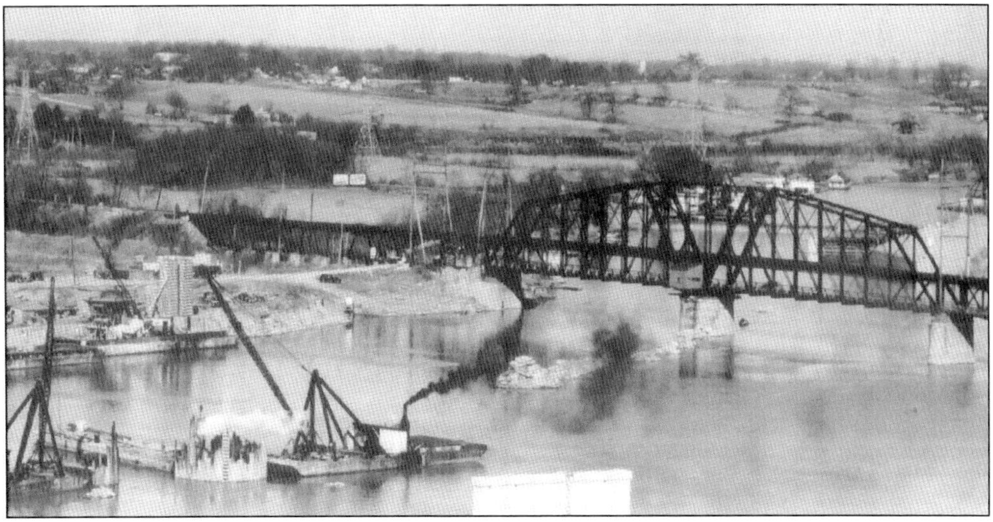

The construction of the piers supporting the new bridge over the Tennessee River is seen here. O'Neal Bridge opened on October 26, 1939, as a toll bridge. It was only a toll bridge for a short period. The last toll was paid on January 7, 1941.

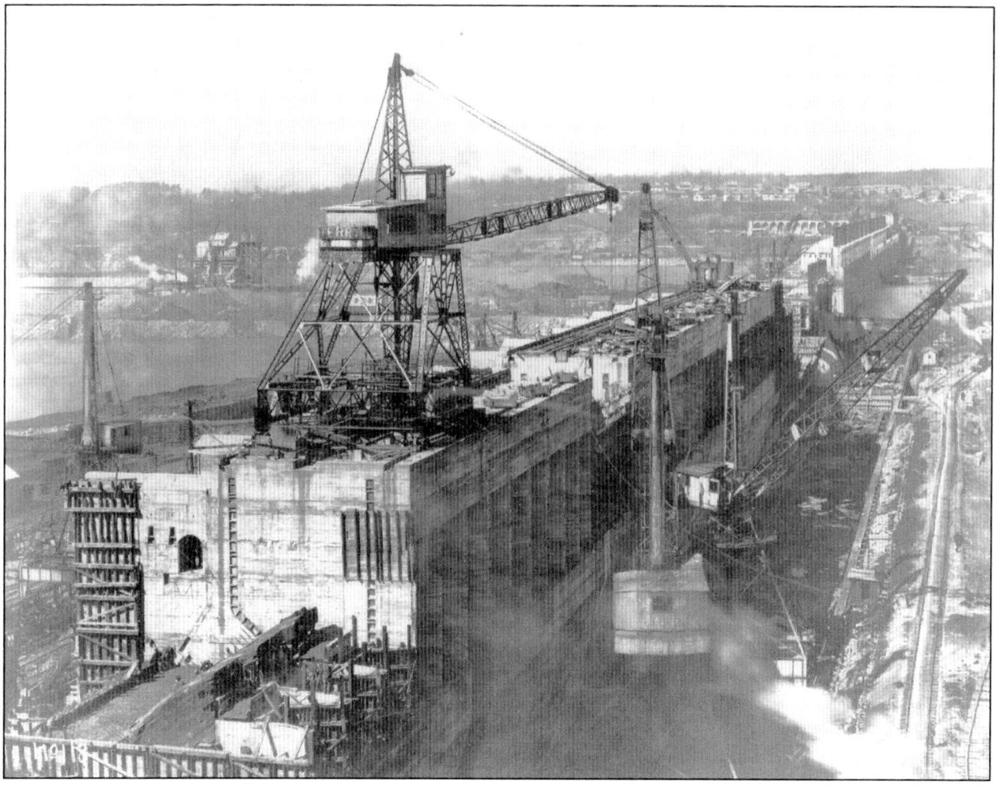

The fear of the possible loss of nitrates if the United States became involved in World War I led the government to authorize construction of two nitrate plants, two coal-fired steam plants, and one hydroelectric plant. Wilson Dam was started in 1918. This is a rarely seen view of the back water side of Wilson Dam in 1923.

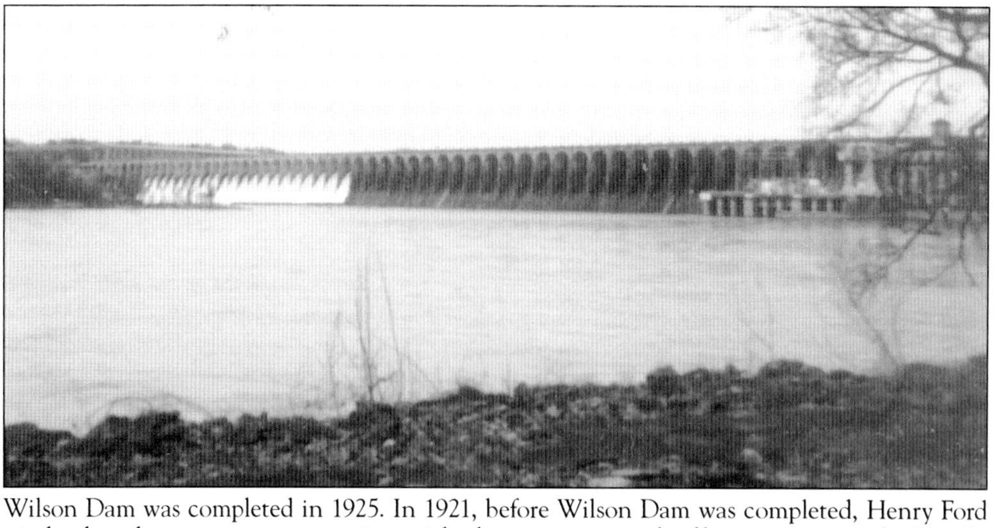

Wilson Dam was completed in 1925. In 1921, before Wilson Dam was completed, Henry Ford tried to buy the government operations with plans to move much of his operation to the Shoals. Causing some uproar in Washington, DC, Ford withdrew his offer three years later. When the government formed the Tennessee Valley Authority, the nitrate plants, steam plants, and dam became a major part.

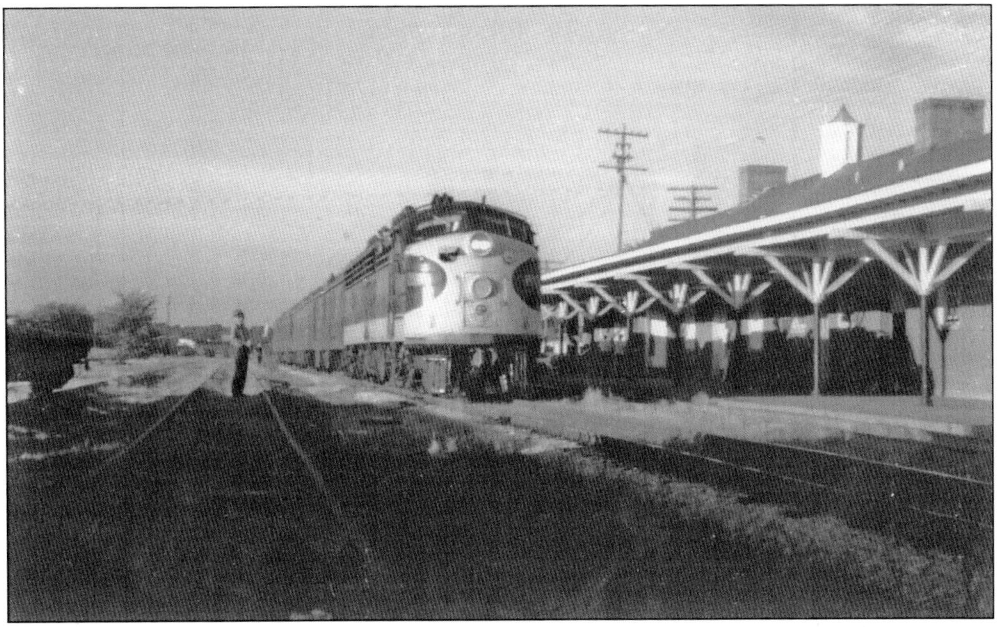

This is train No. 35 sitting at the Muscle Shoals Station in Sheffield. This is the passenger design diesel-electric E series locomotive that would replace steam locomotives. Passenger trains were the first to go to diesel-electric power. The clean operation of diesel-electric locomotives made it unnecessary for passenger trains to change to electric engines before entering highly populated areas.

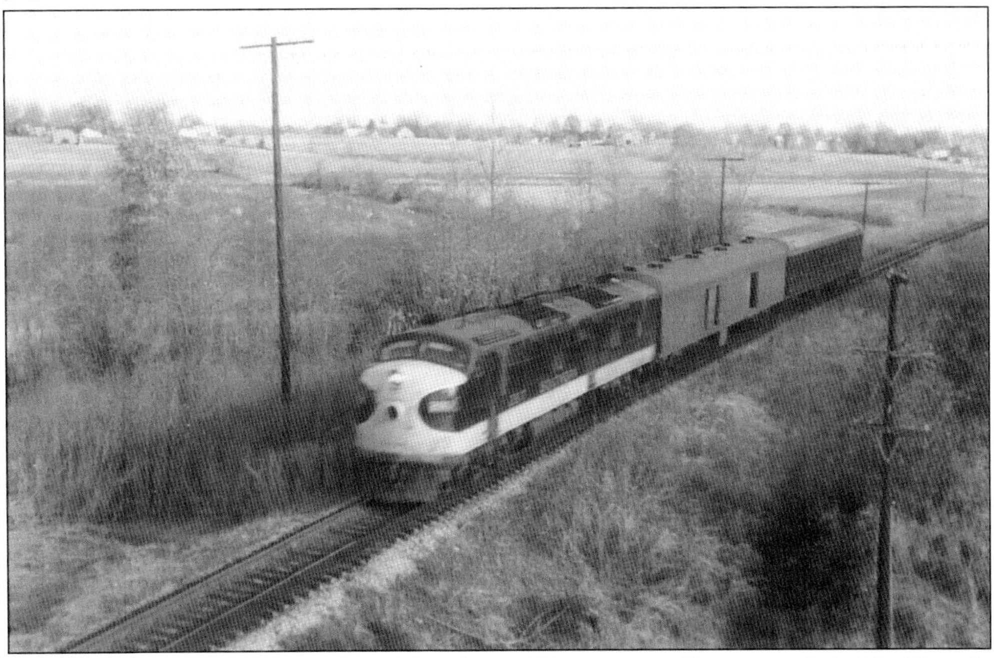

This is train No. 36, which ran from Memphis to Chattanooga, Tennessee, daily. No. 36 made stops at all stations between Memphis and Chattanooga, including the Muscle Shoals Station. Nos. 35 and 36 were also the mail trains, picking up and delivering mail to each stop along the route. These trains ended service for the Shoals Area on March 30, 1968.

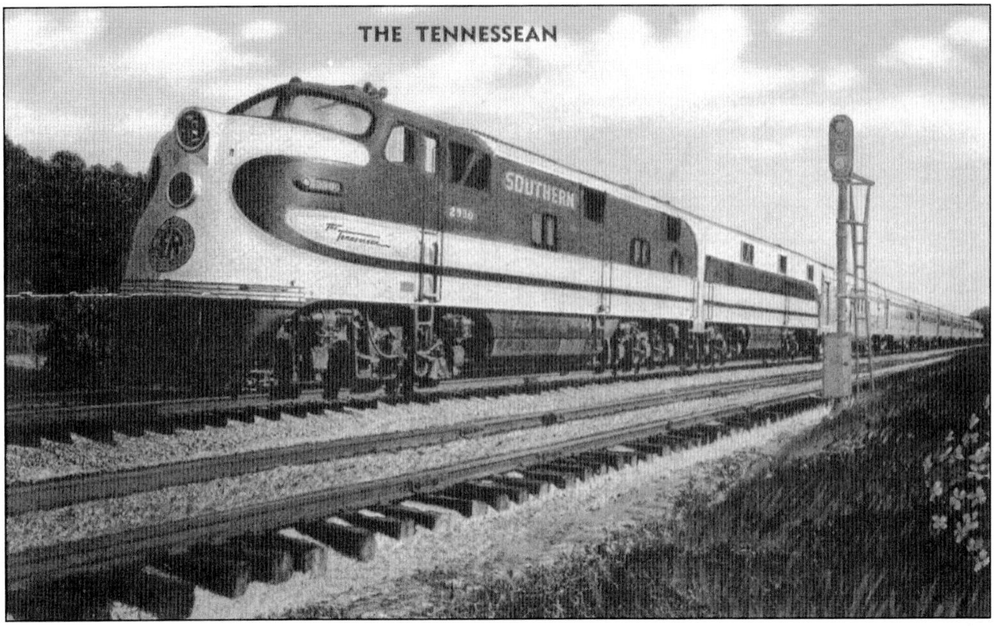

The *Memphis Special* was the passenger train that served this area for many years. The *Memphis Special* was replaced by the *Tennessean*. The *Tennessean* was the streamline passenger train that served the Shoals Area. The train ran daily connecting the Shoals with Washington, DC, and Memphis, Tennessee. This train only stopped at the larger stations and would reach speeds in excess of 80 miles per hour.

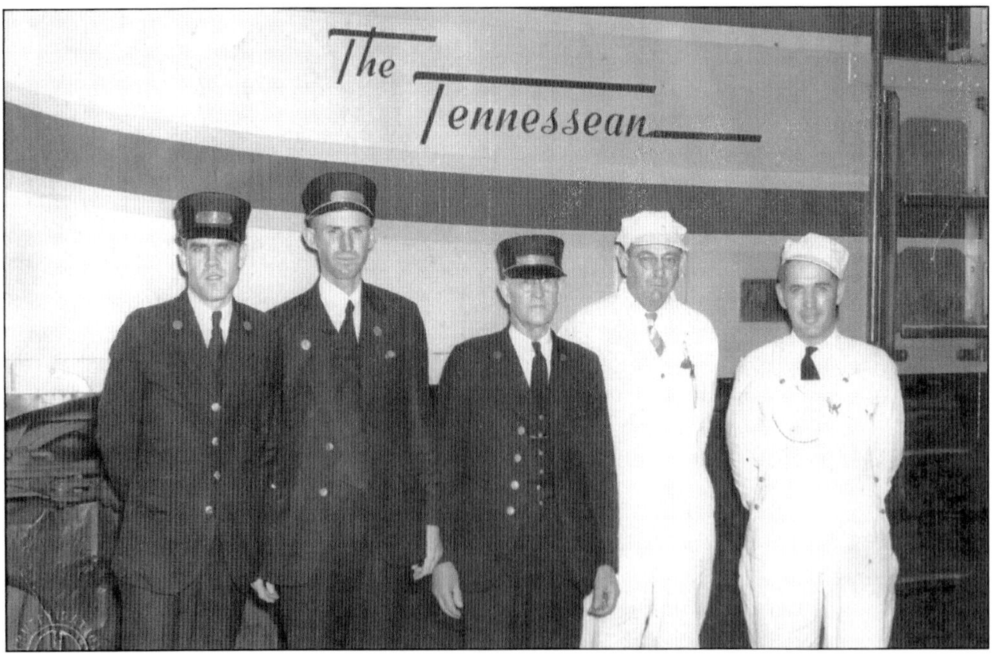

The *Tennessean* made its first exhibition trip in May 1941. The inaugural crew of Southern Railway System's only streamliner to serve the Shoals included S.H. "Harry" Young as flagman, L.E. Blasingame as baggagemaster, R.I. Sanders as conductor, Louis Bradley as engineer, and J.O. Lambert as fireman.

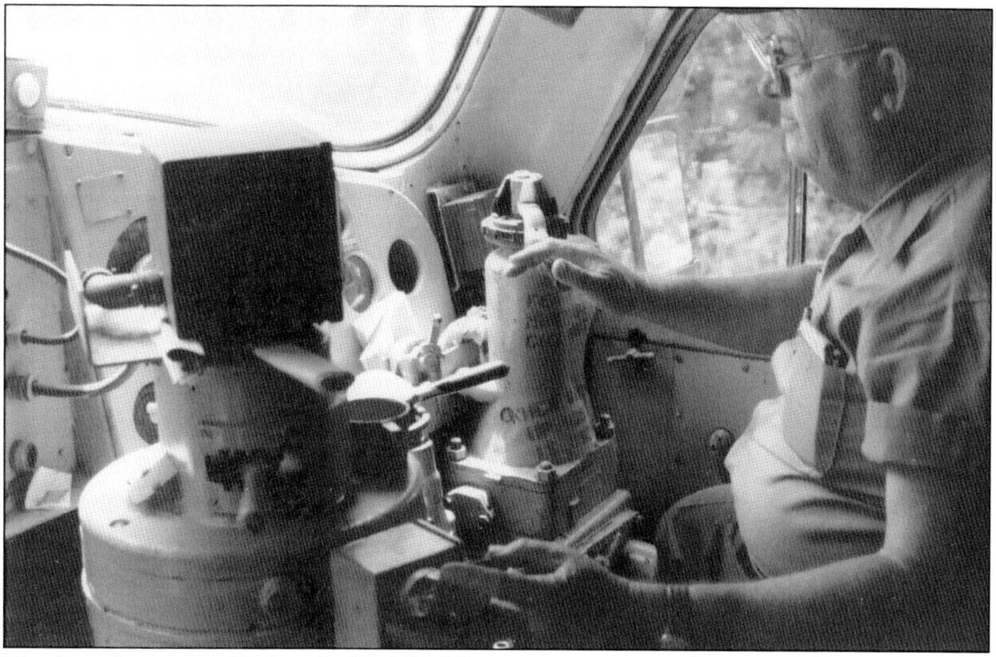

The days of passengers "Riding the High Rails" were coming to an end. Automobiles were becoming the means of travel for America. Trains like No. 36, seen here leaving Muscle Shoals Station in October 1966, were to be a thing of the past. On January 29, 1967, trains Nos. 45 & 46, known as the *Tennessean*, were discontinued.

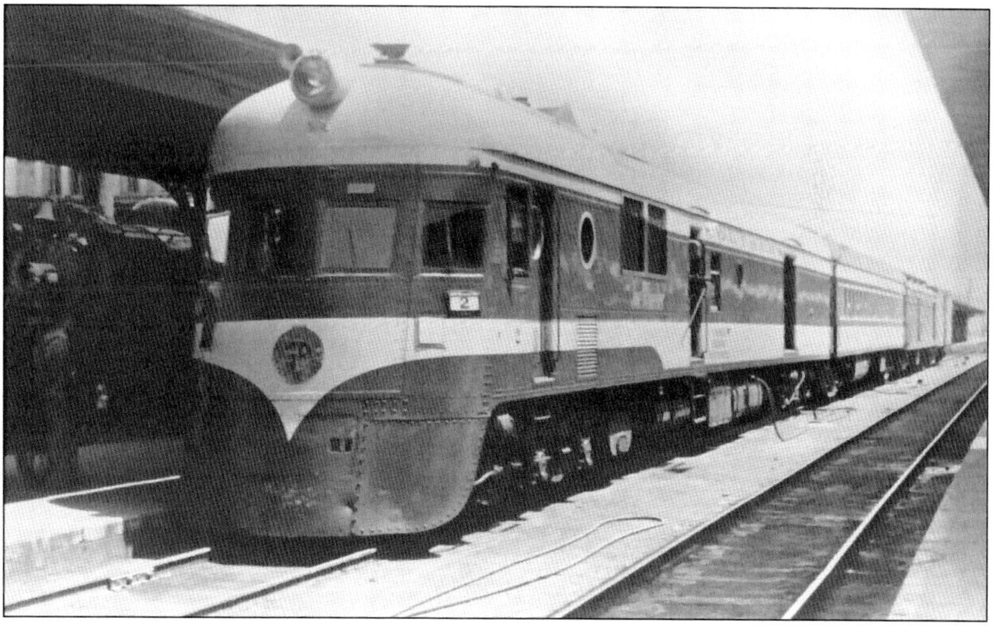

The *Joe Wheeler*, named in honor of Confederate general Joseph Wheeler, was the first diesel-electric train to operate in Tuscumbia. The train left Tuscumbia every morning at 5:17 a.m. to arrive in Chattanooga at 10:15 a.m. and then left Chattanooga at 4:00 p.m. to arrive home at Tuscumbia at 9:12 p.m. The success of the *Joe Wheeler* and others like it prompted the Southern Railway to modernize with diesel-electric trains.

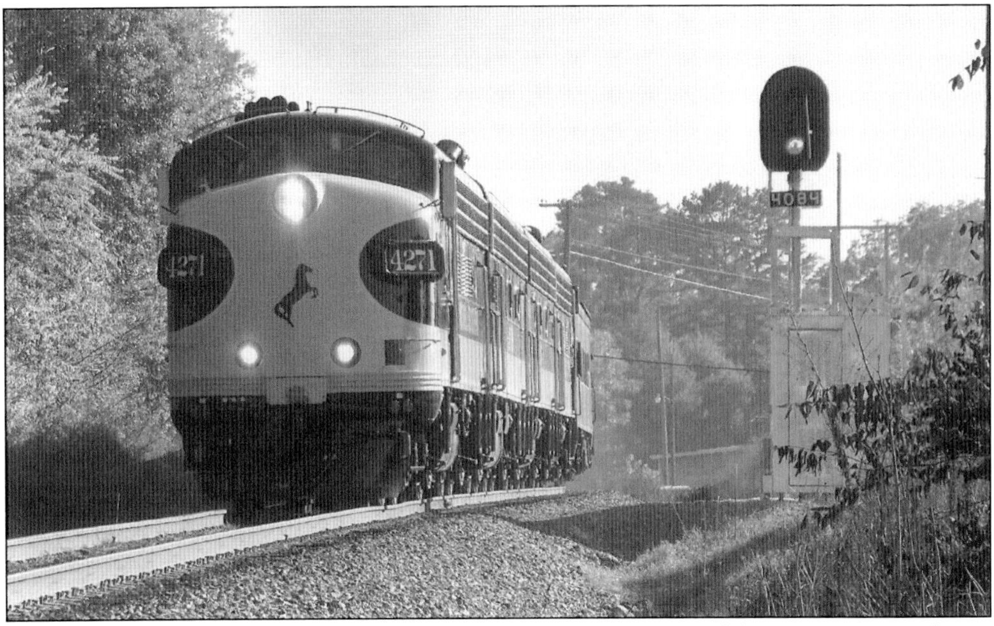

Norfolk Southern Railway's Executive Train, seen here going west of downtown Tuscumbia as it turns on Lilly Pond Curve, is the last of the F series locomotives operating on the line. The F series was often referred to as the "Covered Wagons." They were the locomotives that proved that diesel-electric trains could do the work of steam locomotives.

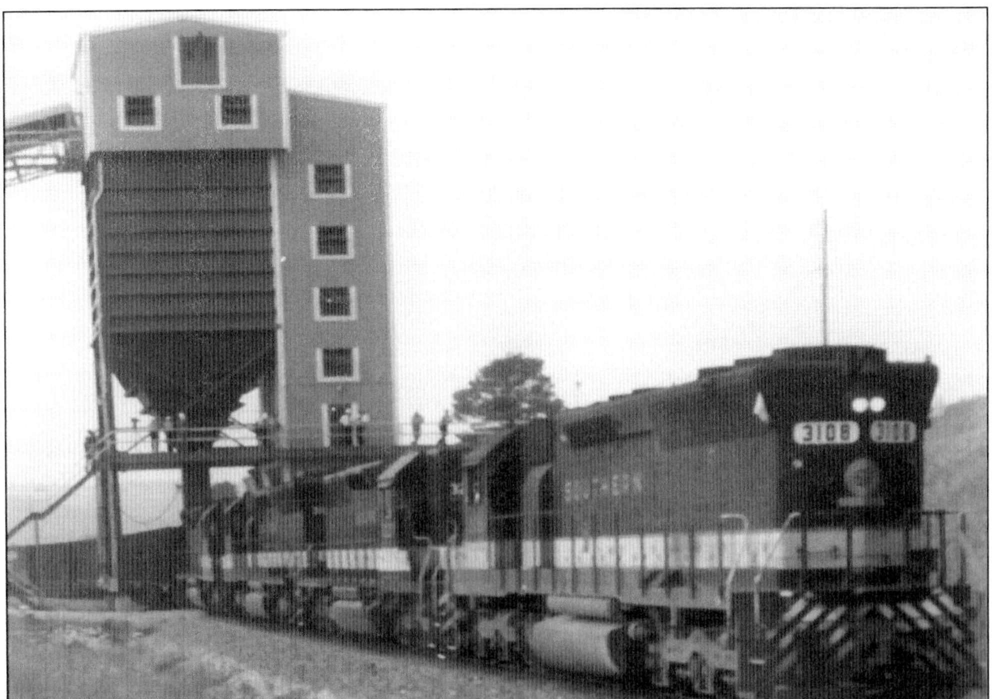

This is the coal loading facility just west of Tuscumbia at Pride Station. Coal would be delivered to the facility by barge traffic, mixed, and loaded onto railcars. The train would make a continuous pass under the transloader as it loaded the cars without stopping. This operation has been closed.

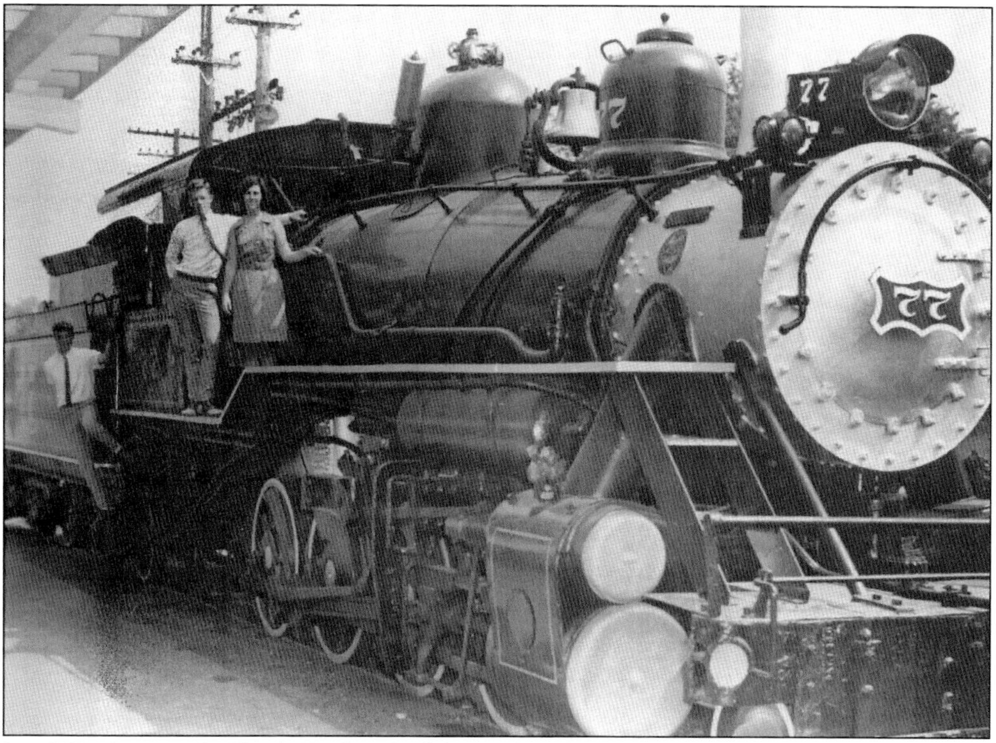

In 1968, the Muscle Shoals Railroad Club purchased engine No. 77 for excursion runs. It is pictured here in the Muscle Shoals Depot in Sheffield with Deshler High School students (from left to right) Steve Henninger, Mike Hunt, and Pat O'Steen.

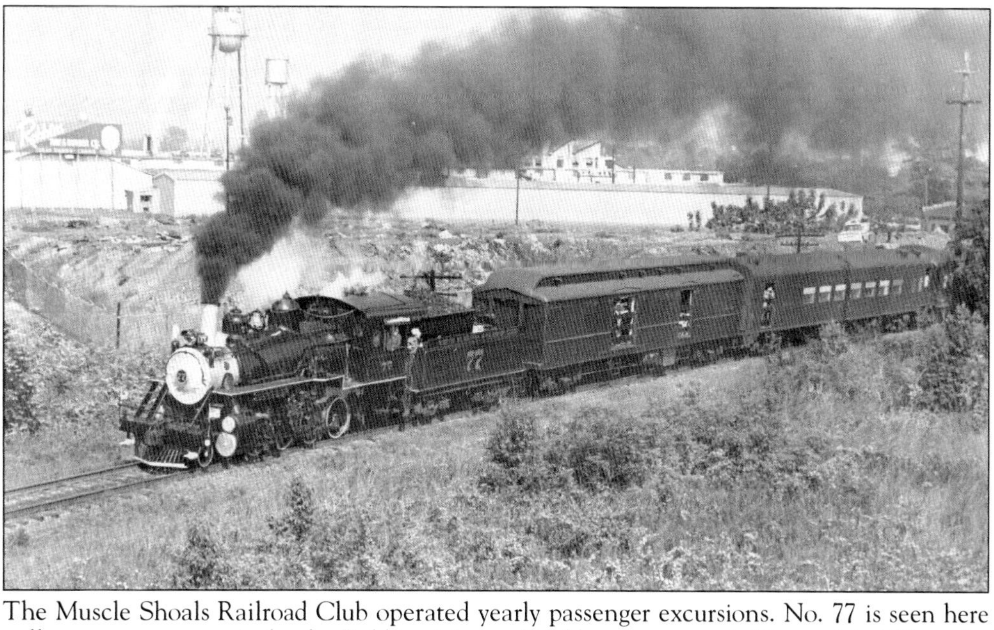

The Muscle Shoals Railroad Club operated yearly passenger excursions. No. 77 is seen here pulling a passenger train by the Robbins Tire and Rubber Company in Tuscumbia. When the Muscle Shoals Railroad Club dissolved, No. 77 was moved to Huntsville and later sold to a company in Canada.

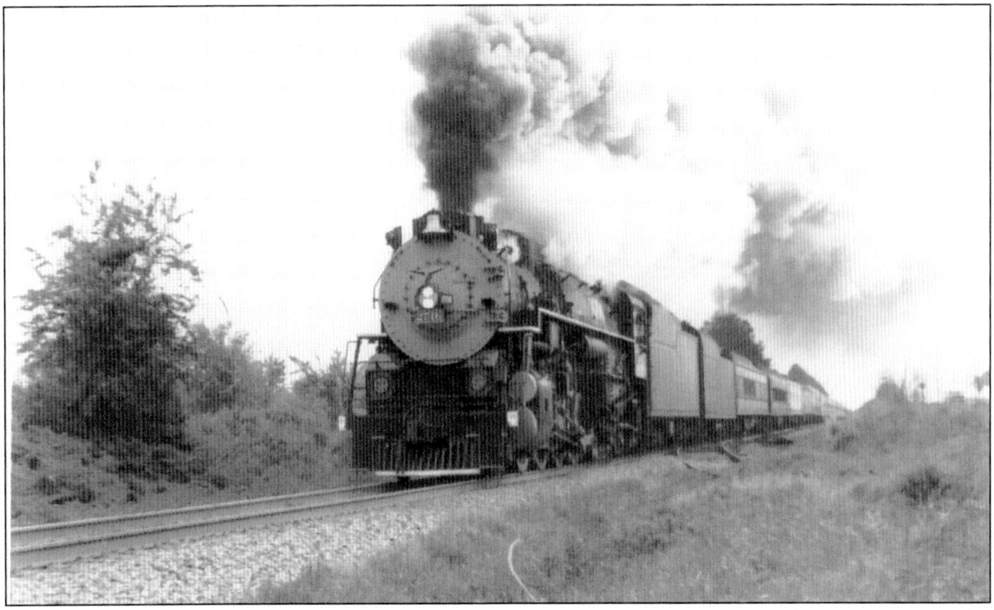

A common expression on the Southern for years when passing the Lilly Pond area was "going by Buttermilk's." Engineer John H. "Buttermilk" McWilliams (the author's father) lived next to the track, and his home was used for location identification. This excursion is pulled by engine No. 2716 with Buttermilk as engineer. Buttermilk is "going by Buttermilk's."

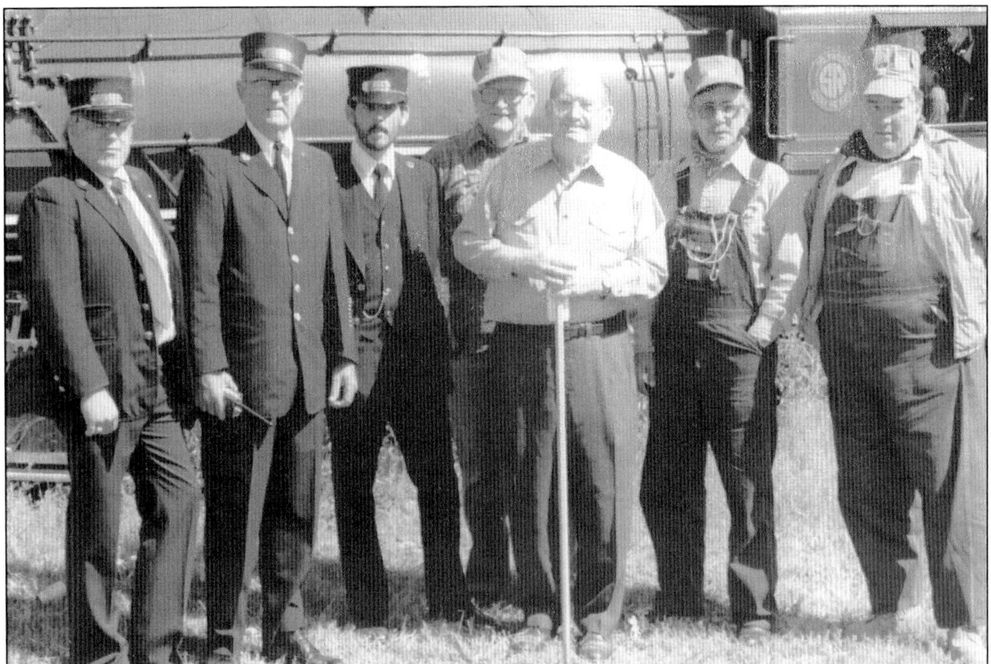

In 1985, engineer John H. McWilliams (with cane) became ill with cancer and was unable to operate the excursion for that year. As a tribute, the excursion with engine No. 4501 had train orders to "stop at Buttermilk's." Railroad officials went to his home and brought him out to the train, where the crew and officials paid a tribute before heading on toward Memphis.

Three

Alabama's Oldest Commercial Buildings

The railroads made Tuscumbia a boomtown in the 1830s. Tuscumbia doubled in size from 1832 to 1834 with the operations of the Tuscumbia Railroad Company and the Tuscumbia, Courtland & Decatur Railroad Company. These railroads built their shops downtown and at Tuscumbia Landing.

The downtown area grew rapidly. Many commercial brick buildings were constructed, many of which remain today. Tuscumbia has some of the oldest commercial buildings remaining in the state of Alabama. There are still businesses occupying commercial buildings built in the 1820s, 1830s, and 1840s. The beautiful Colbert County Courthouse, originally built in 1882, has been featured representing courthouses of Alabama.

Tuscumbia Landing, with all its operations and buildings, was destroyed by Union troops during the Civil War. These operations were never rebuilt. Even with this loss, the downtown area prospered during the late 19th century and early 20th century. Like many small towns in America, the downtown area suffered with the growth of malls. The downtown area has begun to make a recovery. Many of the old buildings have been restored.

This chapter covers the growth of Tuscumbia during this period, and the restoration and growth today.

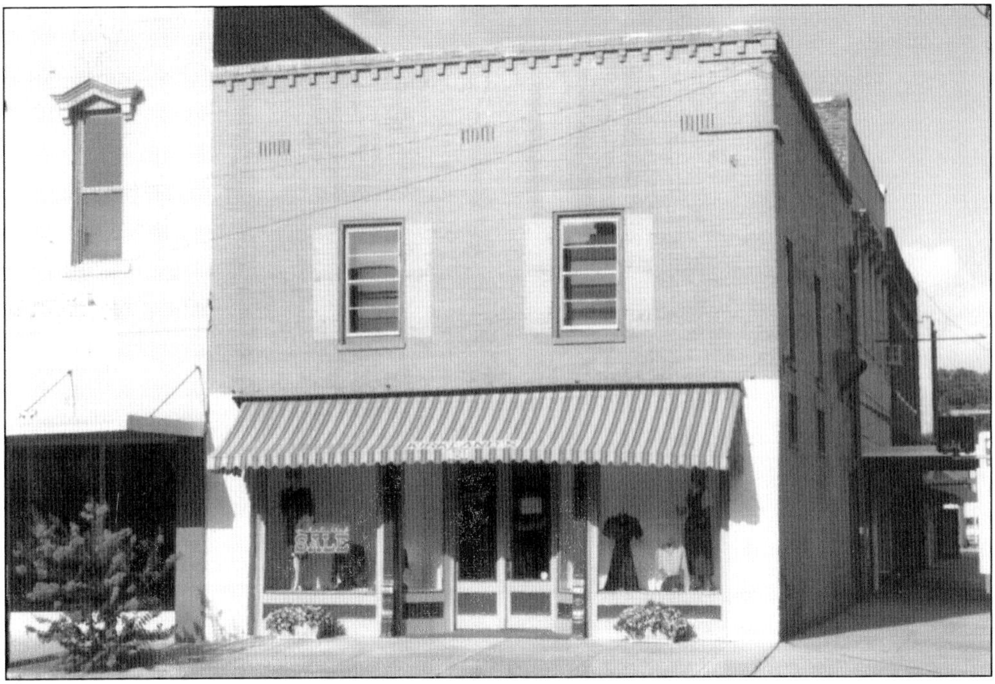

Pictured here is Kirkland's Dress Shop, owned by Ona Mae Kirkland. This building is thought to be the oldest commercial building in the state of Alabama. It was built in 1824 as part of a row of commercial buildings known as Mechanics Row. It was originally Sutherland's Store. The Sutherlands received their fame in the Battle of the Alamo.

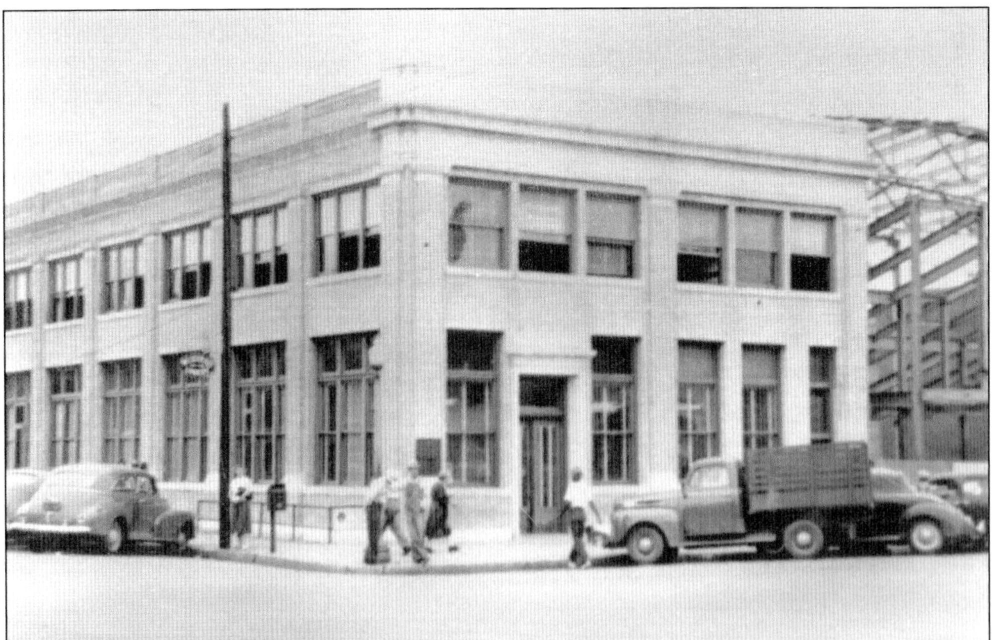

This is the First National Bank Building on the southeast corner of Fifth and Main Streets. The building later became Colonial Bank. Bank Independent bought Colonial Bank, and this location was closed. The building under construction to the south is the Tuscumbian Theater.

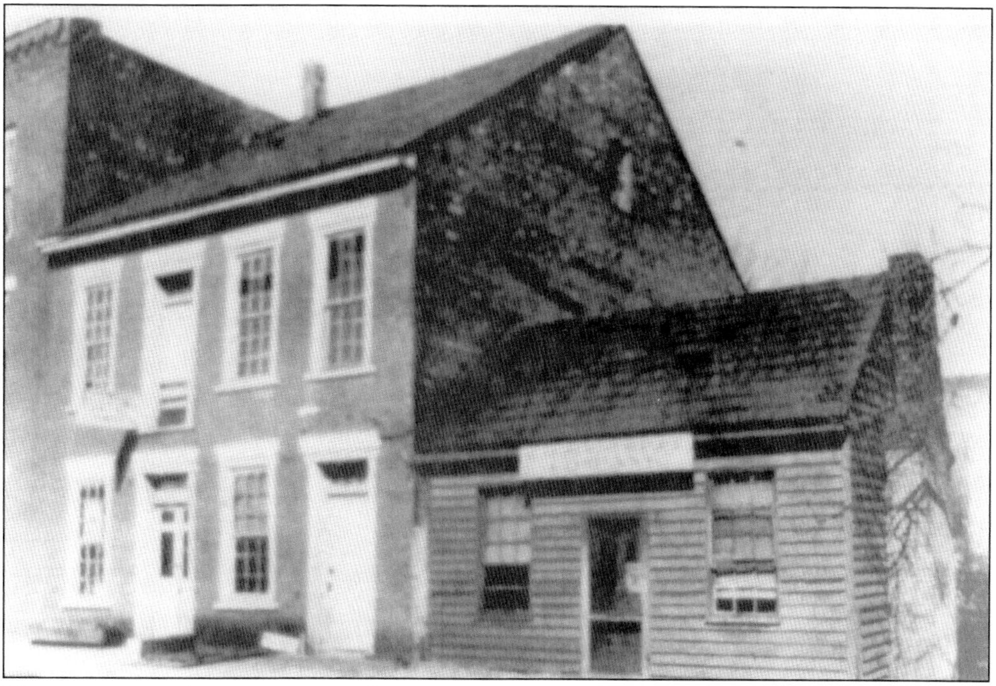

The structure in the center was built by Capt. Samuel Keaghy in 1825 and is the second oldest commercial building in Alabama. Captain Keaghy's store was on the ground floor, and his residence was on the second floor. His assistant Mr. Downs lived in the small building next door.

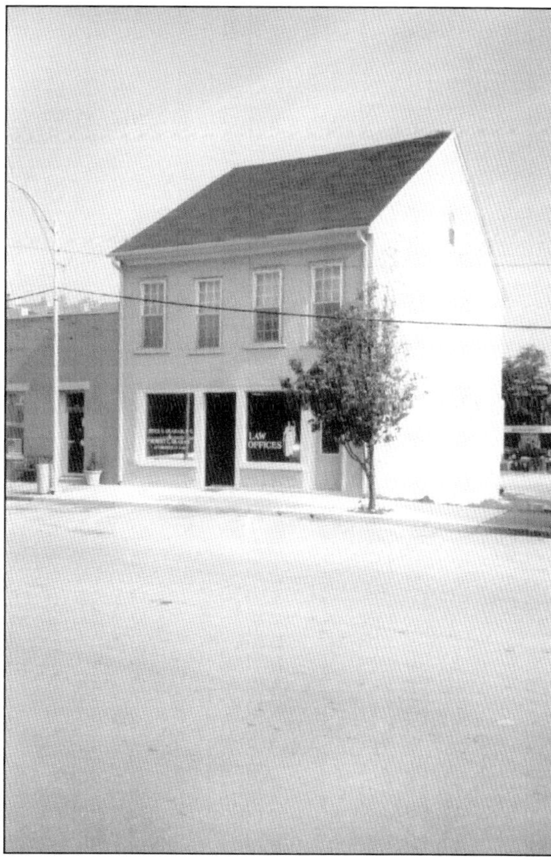

In this picture of Captain Keaghy's store taken around 1980, the small, attached building has been removed, and a stucco compound has covered the brick. The small building had been the police station for years. Police patrolling Tuscumbia would drive by the building regularly to see if there had been a call. If someone had called for assistance, the outside light would be on and the officer would stop and get his instructions.

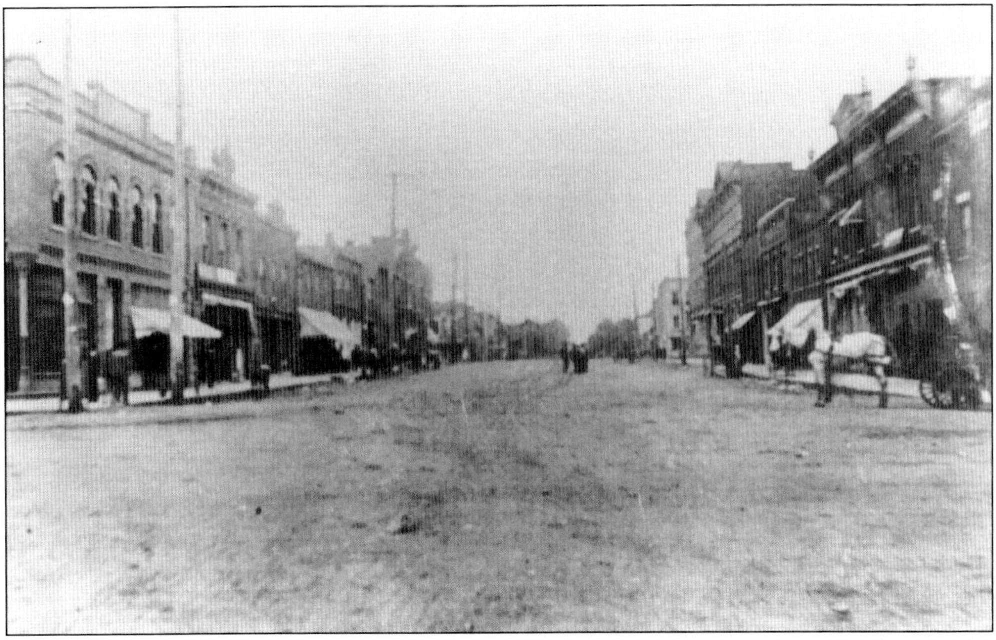

This is a view from Sixth Street around 1905. The picture was taken looking north from the intersection of Sixth and Main Streets. Much of the west side of Main Street, seen here on the left, remains the same today. The Kirk Isbell and the Bickley Buildings, the three-story buildings on the right rear, were destroyed by fire.

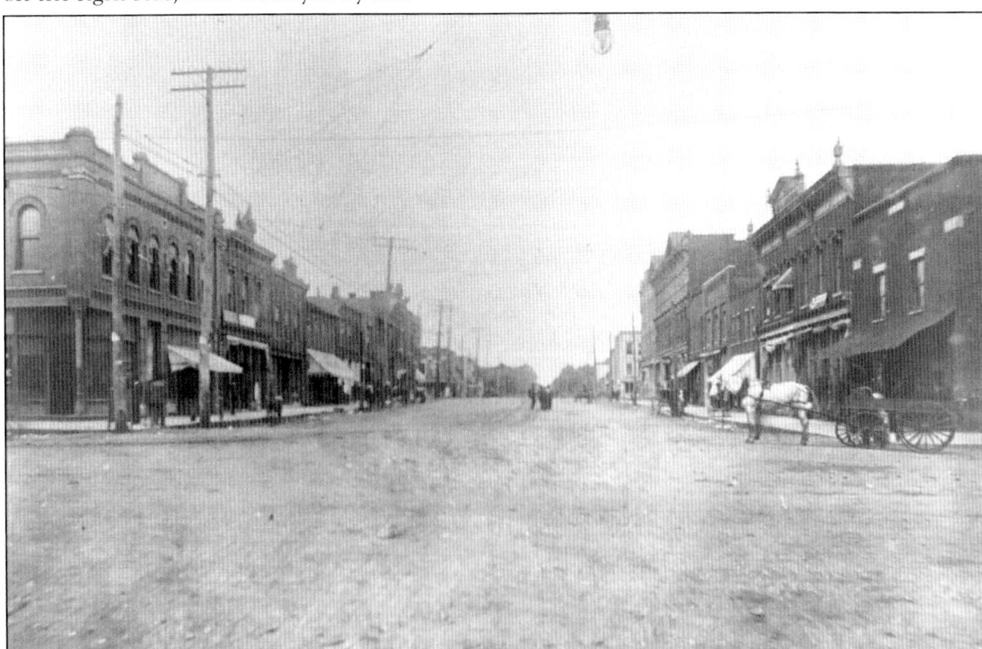

This is another view of Main Street just a few years later, probably around 1910. The three-story buildings on the right have burned down since this picture was taken. The Kirk Isbell and the Bickley Buildings burned on July 7, 1914. The old Horne House Hotel burned around 1955 and was rebuilt as a two-story building.

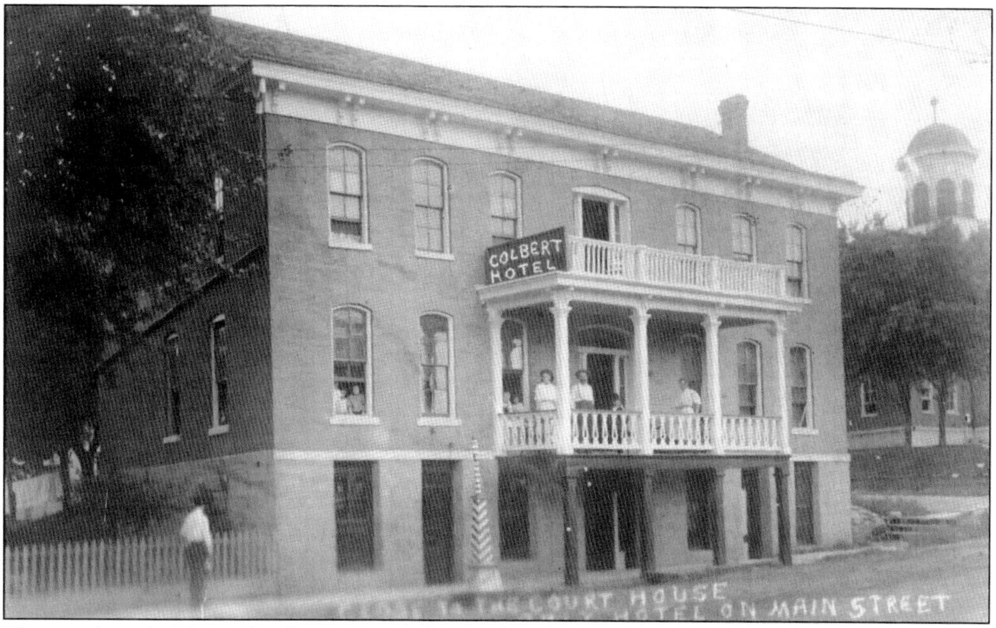

This unidentified home has been changed into a hotel and boardinghouse. The handwritten note on the picture states that the hotel was near the courthouse on Main Street. The building in the background appears to be the Deshler Female Institute. The David Deshler home was next to the school and was used as a boardinghouse before being destroyed in 1874 by a tornado.

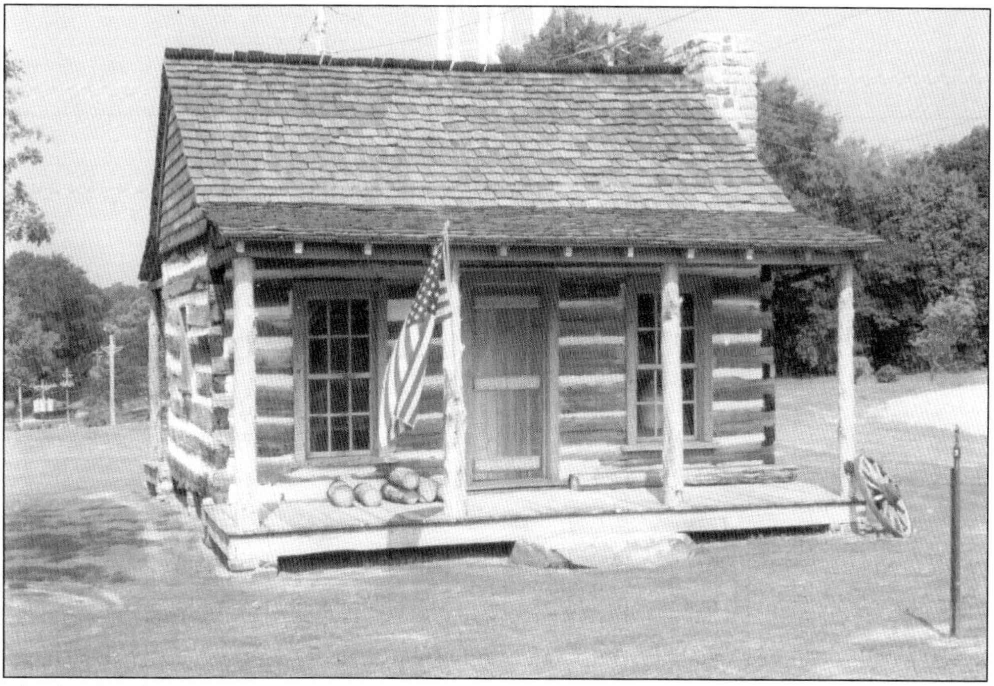

The first hotel in Tuscumbia was a series of log cabins. These cabins were run by Michael Dickson. This log cabin was originally across the street from its present location and was owned by Charley Carmichael. Carmichael donated the cabin to the Colbert County Landmarks Foundation. The foundation had the cabin placed at this location.

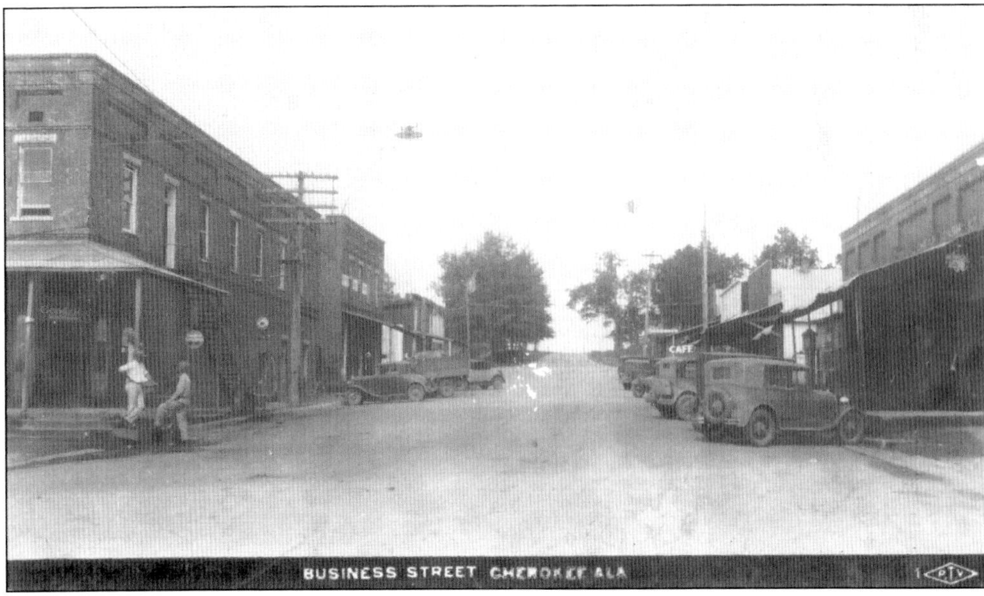

Colbert County was established by the Alabama legislature in 1867 from the northern half of Franklin County, only to be repealed in 1868. Colbert County was reestablished in 1870. A vote was taken to decide if Tuscumbia or Cherokee would be the county seat. This is a picture of Cherokee in 1934. All the buildings on the right burned in a fire in the 1960s.

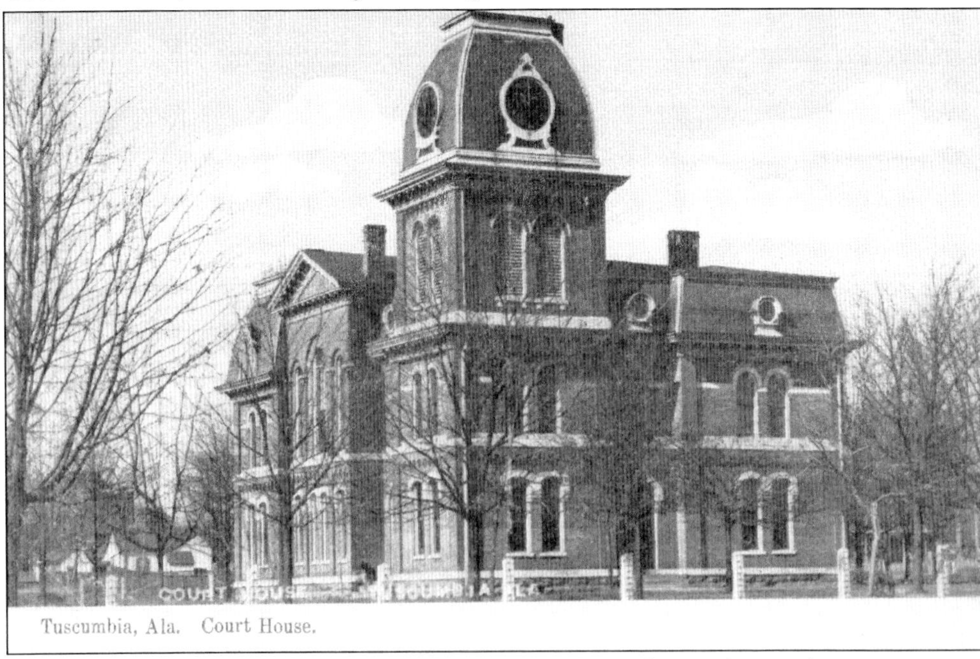

Tuscumbia was chosen the county seat. Prior to construction of a courthouse, the commissioners met in different places around town, such as the hotel or Masonic Lodge. In 1881, the county purchased the city block on the west side of North Main Street between Third and Fourth Streets. The large house on the block was divided into two parts, and moved to other locations as individual homes. One of these homes still stands today as the old McWilliams Home on the western edge of town.

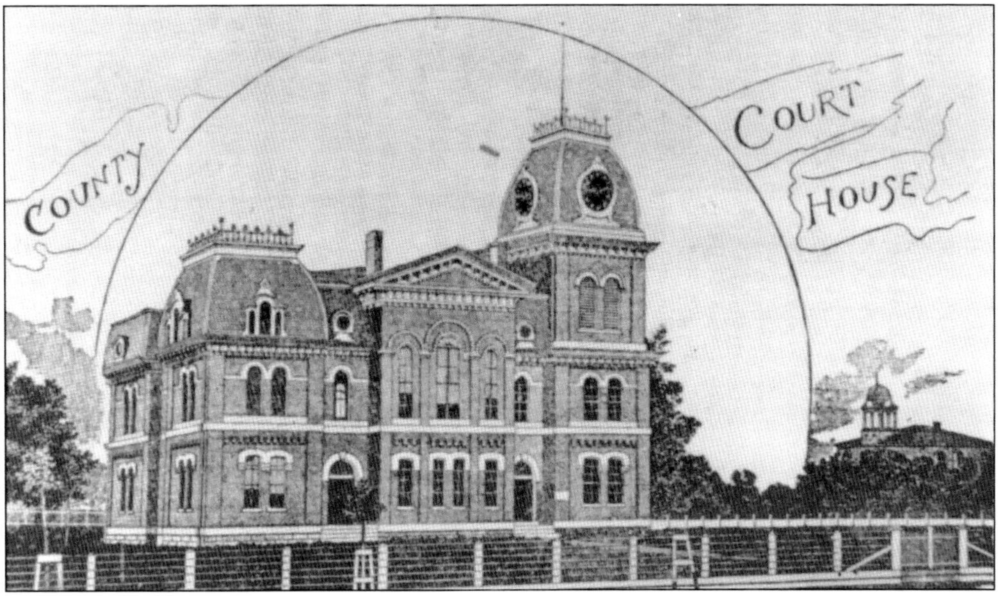

Former governor Robert Burns Lindsay was the speaker for the ceremony of laying the cornerstone on August 22, 1881. Colbert County began to occupy the new courthouse a year later on August 29, 1882, although construction was not completed. The landscaping was completed in November, and George Black finished the clock just before Christmas.

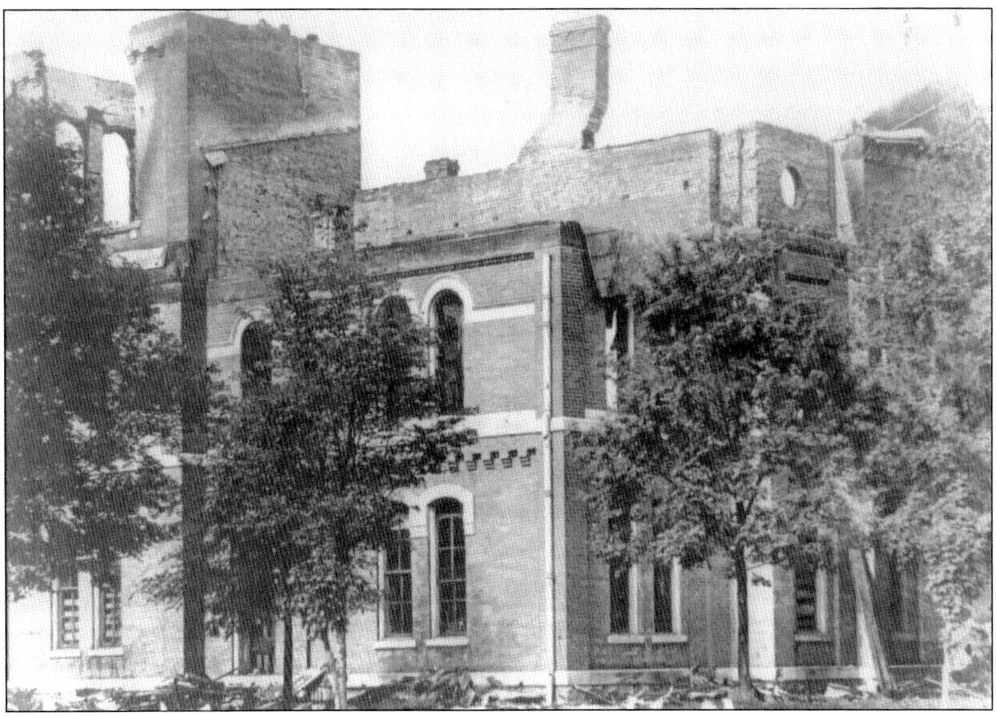

On the morning of May 14, 1908, A.M. Steele gave the alarm that the courthouse was on fire. Citizens aided the fire department by forming a paper brigade and saving all the courthouse records, books, and other important papers. The interior of the courthouse was completely gutted, leaving nothing standing but the walls.

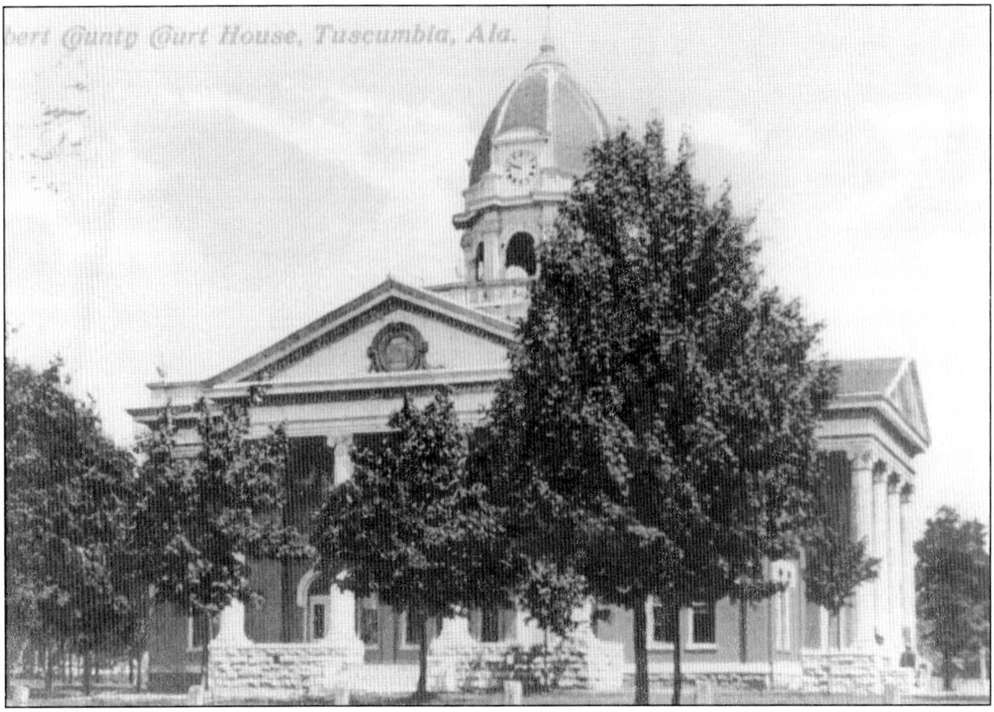

The solid brick exterior walls were not heavily damaged. The decision was made to reuse the exterior walls of the old courthouse. The new courthouse was to have four columned porticos, one on each side. The clock tower was moved from the southeast corner of the structure to the center of the courthouse in a beautiful dome.

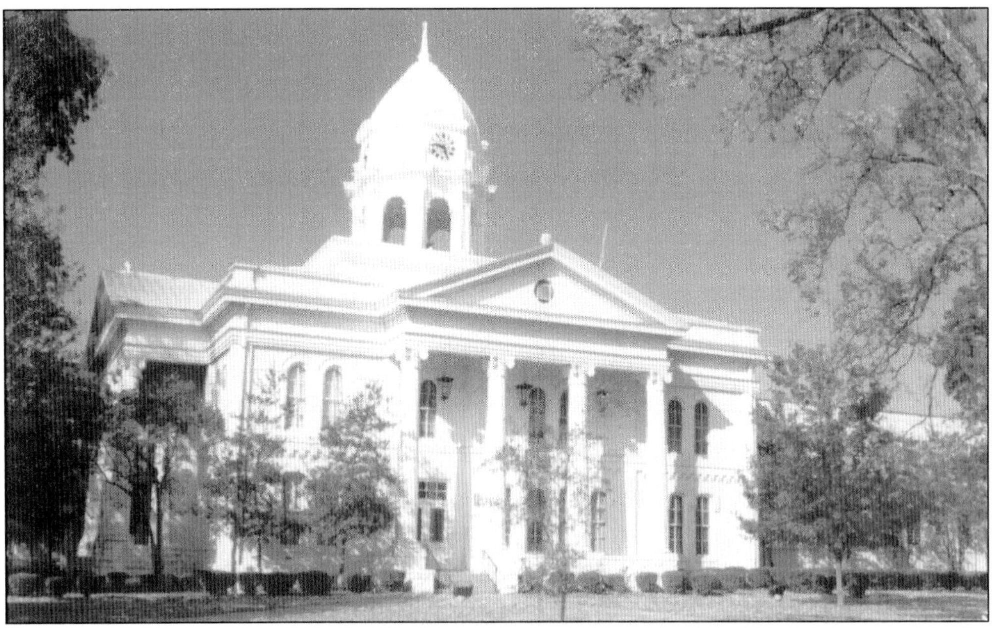

The courthouse was painted white to cover some of the stains left on the brick by the fire. There have been two major additions to the courthouse. In 1948, an addition was made to the north side. The west wing was added in 1975, and the interior was remodeled in 1976.

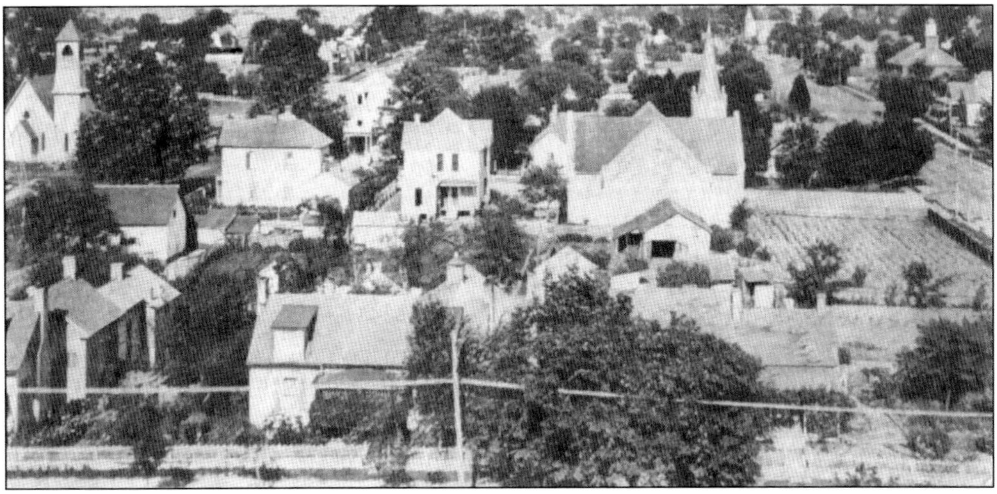

The top of the courthouse offers a beautiful view of Tuscumbia. Looking east, this picture was taken around 1900. The First Baptist Church is in the center. St. John's Episcopal Church is on the left, and First Presbyterian Church is in the right background. The street to the right is Fourth Street.

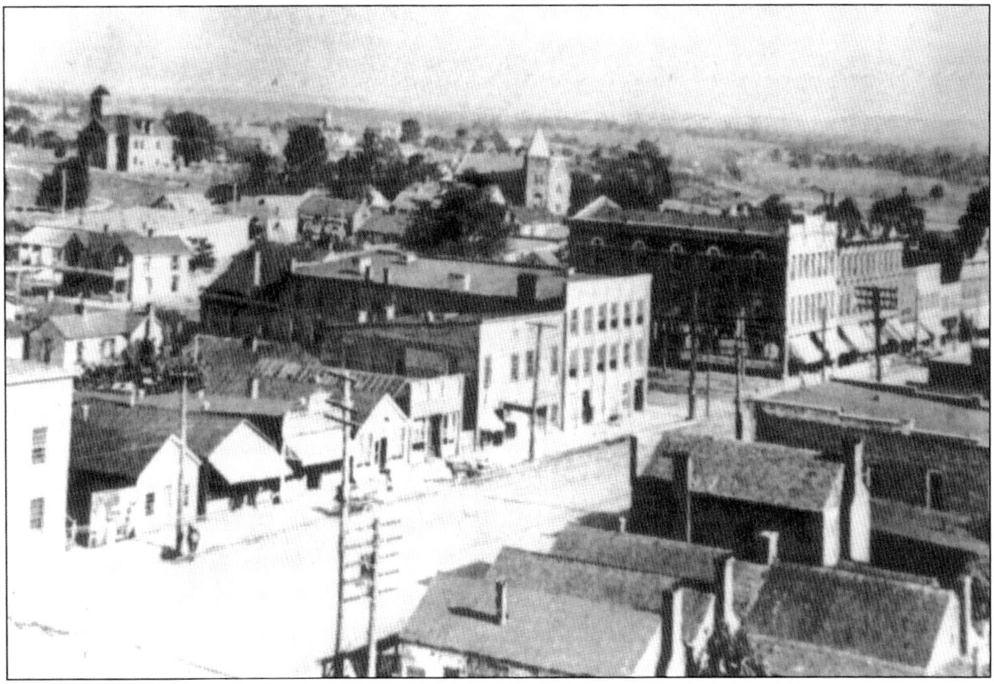

This c. 1900 photograph was also taken from the top of the courthouse facing southeast. It offers a good look at the buildings along the east side of Main Street. Most of these buildings are gone today. The three-story buildings were lost to fire. The school in the foreground is the Tuscumbia Public School building, and the Methodist church is in the center.

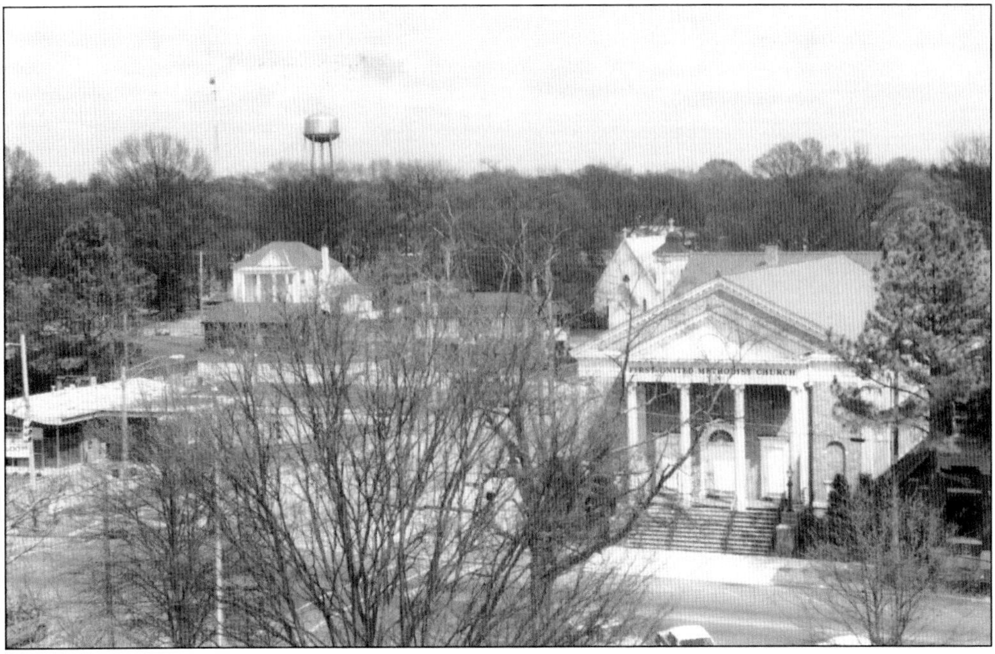

This view, looking northeast from the courthouse, was taken around 1980. It shows the First Methodist Church and St. John's Episcopal Church. The house with columns in the background is the Bell House. Deshler Female Institute was to the left, where the service station is located.

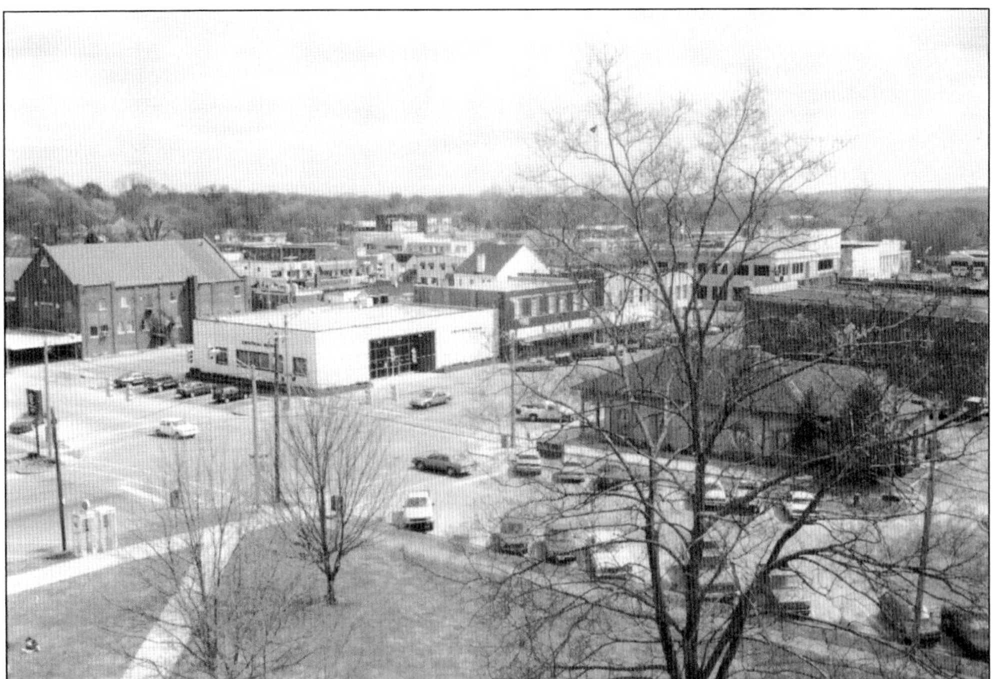

This is a view from the top of the courthouse around 1980. Many things have changed in the downtown area since 1900. Most of the buildings on Main Street have been replaced with more modern buildings. Many of the little shops that used to be found all over town are gone.

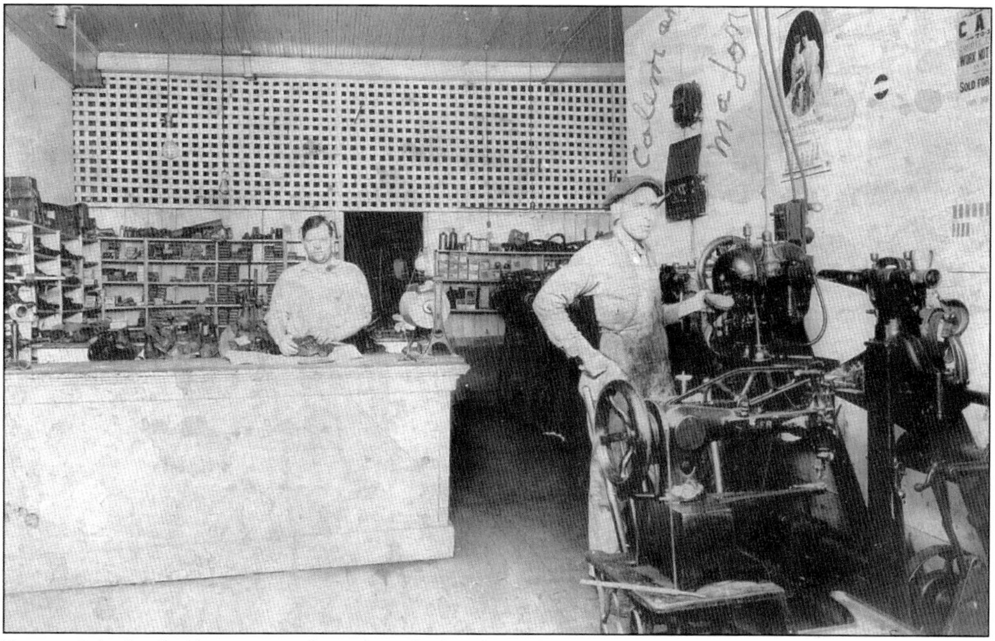

Emery Schultz (left) is pictured inside Schultz Shoe Shop. The gentleman on the right is Coleman McDonald. In today's throwaway world where shoes are just thrown away, there seems to be little need for shoe shops. The days when one would take his or her shoes in to have new soles or half soles are just about gone.

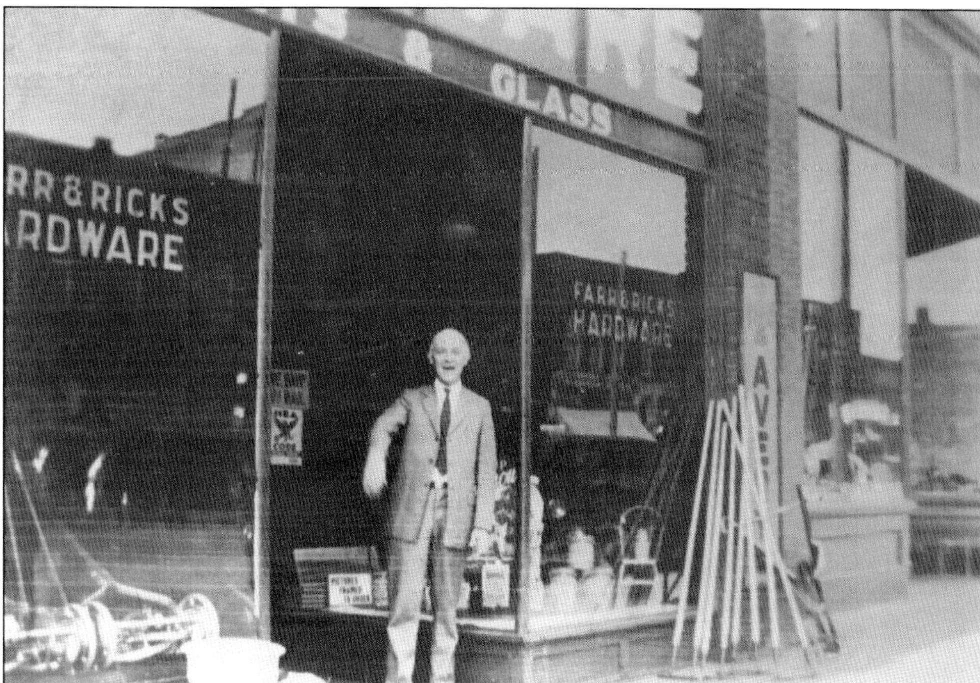

Charles Ricks is seen here in front of the Farr and Ricks Hardware Company. Hardware stores and general mercantile stores were a common business in town for years. In 2005, the last hardware store closed in Tuscumbia when David and Bonnie Walker closed C.W. Hardware on Sixth Street.

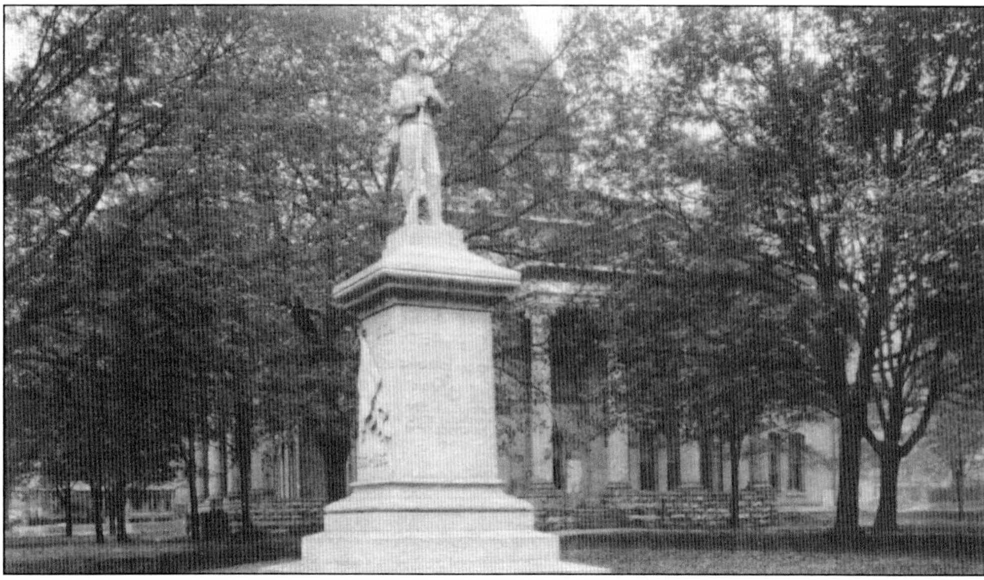

The Civil War, known to many Southerners as the War Between the States, devastated Tuscumbia. Union armies burned many buildings, including Tuscumbia Landing. This destroyed Tuscumbia's commerce. To commemorate the soldiers who fought, the Daughters of the Confederacy raised money to place a statue of a Confederate soldier on the lawn of the courthouse.

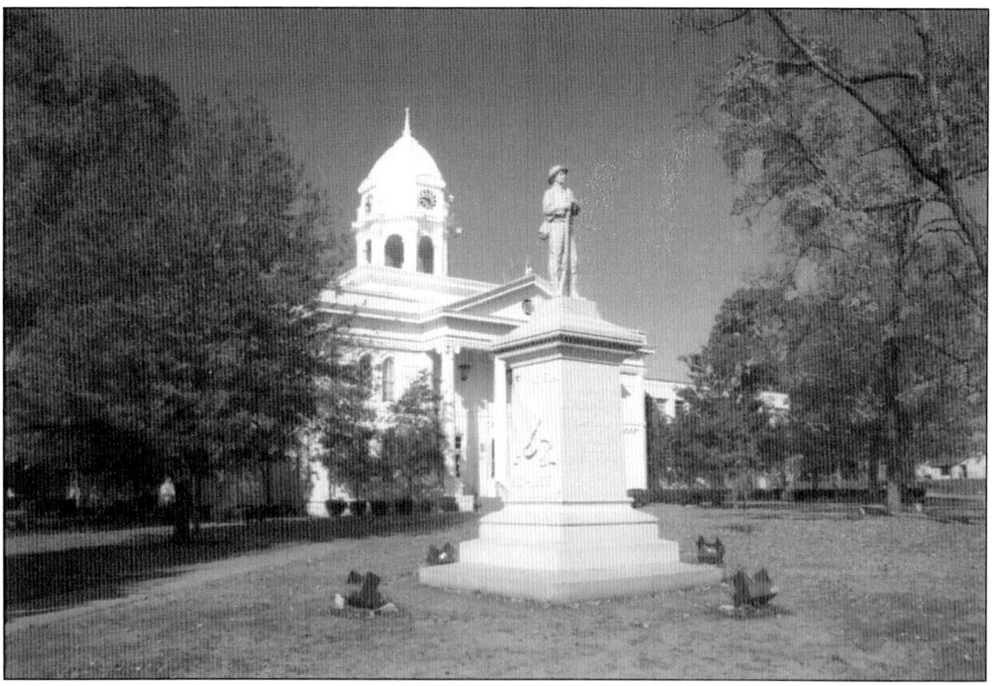

There had been a race between Lauderdale County and Colbert County to see who could raise the money the quickest to build a statue. Lauderdale County was able to raise the money first. Colbert County, not to be outdone by her neighbor, decided they would try to build a larger and better-looking statue.

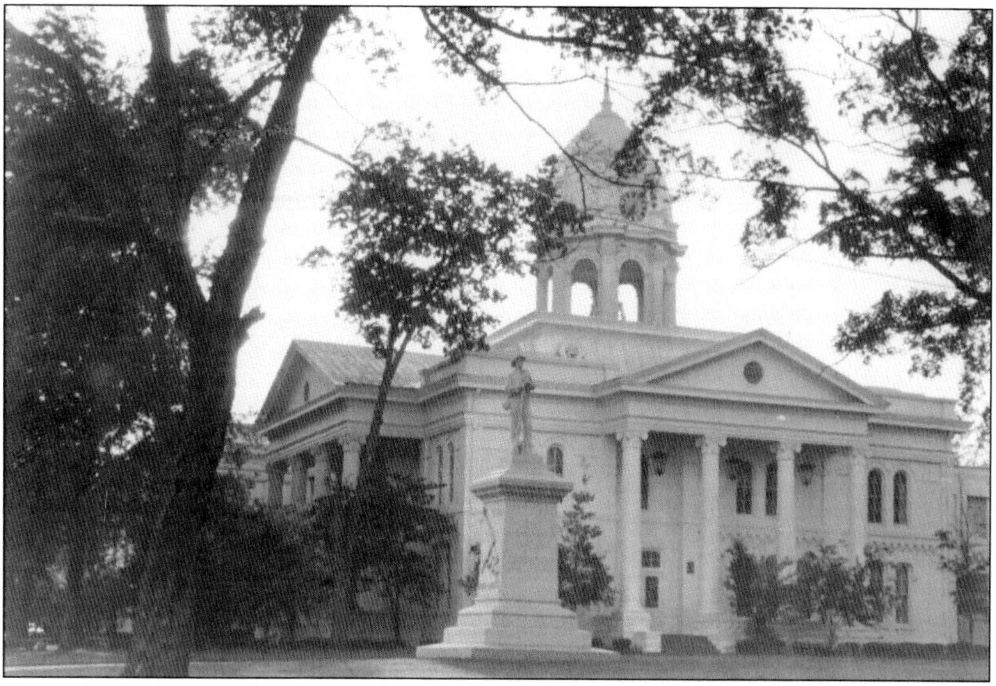

Tuscumbia lost many of its historic buildings during the Civil War. Many of the records were burned. Many young men from the area lost their lives. Out of the ashes of war grew a new county with a beautiful courthouse.

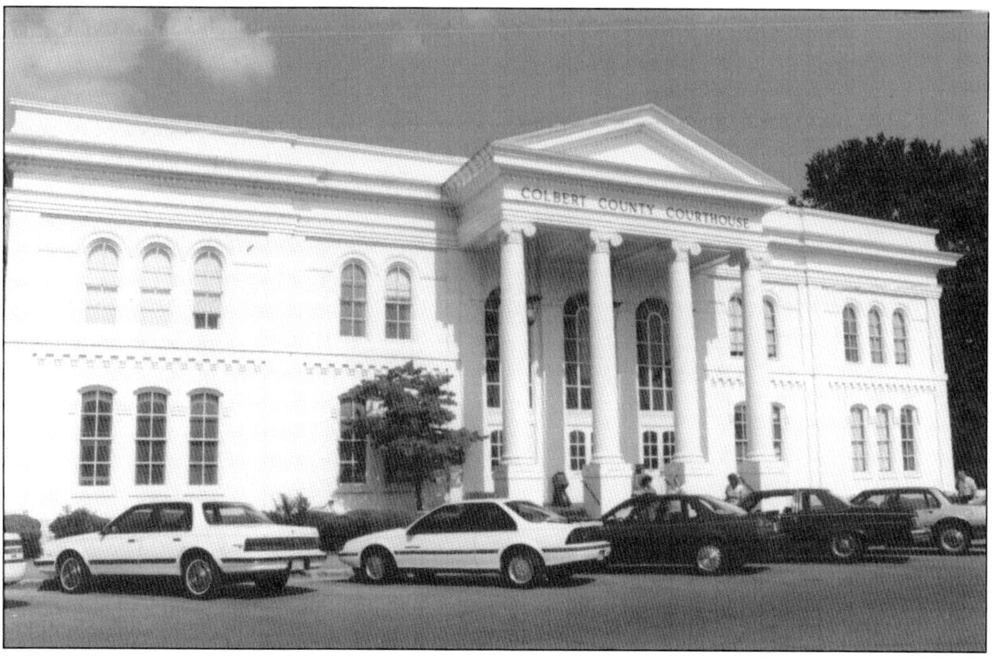

Many counties have chosen to tear down their old courthouses and build newer ones as they grew. Colbert County chose to expand its courthouse with a similar design for the addition. The west wing, pictured here, was constructed in 1975. It is the main entrance to the courthouse today.

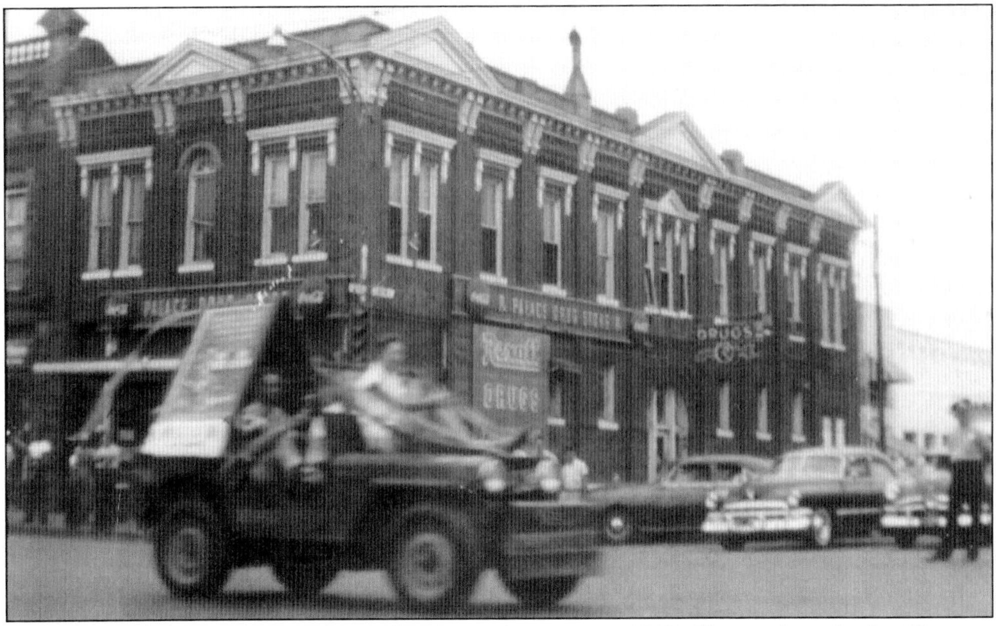

Guido Llueddeman came to Tuscumbia from Germany in 1865. He purchased a building on the corner of Fifth and Main Streets. Llueddeman's Store became very successful. In the 1880s, Guido Llueddeman tore down the old building and built the building known as the Palace today. When Llueddeman retired, he sold the business to his partner James N. Sampson and moved to Oregon.

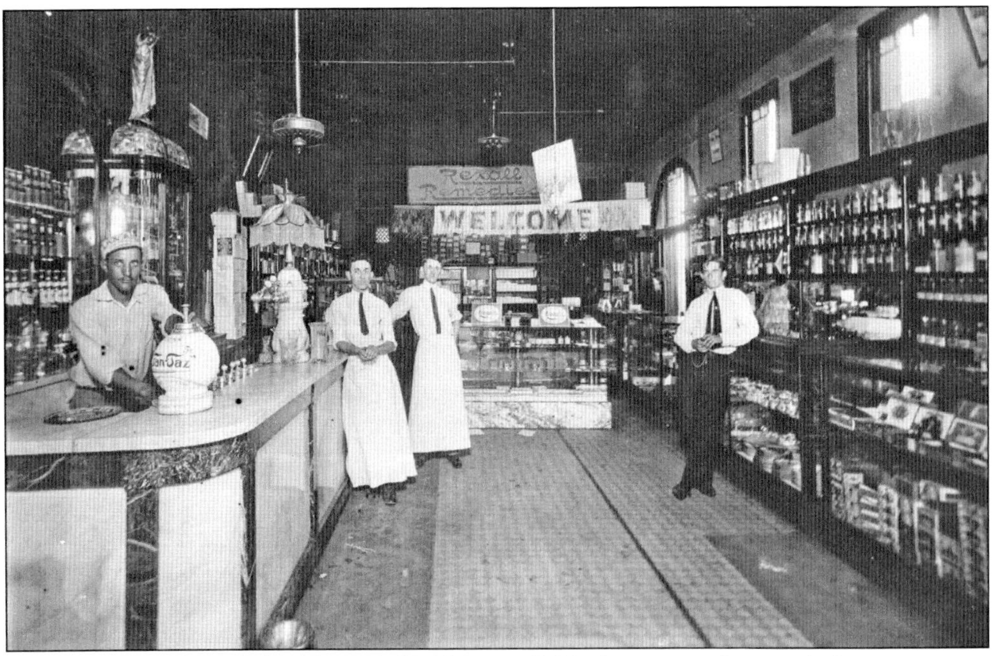

W.R. Sevier purchased Llueddeman's building in 1906, changing it from a clothing store to a drugstore. He formed the Palace Drug Company and installed a soda fountain. The Palace Drug Company operated from 1906 to 1908. The business was sold to Robert Hyde, who renamed it the Palace Drugstore.

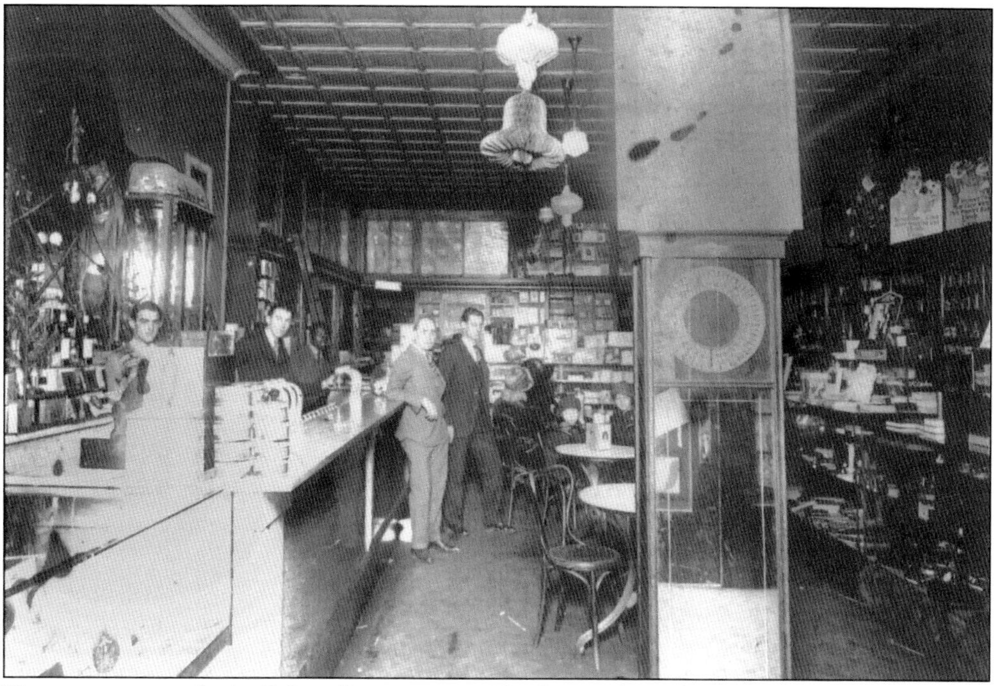

This is a view inside the Palace Drugstore in 1924. Pictured are, from left to right, clerks James L. Mays and John L. Neyman, porter John Downs, owner Robert E. Hyde, and pharmacist John Seay. The customers are unidentified.

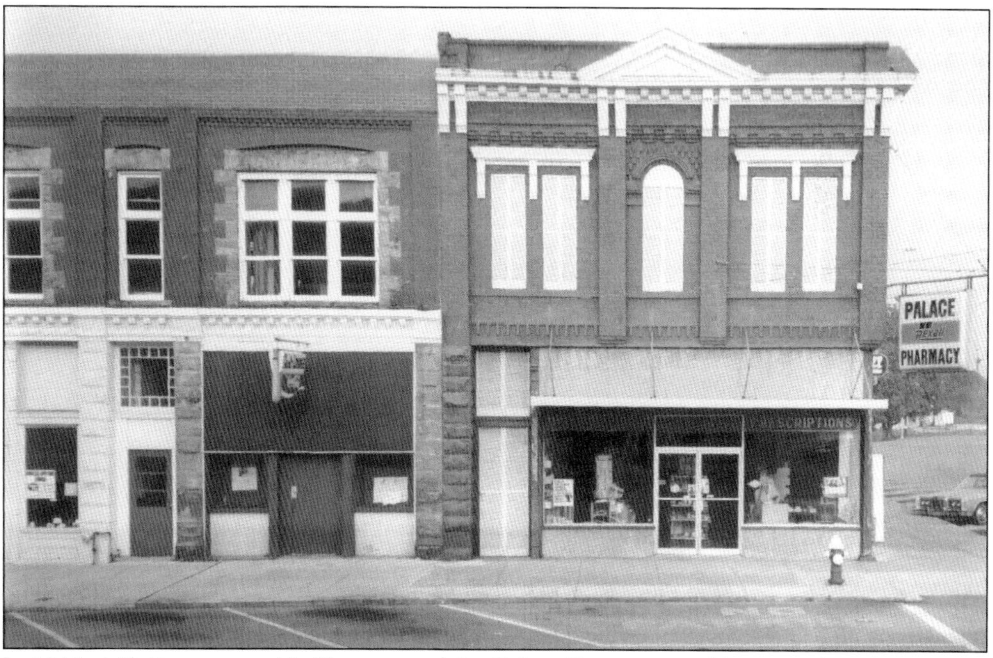

In 1944, A.E. Ray acquired half interest of the Palace Drugstore and became the sole owner in 1957. He operated the business until his retirement around 1990. The building was vacant until Harvey and Joyce Ann Robbins purchased it in 1999. The Palace Ice Cream and Sandwich Shop operates out of the building today.

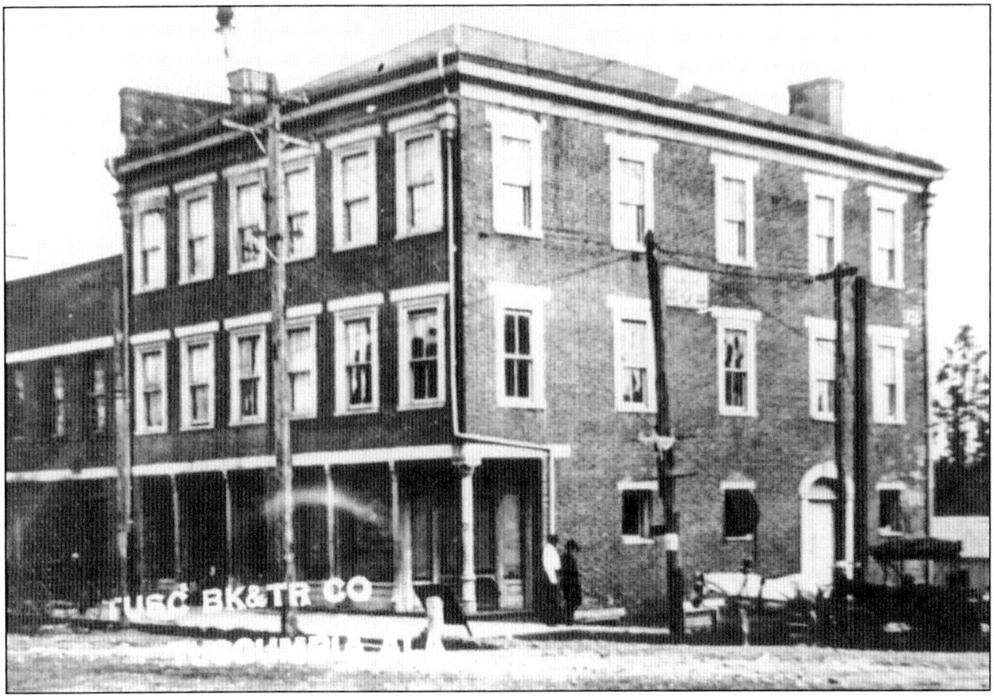

One of the earliest organizations in Tuscumbia was the Masons. The first recorded meeting was in the 1820s in the one room schoolhouse on the mound at the head of the spring. In the 1830s and 1840s, the Masons ran a lottery to help raise funds to build a lodge. The lottery drawing was a two-day event.

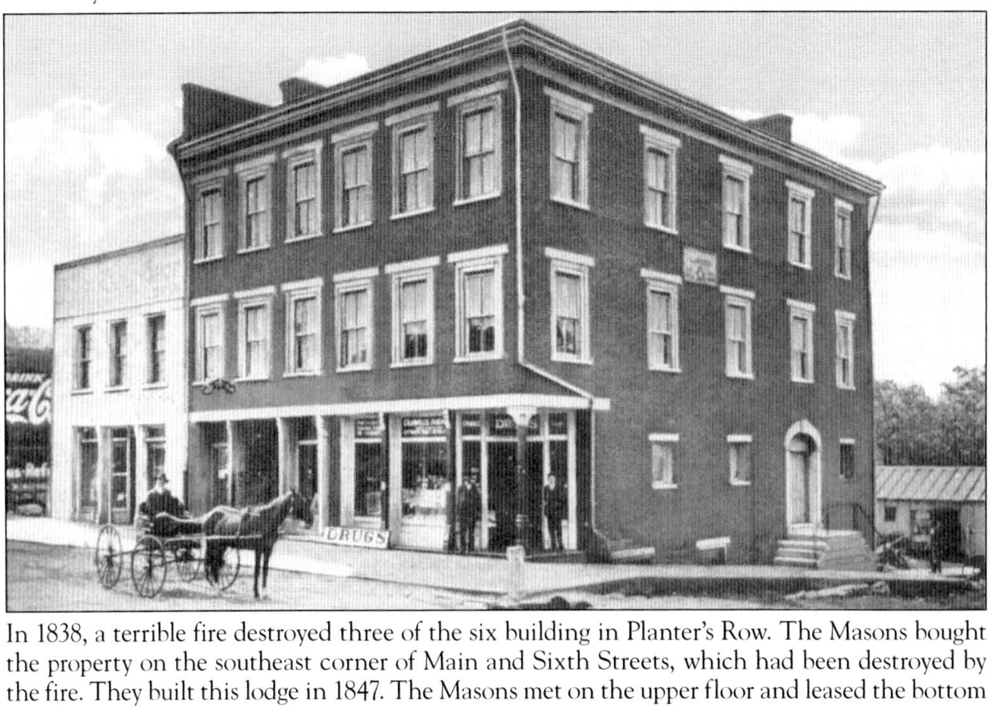

In 1838, a terrible fire destroyed three of the six building in Planter's Row. The Masons bought the property on the southeast corner of Main and Sixth Streets, which had been destroyed by the fire. They built this lodge in 1847. The Masons met on the upper floor and leased the bottom two floors.

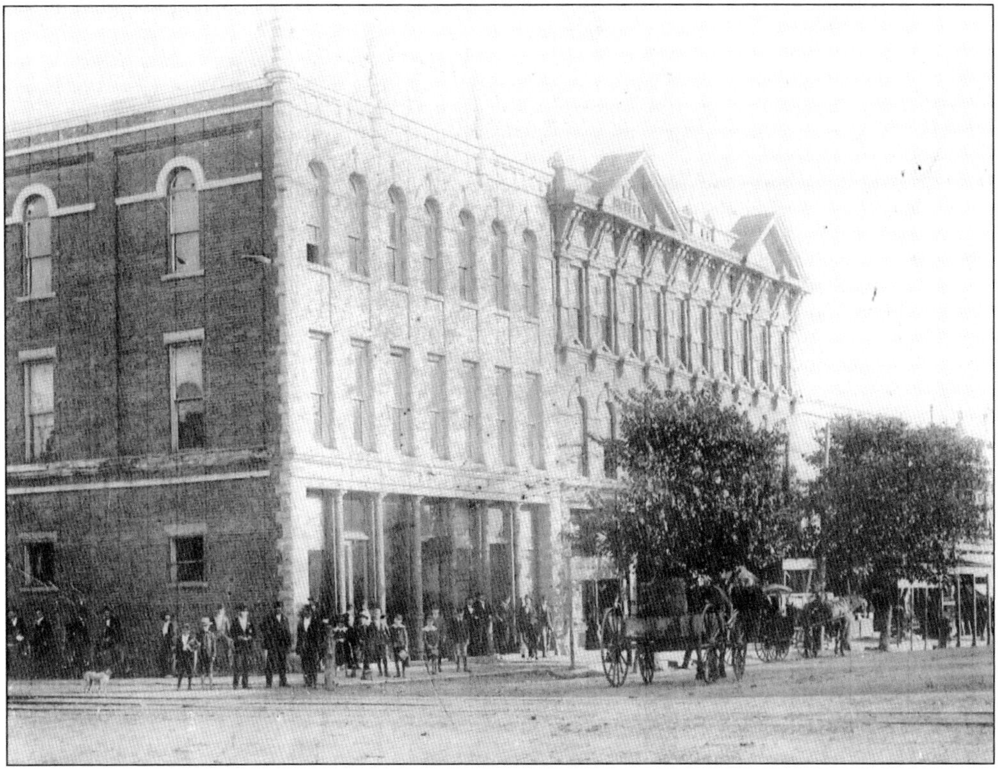

The Kirk Isbell Building and the Bickley Building were built in the late 1800s. They were built on the southeast corner of Main and Fifth Streets across from the Palace Drugstore. Many businesses leased space in these buildings, as they became some of the busiest in town.

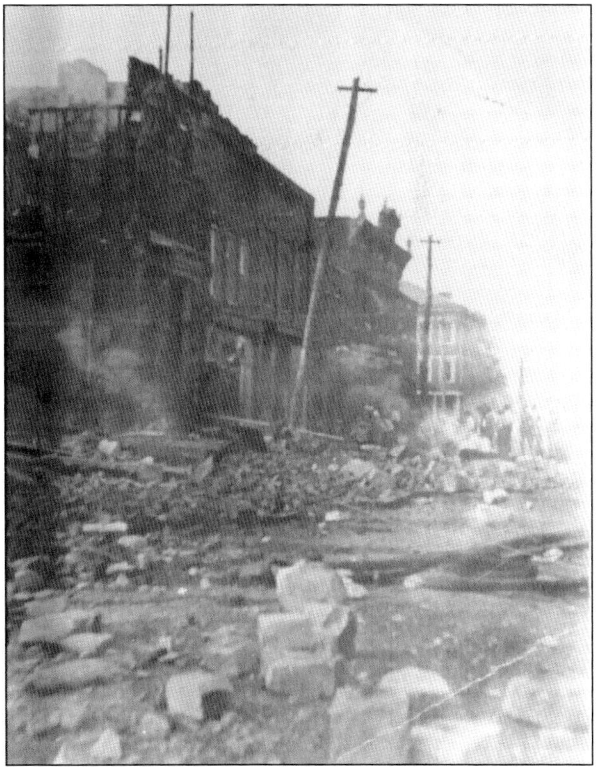

On July 7, 1944, the fire department was alerted about a fire on Main Street. The Kirk Isbell Building and the Bickley Building were engulfed by fire. The fire was too far gone to save these buildings, but the fire department was able to keep it from spreading. The fire destroyed almost half a city block.

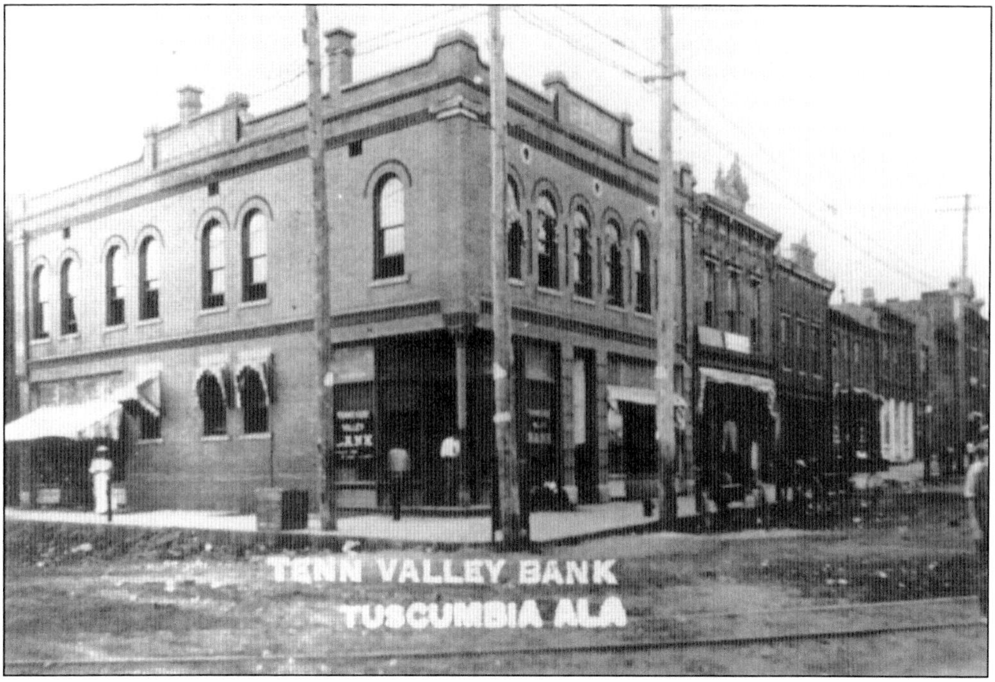

This is a photograph of the west side of Main Street between Sixth and Fifth Streets featuring the Tennessee Valley Bank. This picture was taken some time after 1903, as indicated by the streetcar tracks turning the corner. The power lines used by the streetcars are also visible.

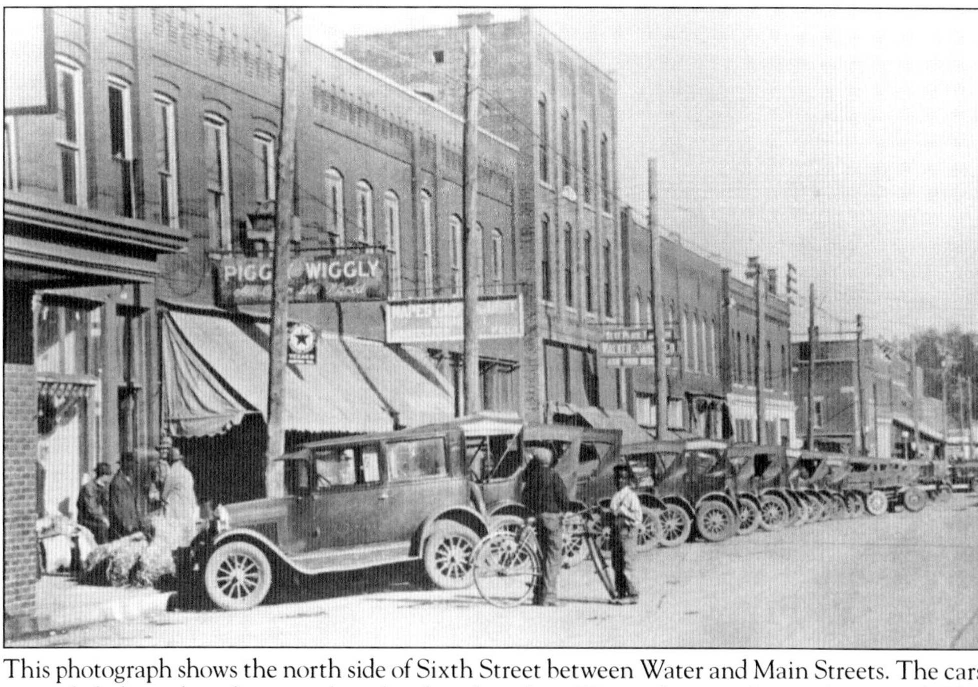

This photograph shows the north side of Sixth Street between Water and Main Streets. The cars not only help to date the scene but also show how busy Tuscumbia was during this period. The Piggly Wiggly store is in the foreground. The three-story building in the center is the Walker James Company Building.

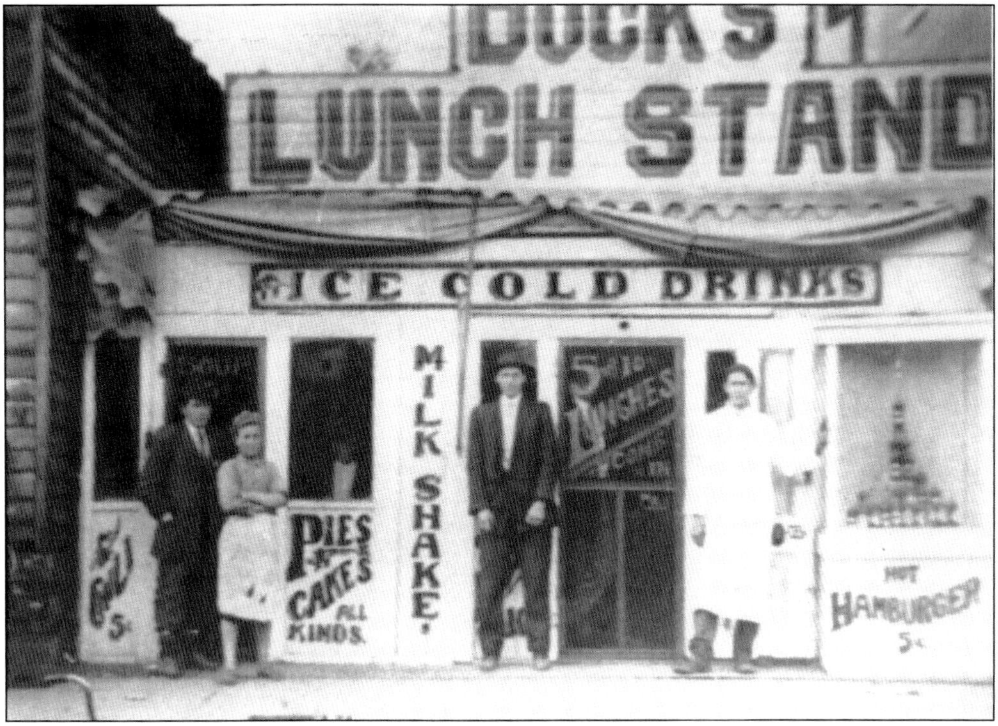

The life and landscape of Tuscumbia were changed forever by a visit to the World's Fair, or so the story goes. When "Dock" came home, he introduced a new taste to town—the hamburger—opening Dock's Lunch Stand on the north side of Sixth Street.

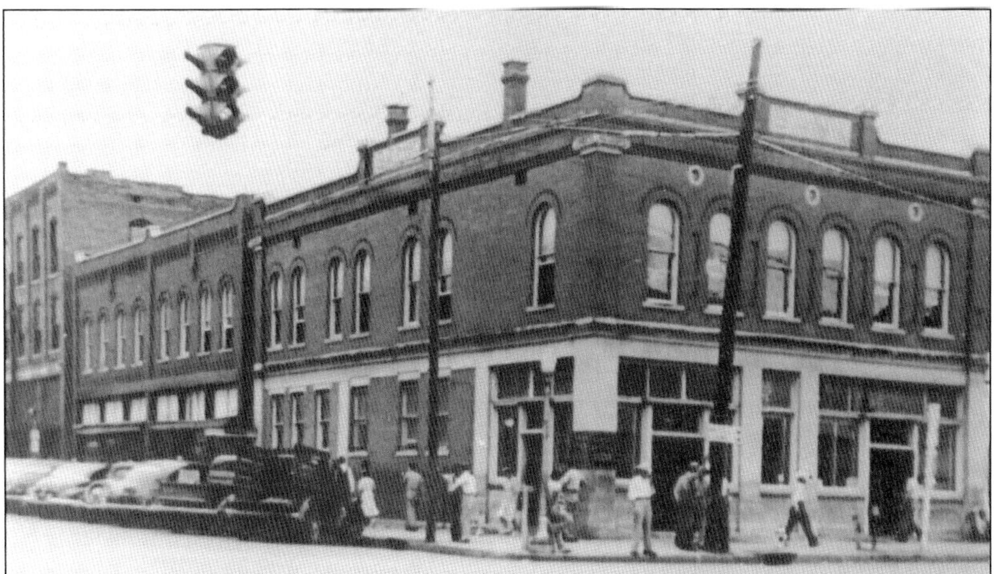

This view of Tennessee Valley Bank also shows the buildings to the west. The James and Walker Building is the only 20th-century three-story building remaining in town. Notice the streetlights were in the center of the intersection. Streetlights were moved from the center of the intersections to the sides for a few years but were moved back to the center in 1985 due to the number of wrecks.

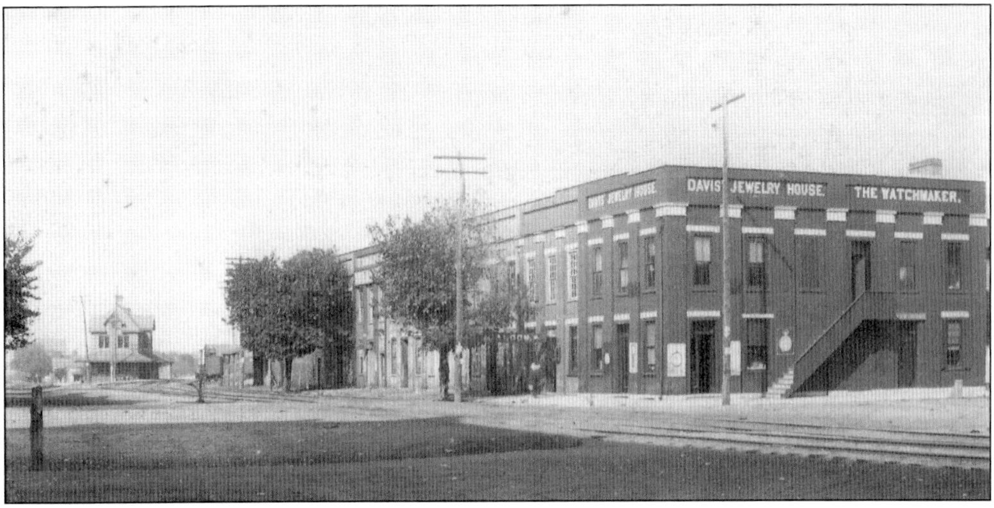

These seven buildings, collectively known as Commerical Row or Seven in a Row, were built around 1830. They were built to front the Tuscumbia Railroad Company tracks. The tracks seen in the upper picture are those of the Memphis & Charleston Railroad, which bought out the Tuscumbia Railroad in 1851. Some of the early businesses were J.T. Abernathy's Dry Goods, Darby D. McClune Dry Goods, Tim Cooley's Boots and Shoe, William H. Reese Commission Business, Bradley and McFarland Dry Goods, and Hugh and Carroll Dry Goods. Although the railroads are gone, Commerical Row still stands today as Alabama's oldest row of commercial buildings.

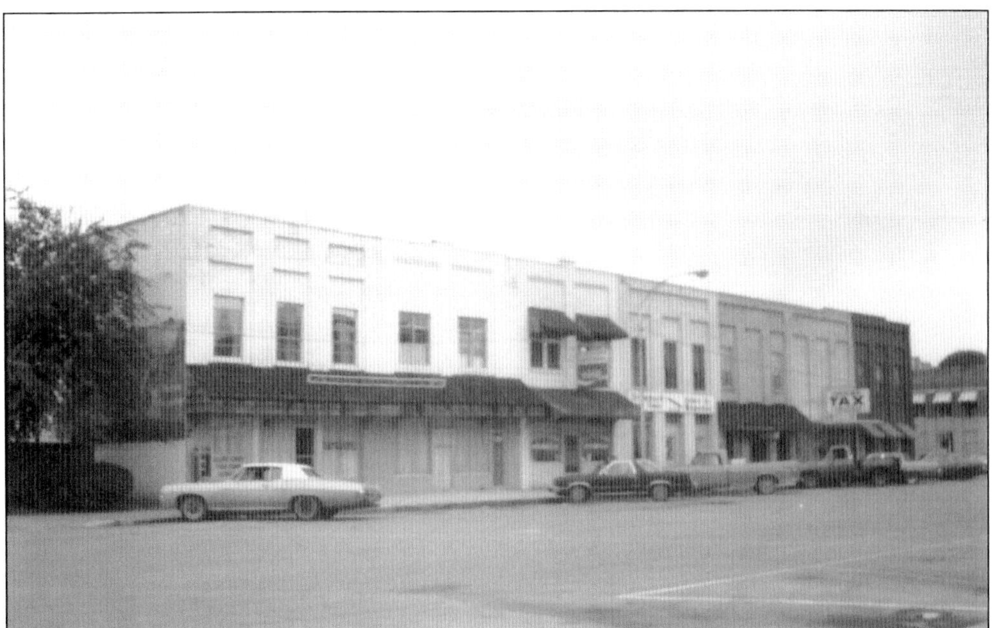

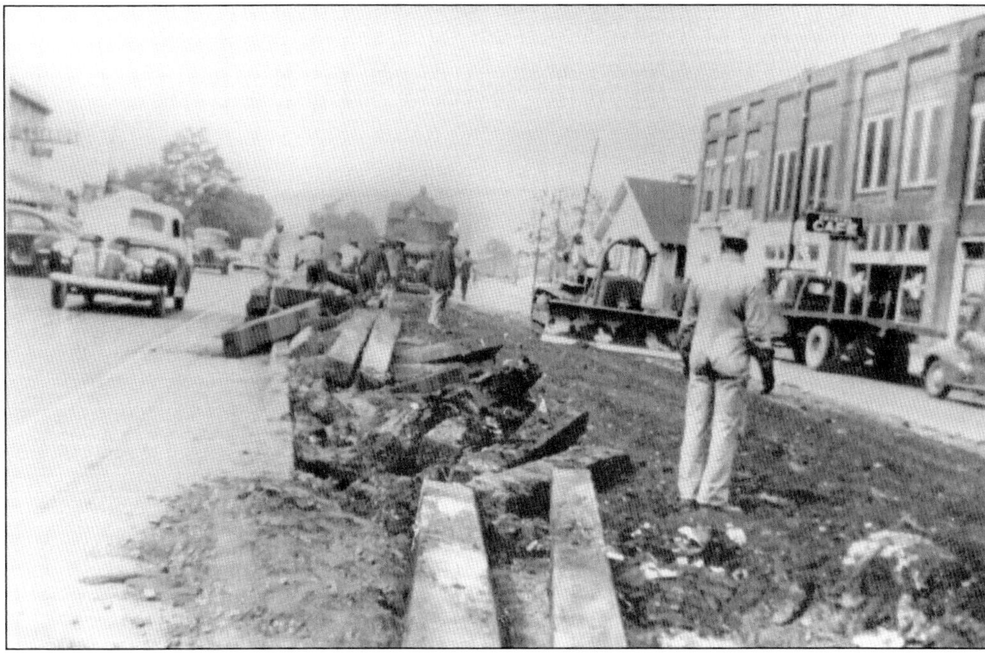

By 1948, all through trains bypassed Tuscumbia, and it had become an inland station. There was no longer a need for the tracks on Fifth Street. The Southern Railway System decided to remove its railroad tracks, but the streetcar tracks remained. The tracks to the depot from the main line remained and were used for freight delivery to Tuscumbia.

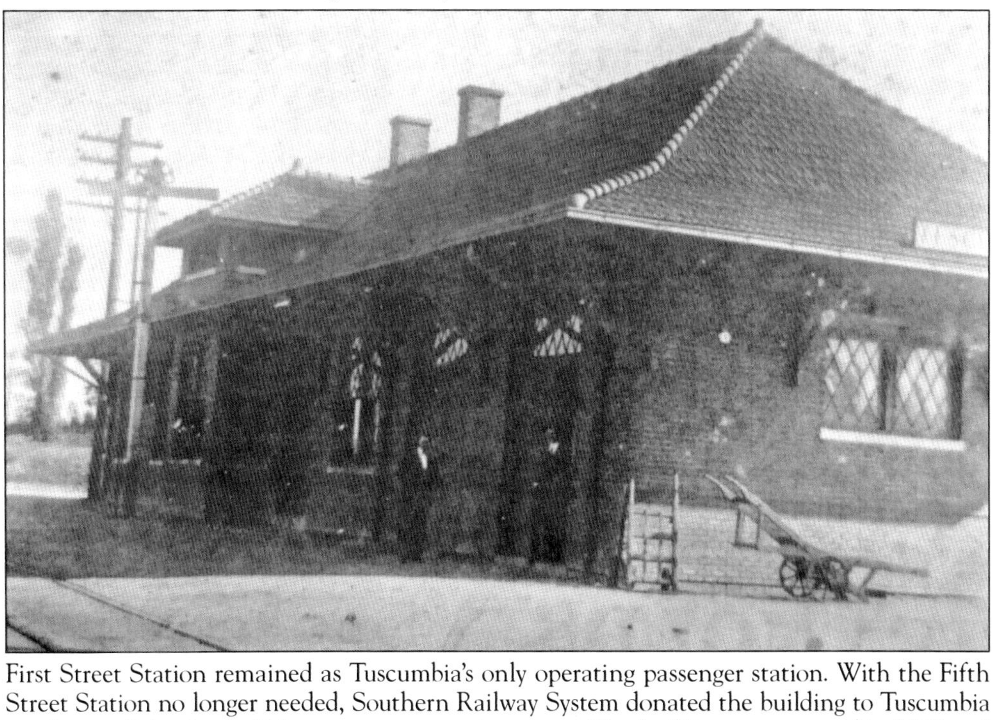

First Street Station remained as Tuscumbia's only operating passenger station. With the Fifth Street Station no longer needed, Southern Railway System donated the building to Tuscumbia on the condition it would become a community center. The building was restored in 2003 and is a railroad museum at present.

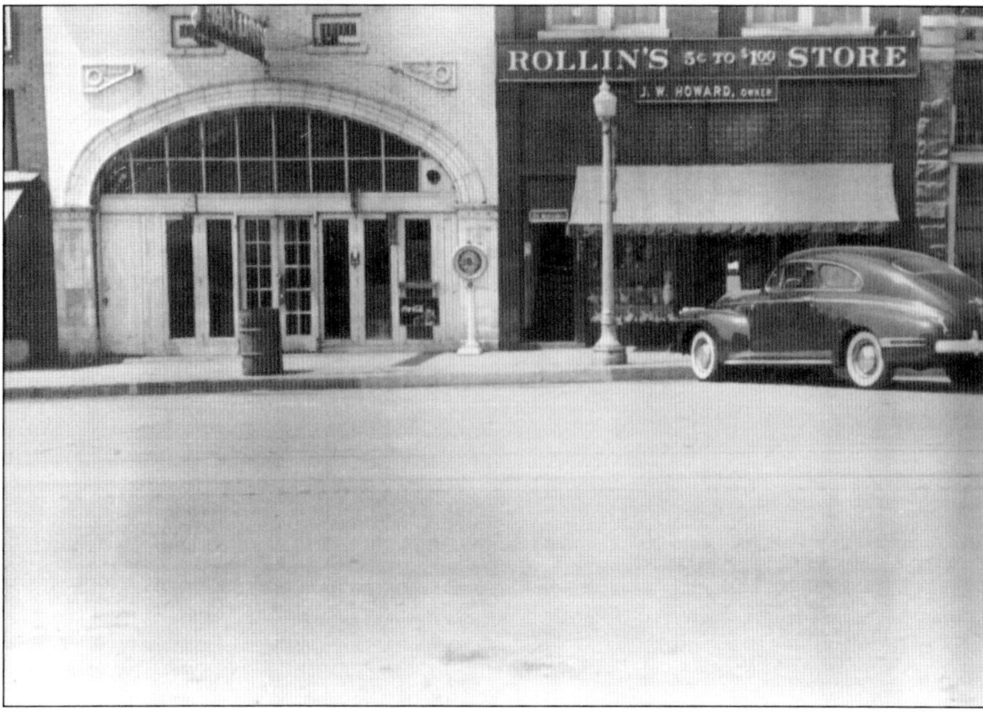

The building with the brick arch was a silent movie theater, the Bijou Theater. The story goes that a tunnel went from the theater to the Parshall House hotel on the corner of Fifth and Water Streets. The basement of the Parshall House was an entertainment center featuring gambling and drinking.

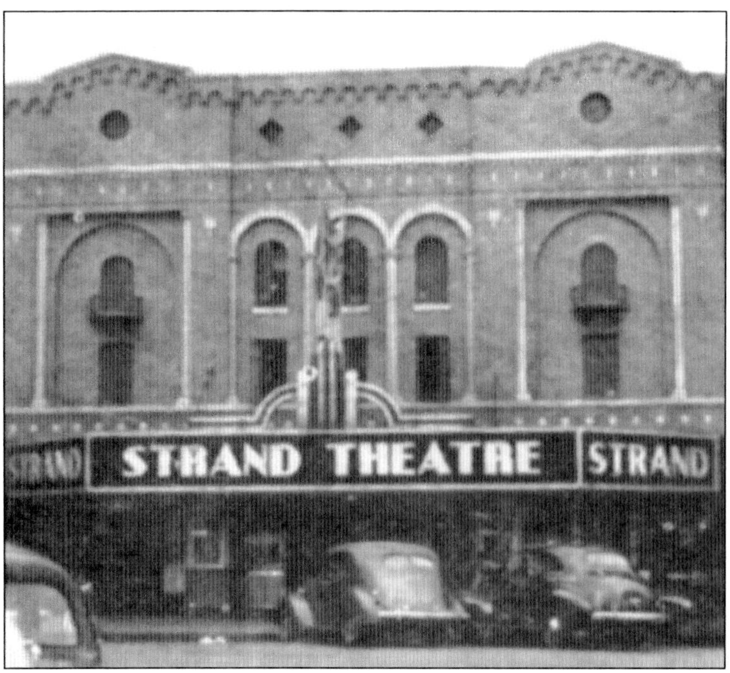

Tuscumbia had two silent movie theaters in the 1920s. They were the Bijou Theater and Pastime Theater. The beginning of "talking pictures" meant Tuscumbia had to have a new theater. The Strand Theatre was a very luxurious building with a stage and movie screen. Gene Autry, the movie actor and singing cowboy, made a personal appearance here.

Tuscumbia was a growing town after World War II. A new air-conditioned theater was needed. This new theater was built in Tuscumbia in 1950. It was named the Tuscumbian. Only the Shoals Theater in Florence was larger. For a couple of years, both the Strand and Tuscumbian were showing movies.

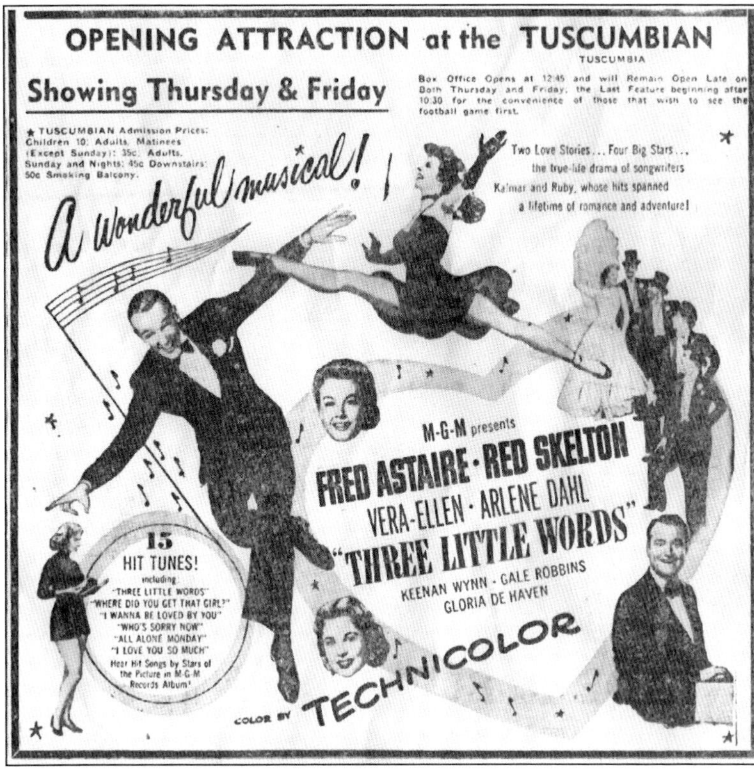

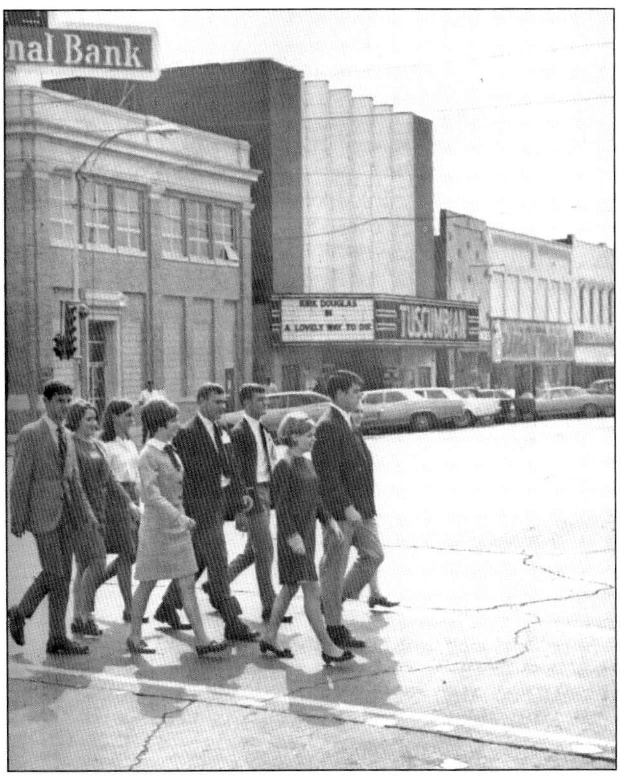

The Tuscumbian was located on Main Street between Fifth and Sixth Streets next door to the First National Bank. Pictured here walking across the street in 1968 are, from left to right, Deshler High School seniors Steve Henniger, Sherri Hill, Linda Fielder, Pam Bassett, Bill Morton, Tommy Whitehead, Elaine Greenhill, Whit Beasley, and Pat Haskins.

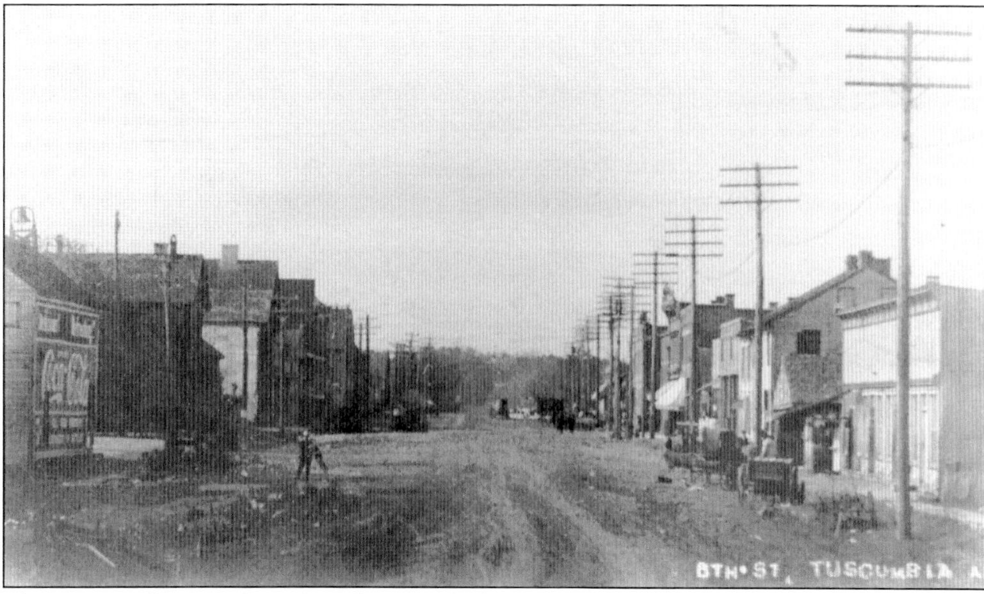

This c. 1900 photograph is of Sixth Street looking west. Located on the corner of Dickson and Sixth Streets, the fire station is the building on the left with the Coca-Cola sign on the side. The building to the right is probably the meat market. In the 1800s, there was a law requiring all meats to be sold at the meat market. Many times Dickson Street was referred to as Market Street because of the market's location.

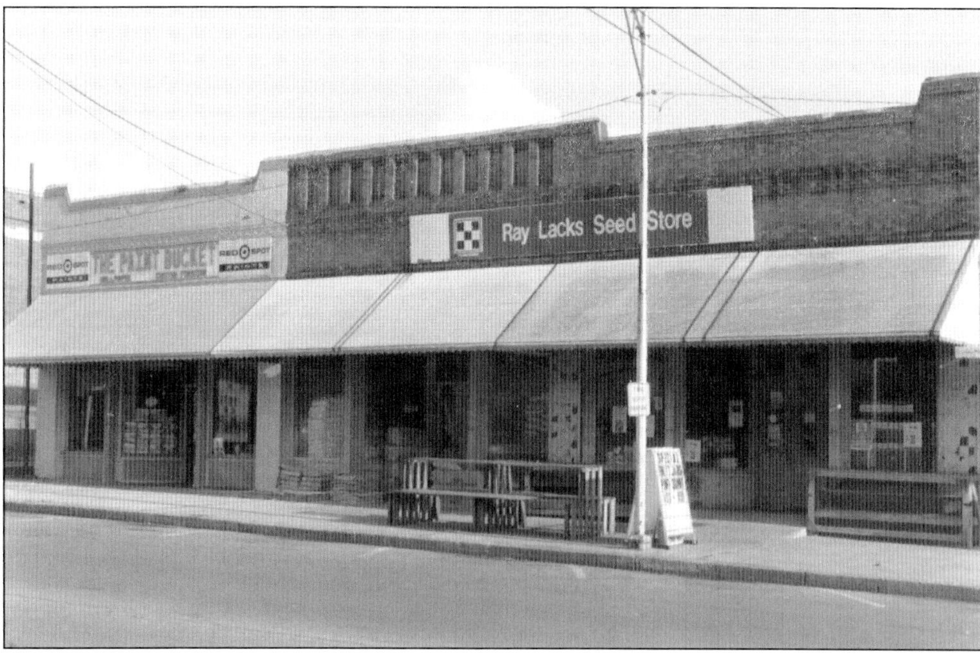

Ray Lacks Feed Store and the Paint Bucket, pictured here around 1980, were located in the area that was originally known as Planters Row. On August 1, 1838, fire broke out in Planter's Row in the Simpson and Hubert Grocery Store, and the fire department had its first major fire. All six buildings were lost, but the fire was contained and did not spread. Three of the six buildings were rebuilt on this location.

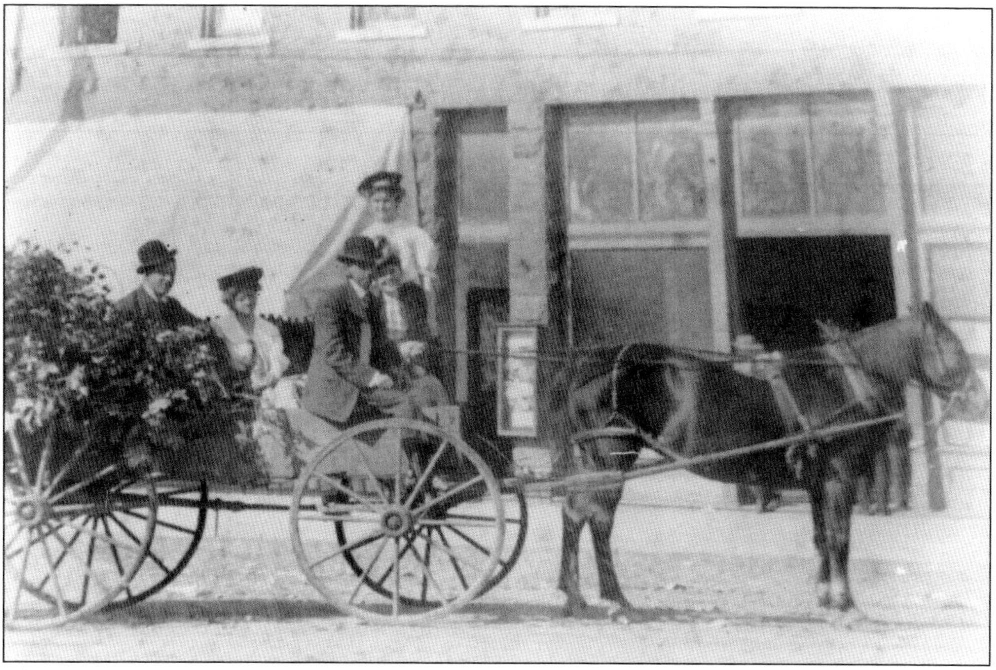

This photograph was taken on Sixth Street between Main and Dickson Streets around 1900. The people are unidentified. The buildings in the background, on the north side of Sixth Street, are still in use today. The post office was in the building to the right for many years.

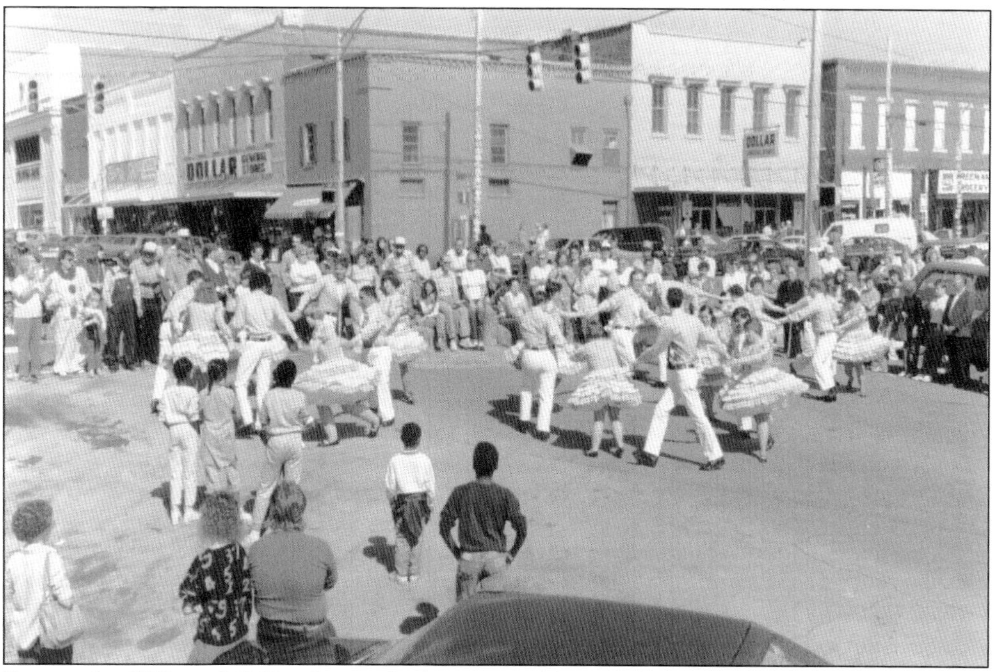

During the 1970s and 1980s, the city had a street celebration known as the Coldwater Fair. The fair featured several live events with stagecoach rides and street vendors. One of the popular events was street dancing. This photograph shows a street dance at the intersection of Main and Sixth Streets.

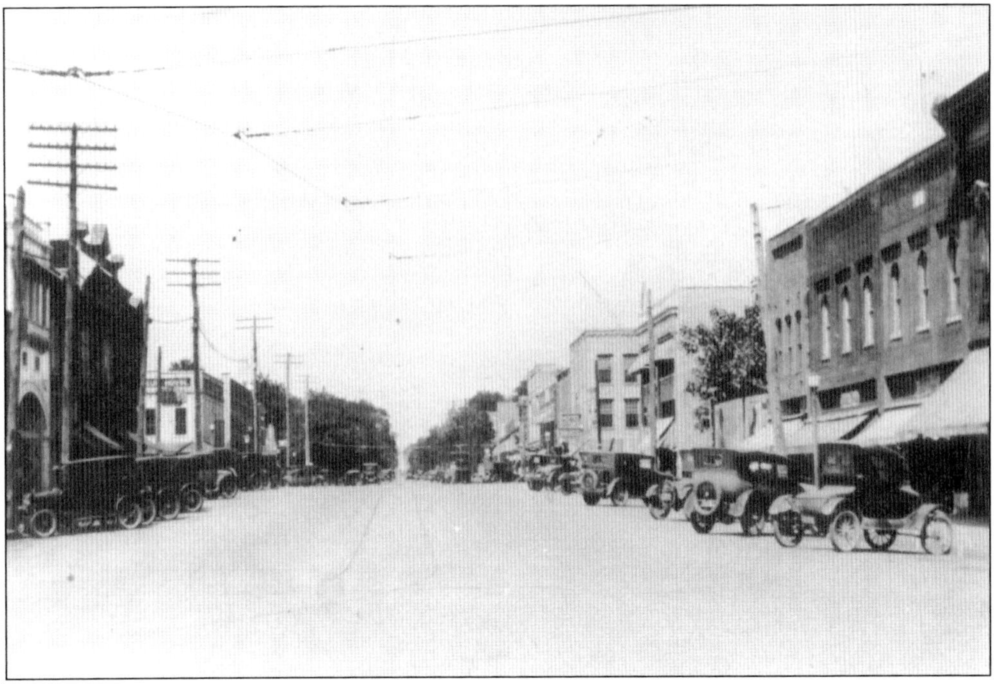

This is a view of Main Street looking north. The automobiles parked on the street easily date the picture. The Fifth Street corner still shows the damage from the fire that destroyed the Kirk Isbell and Bickley Buildings. The open lot where the trees are will be filled when the Tuscumbian Theater is built.

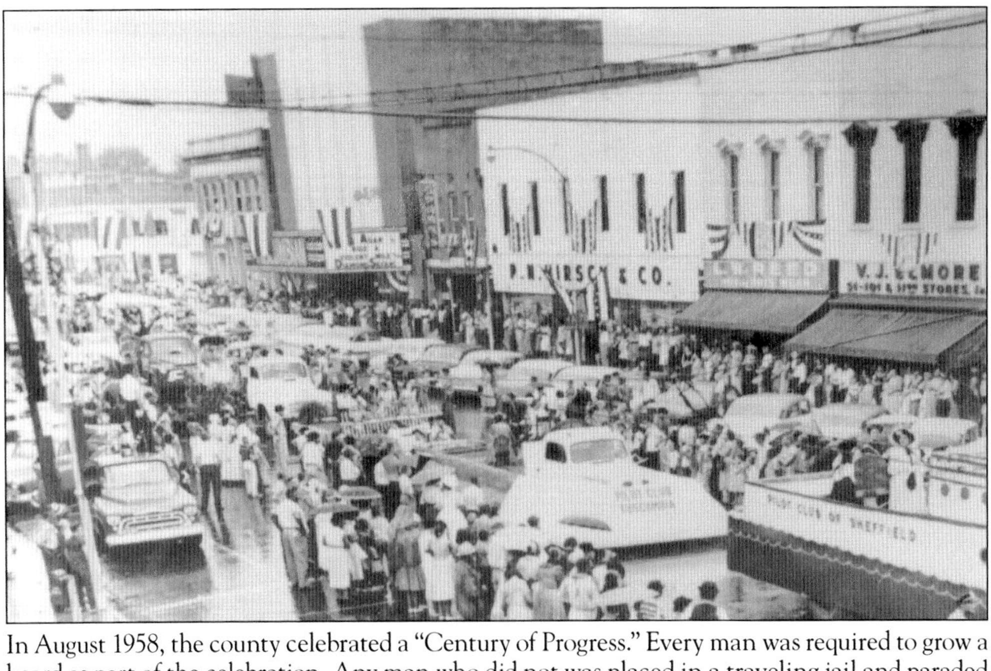

In August 1958, the county celebrated a "Century of Progress." Every man was required to grow a beard as part of the celebration. Any man who did not was placed in a traveling jail and paraded around town until he was able to raise bail money from the crowd. The parade traveled from Muscle Shoals, through Sheffield, to Tuscumbia and then finished at Spring Park.

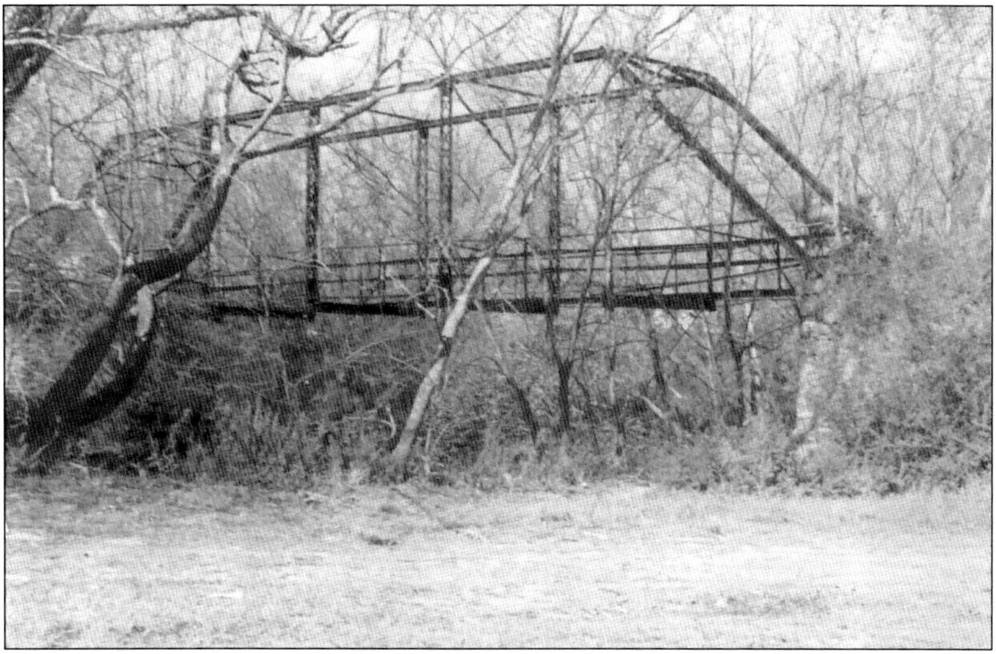

Spring Creek was a major obstacle for anyone trying to go west when the water was high. The ford, located just up creek from the Hindman's Mill dam, would be impassable. The Franklin County Commission decided to build a bridge across the creek around 1830. The original bridge was a wooden structure until this iron bridge replaced it around 1920.

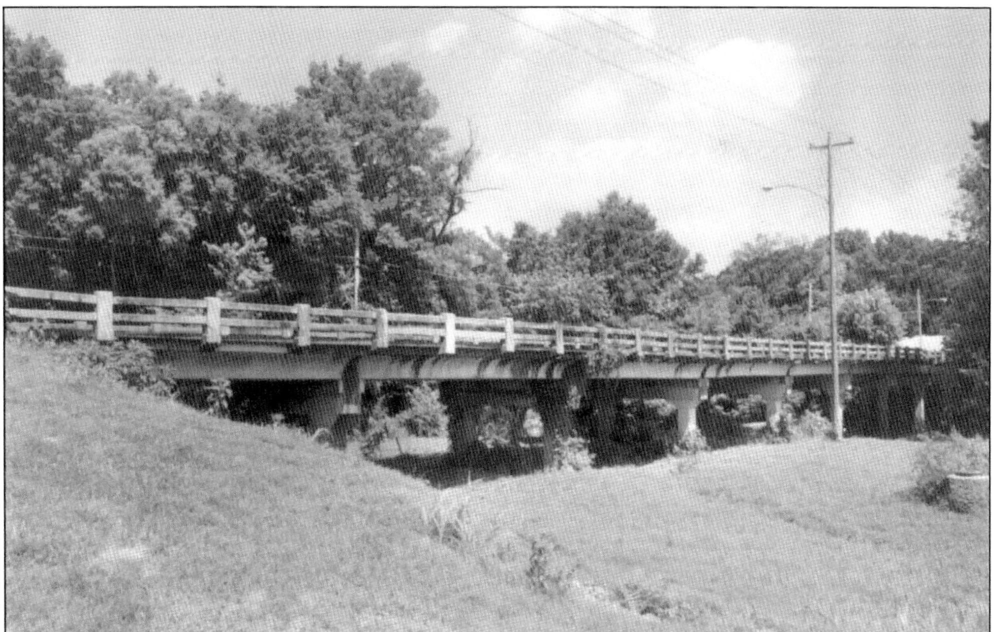

Lee Highway was constructed in the 1920s from Washington, DC, to San Diego, California, passing through Tuscumbia. This new concrete bridge was built as a part of the highway system just west of the County Bridge. The first automobile crossed over the bridge on July 10, 1928. This bridge has since been replaced.

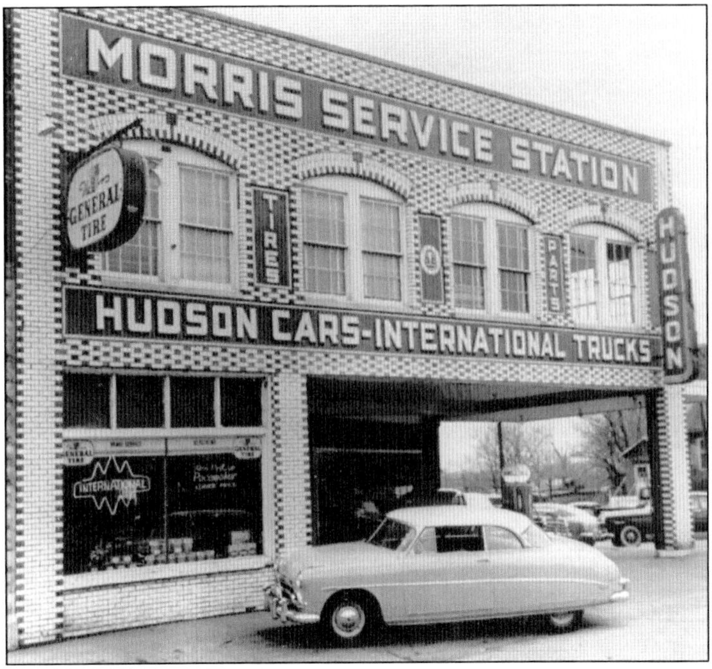

Charlie Morris entered the service station business in Tuscumbia in 1935. He began on the corner of Sixth and Dickson Streets, and prospered. He became a Hudson dealer and built a new store on the southeast corner of Sixth and Water Streets. This building is owned today by Kenny Von Boeckman.

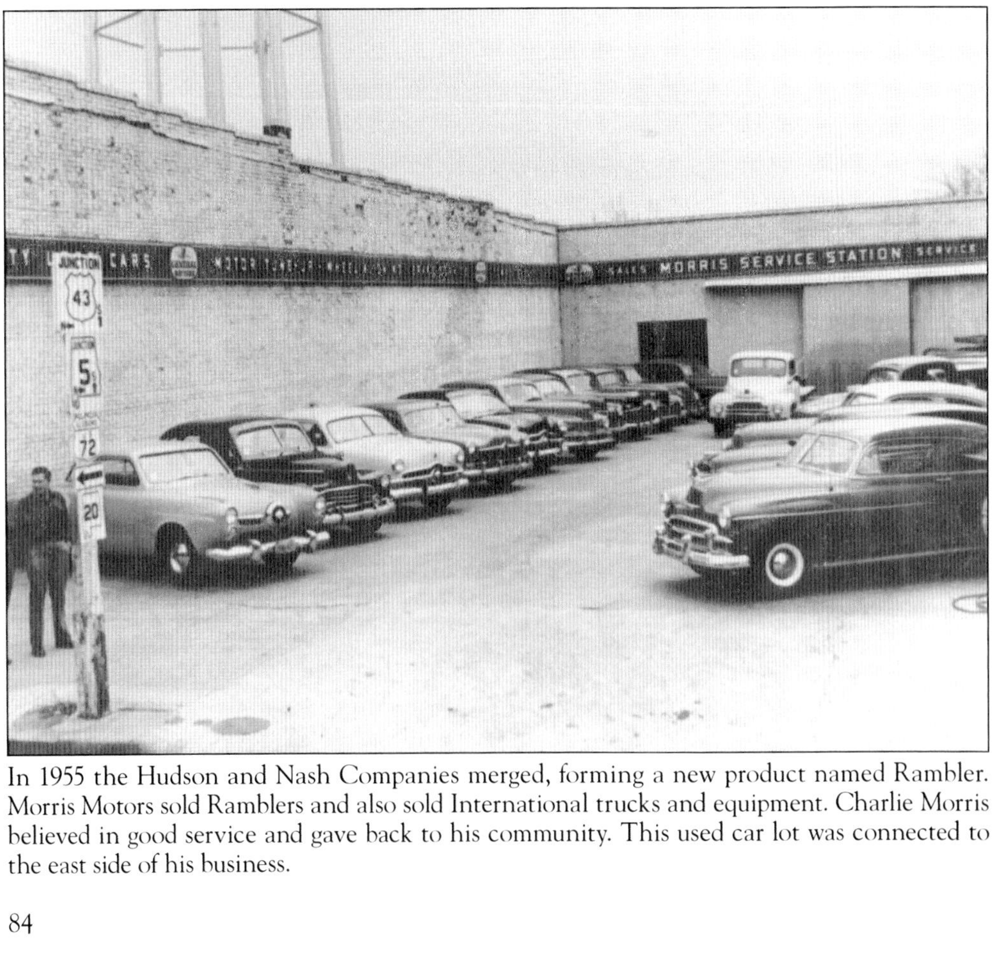

In 1955 the Hudson and Nash Companies merged, forming a new product named Rambler. Morris Motors sold Ramblers and also sold International trucks and equipment. Charlie Morris believed in good service and gave back to his community. This used car lot was connected to the east side of his business.

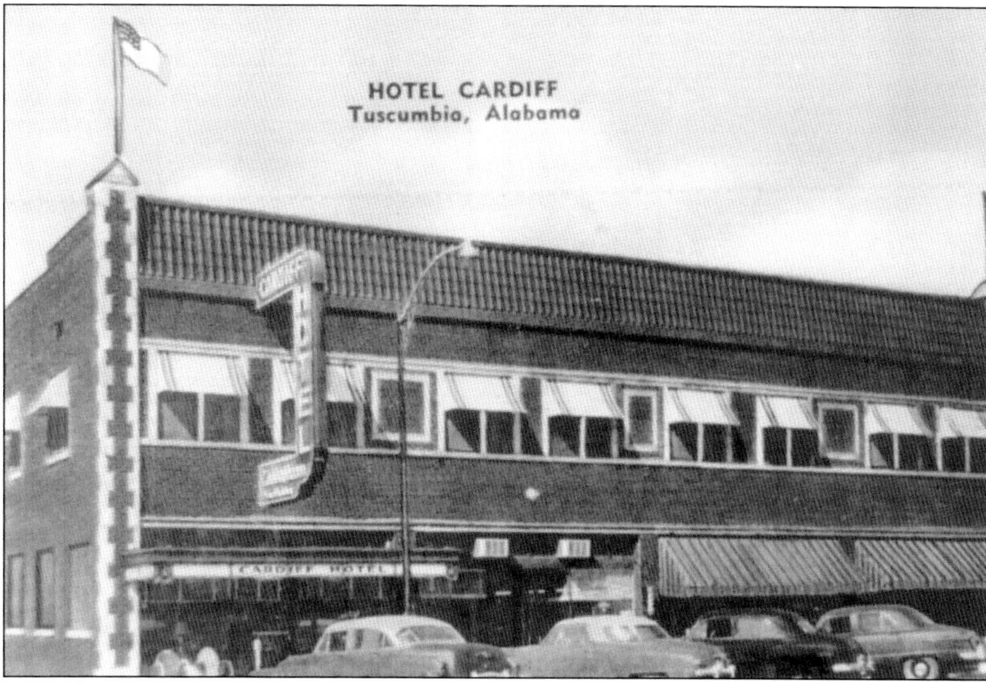

In the first half of the 20th century, roads and railroads passed through town bringing a regular stream of visitors to Tuscumbia. This brought many tourists through the downtown area. The destruction of the Franklin House hotel by fire in 1915 left a need for a hotel downtown. The Cardiff Hotel was built on Main Street, filling the need.

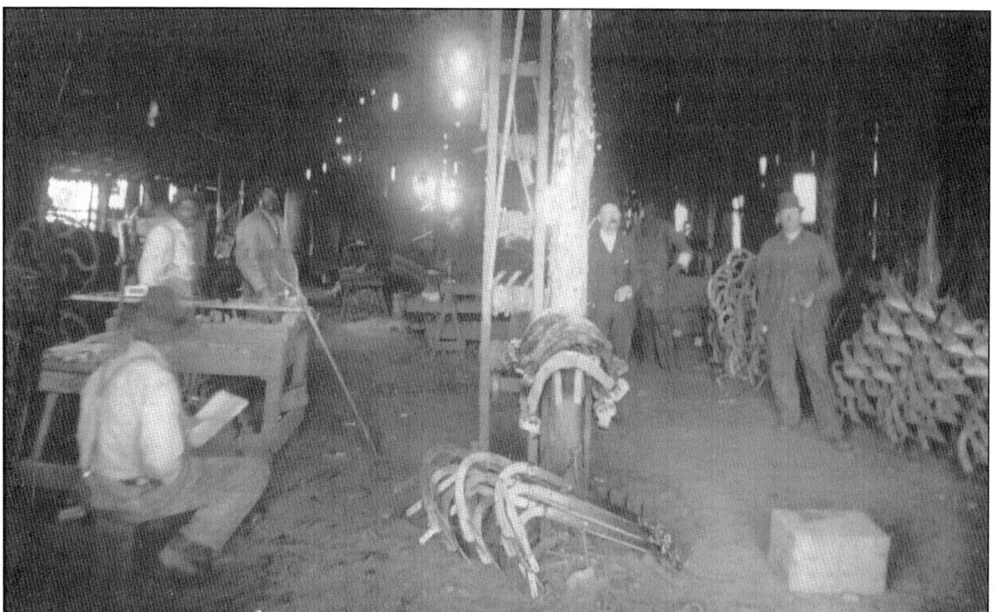

In 1978, C.T. Barton, a Tuscumbia businessman, invented and patented a cultivator. He created Barton Agricultural Works. T.T. Rowland, a Tuscumbia blacksmith, built the cultivators. His shop, the interior of which is pictured here, was located on Water Street between Sixth and Fifth Streets.

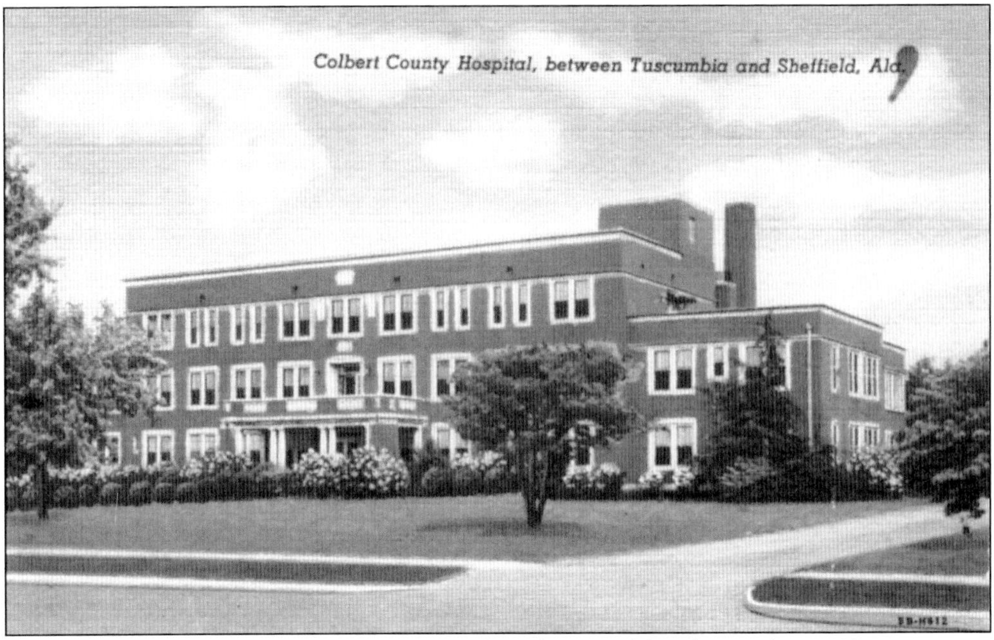

The overwhelming growth of Colbert County brought a need for a hospital. In 1927, an area was chosen on the border of Tuscumbia and Sheffield for the construction of the Colbert County Hospital. The hospital has undergone four major renovations and expansions. Today, the award-winning hospital is known as the Helen Keller Hospital.

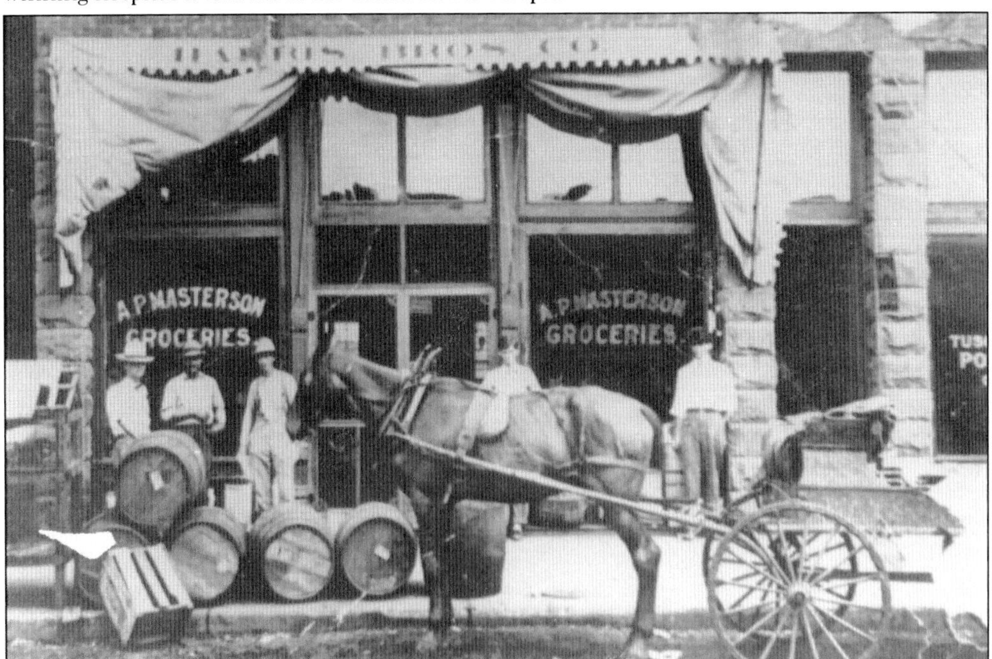

Harris Brothers and Company, located on the north side of Sixth Street between Main and Dickson Streets, sold groceries and produce from this building in 1878. In 1910, Aaron Harris was listed as owner, with P.L. Braden as manager. A.P. Masterson probably purchased the grocery business after 1910. The post office was located next door at this time.

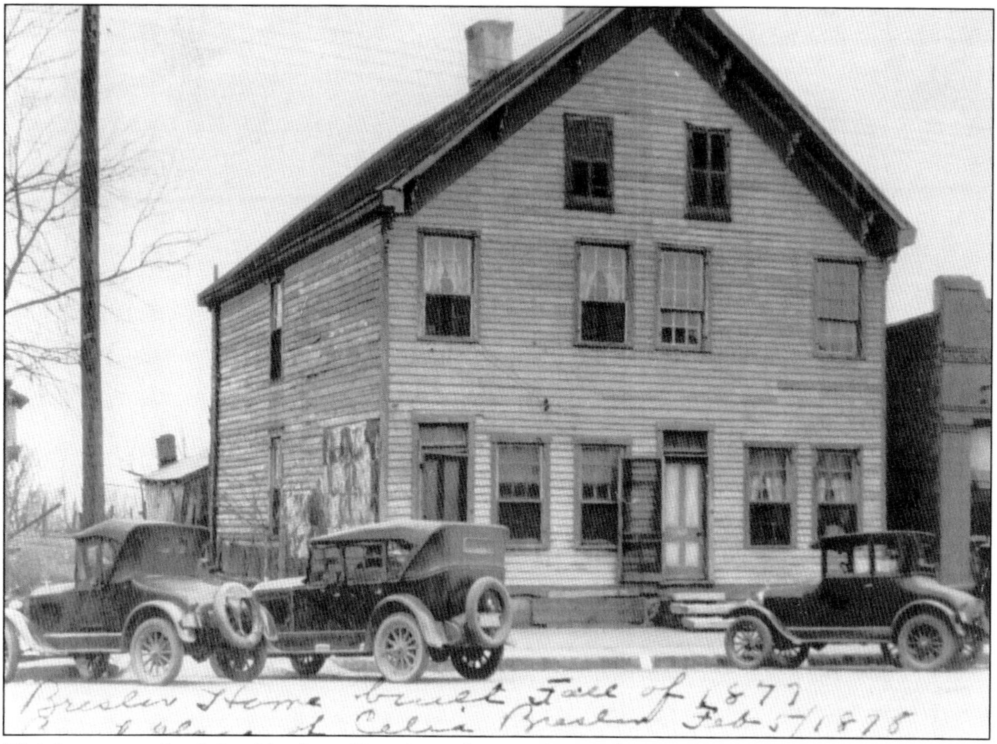

This home was built by Abraham Bressler, a dry goods merchant who also sold hides and furs. In the 1930s, the US Postal Service began to search for a place to build a new post office. A place downtown was needed, and this is the location that was chosen.

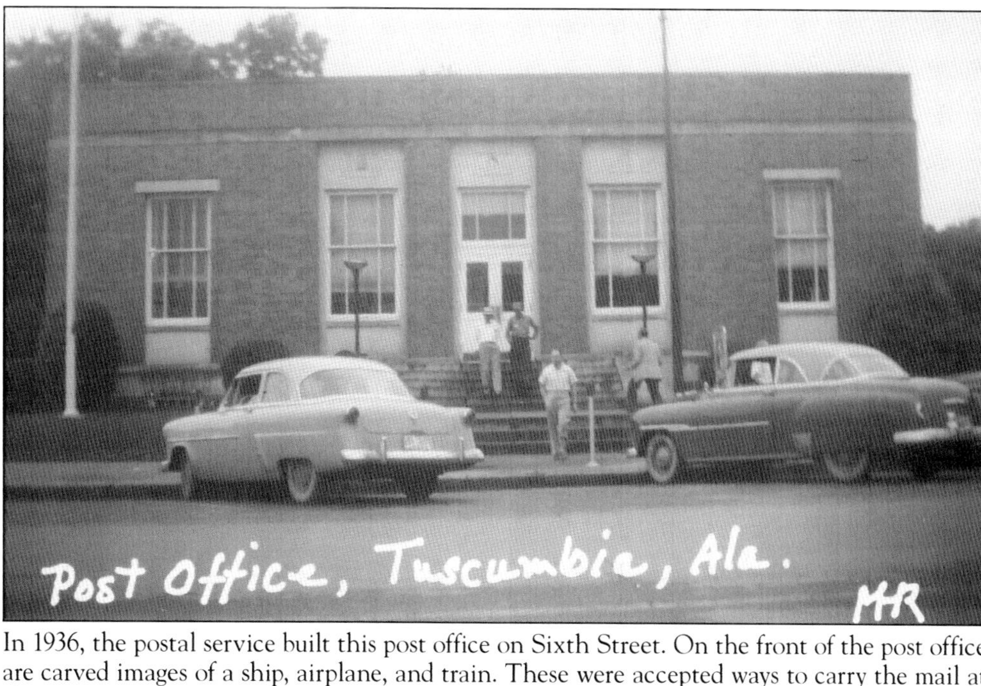

In 1936, the postal service built this post office on Sixth Street. On the front of the post office are carved images of a ship, airplane, and train. These were accepted ways to carry the mail at this time. Passenger trains usually carried a postal car to help with mail delivery.

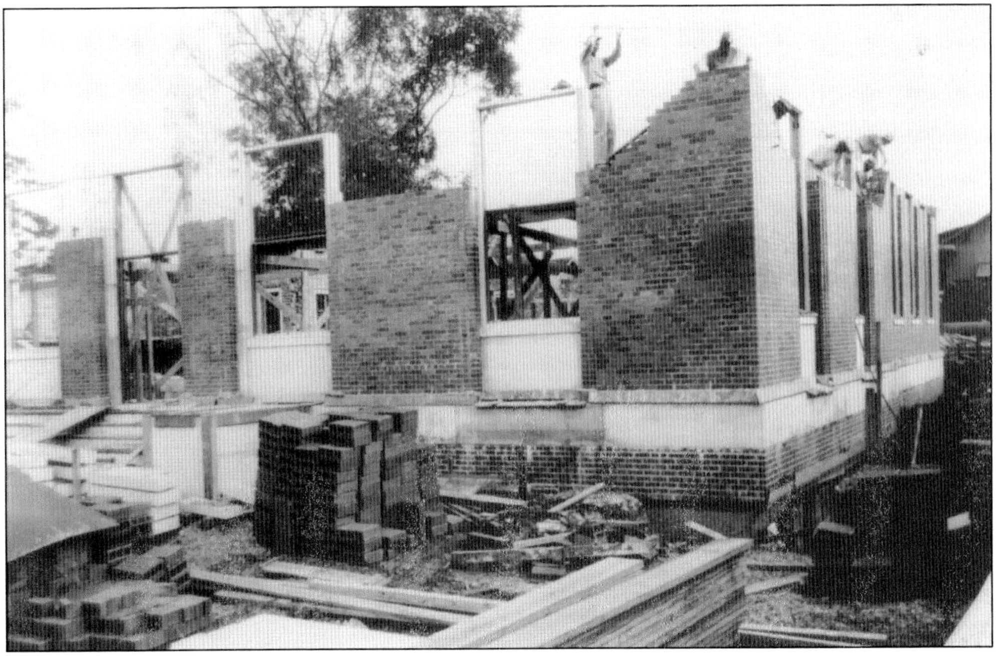

The first postmaster for Tuscumbia was Col. William McDonald, who served under Gen. Andrew Jackson and was known by the nickname "Bully McDonald." The postal service was much different in the 1800s. Whoever was chosen as postmaster, usually a merchant, would have to host the post office in his store.

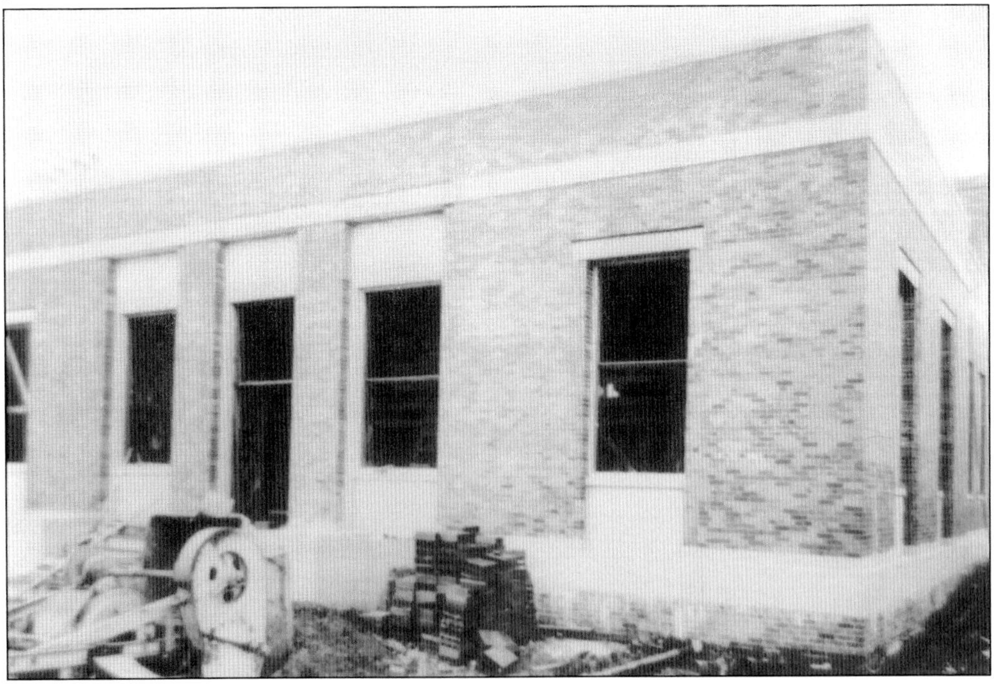

At this time, there was no home mail delivery; the mail recipient's name was printed in the newspaper. The person would then pick up their mail at the post office. A growing town with mail delivery needed a post office to work out of. Notice the exterior walls are solid brick.

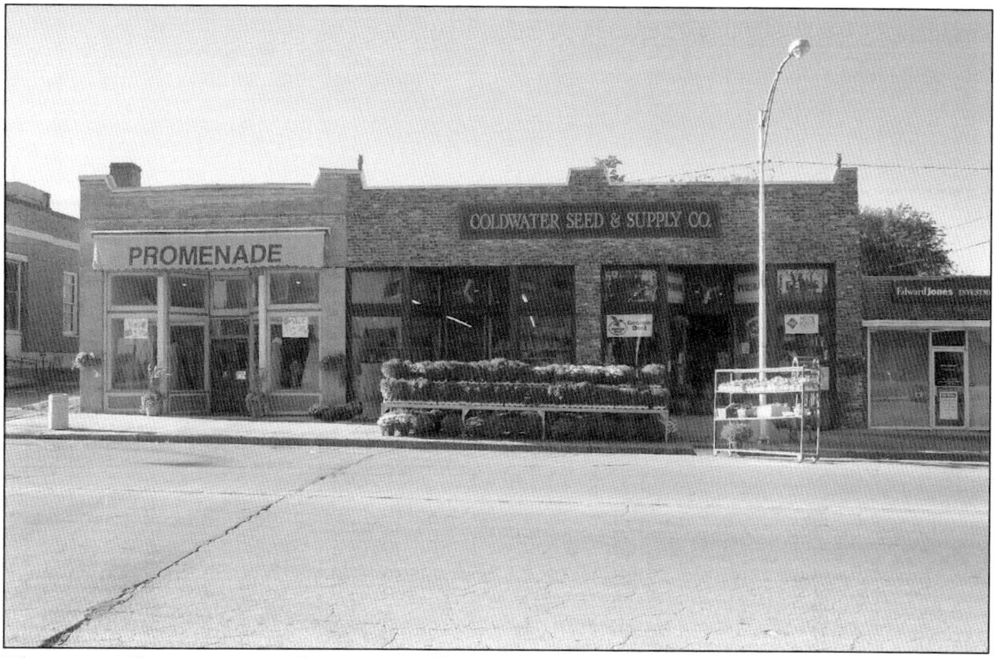

The new millennium was to bring many changes to downtown Tuscumbia. The old Lacks Feed Store was remodeled. Dwight James moved into the building and renamed it Coldwater Seed & Supply Company. Rebekah Underwood moved her business, Promenade, into the building next door.

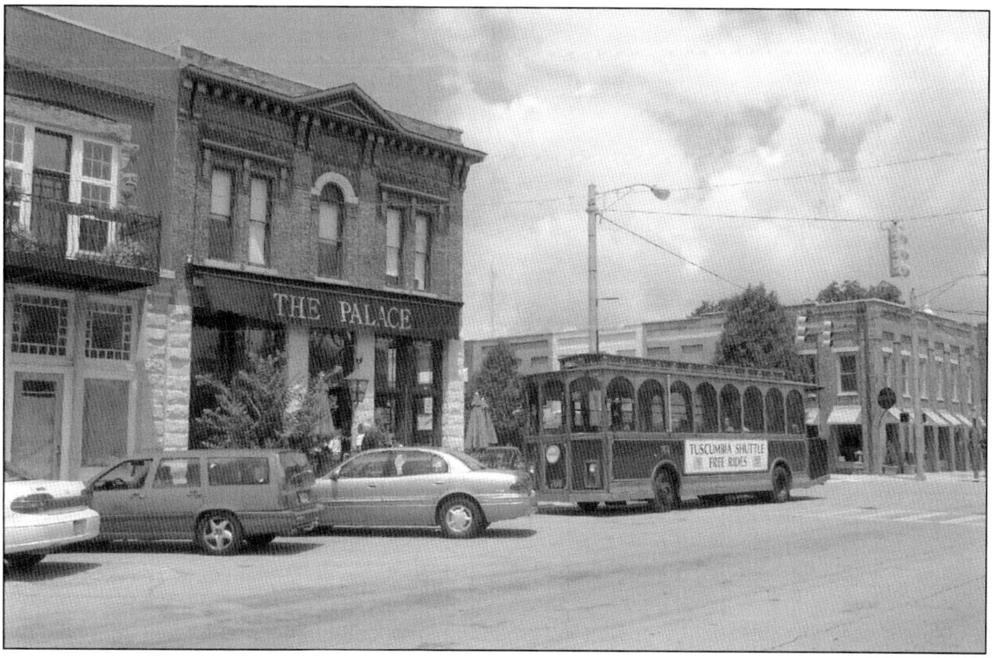

Harvey and Joyce Ann Robbins bought the abandoned Palace Drugstore building. The old drugstore and soda shop was prominent in their high school memories, so they decided to restore the building back into a soda shop. Today, the Palace Ice Cream and Sandwich Shop occupies the building.

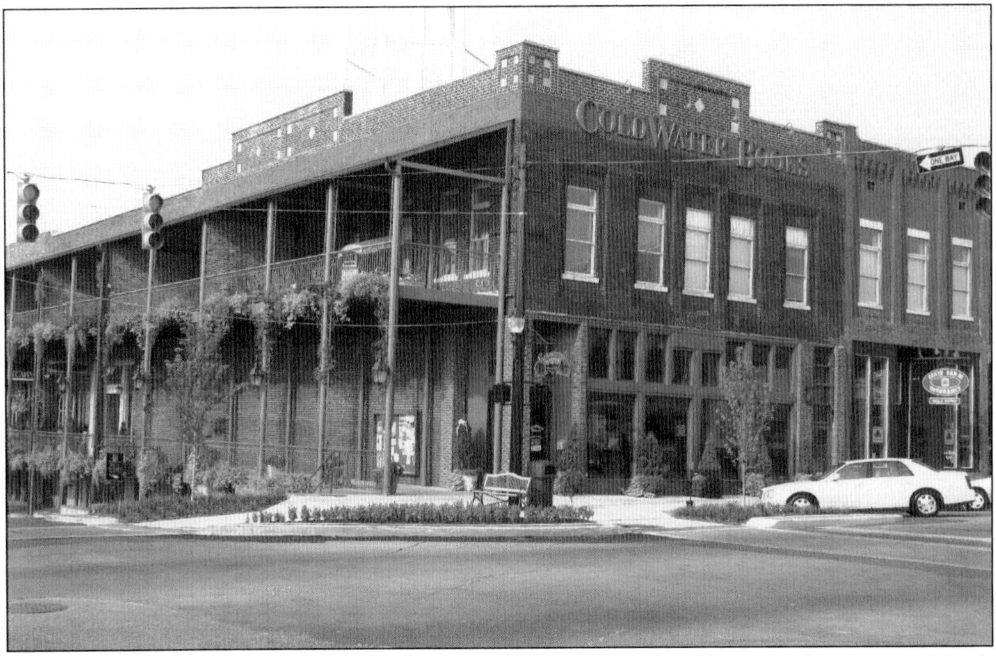

Robbins Property Development decided to remodel the series of buildings on the corner of Sixth and Main Streets. Apartments were built in the second stories, while businesses occupy the lower floors. When this structure was built around 1900, the basement floor contained cots. Visitors to Tuscumbia could pay a dime to sleep on one of the cots.

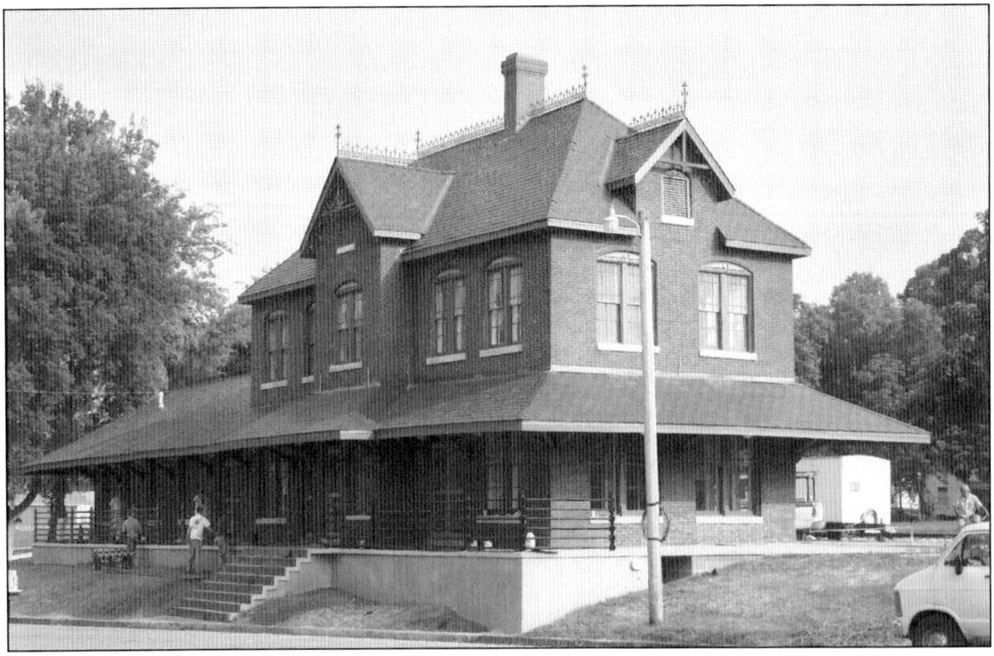

The old 1888 Memphis & Charleston Railroad depot underwent major restoration work in 2004. The building was restored to its days of grandeur when it was the pride of Tuscumbia and the main station for the railroad. In its heyday, over 30,000 people would buy tickets here each year. Today, the building contains the Tuscumbia Railroad and Transportation Museum.

Four

EDUCATION

The formation of a new town on the frontier in 1820 caught the eye of elderly schoolteacher John Anderson. Anderson arrived in town and asked to be the town's schoolteacher. He was asked to write an essay by which he would be judged. He became a very respected teacher and a justice of the peace, thus being able to perform matrimonial ceremonies for some of his students.

The citizens saw the importance of a good education and formed schools for both boys and girls. There were coeducational schools starting in the 1830s. When the state decided to build the University of Alabama, Tuscumbia asked to be considered as the host town. When it became clear that the school was going to Tuscaloosa, citizens approached the Methodist Conference suggesting a college be built near Tuscumbia. This college became LaGrange College and would be the first college in Alabama, incorporated in 1830.

Like most Southern towns in the years following the Civil War, Tuscumbia had a dual school system for white and black children. African American schools were closed in the 1960s, and all Tuscumbia children started attending the same schools.

This chapter covers the Tuscumbia school system as recorded by the camera.

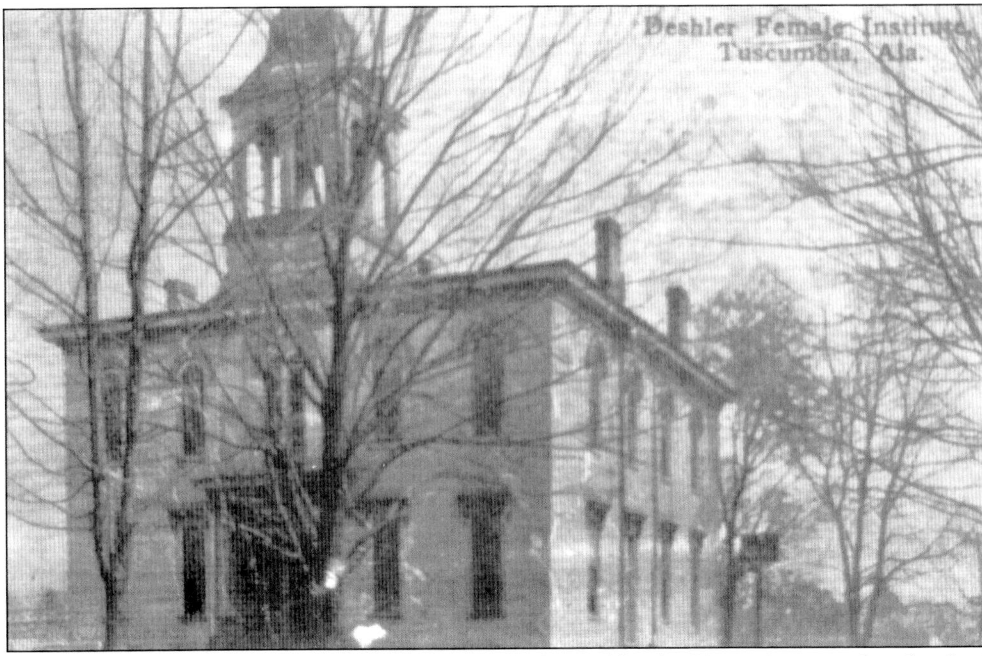

The Tuscumbia Female Institute was reported to be burned by the Union League after the Civil War. Because of the absence of a school for women, David Deshler willed to Tuscumbia the city block his home was on to build a school. The school was named in honor of his son Brig. Gen. James Deshler, who was killed at Chickamauga fighting for the South.

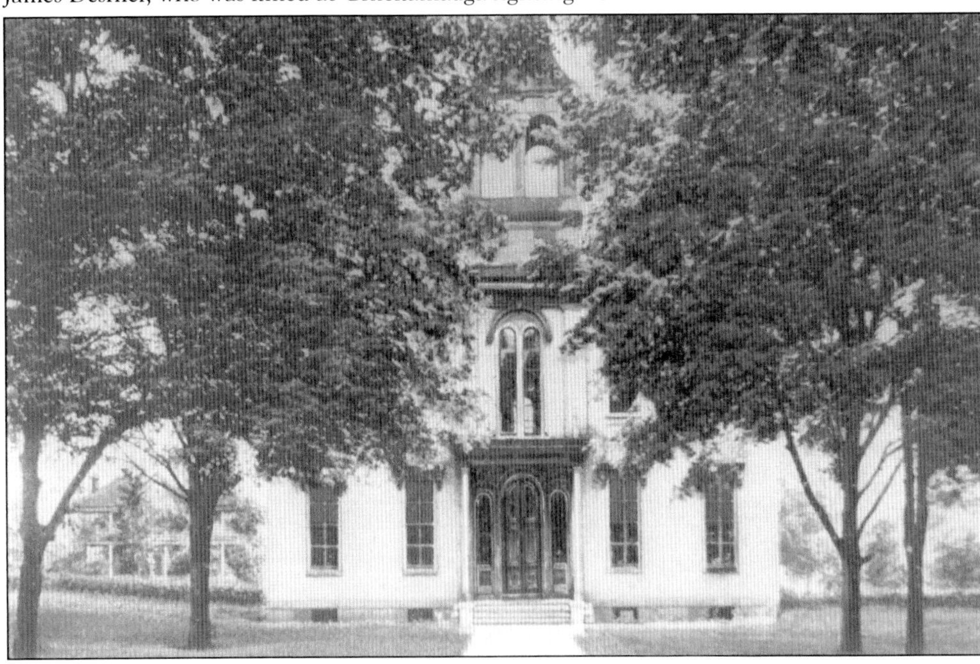

The Deshler Female Institute opened in September 1874, only to have a tornado destroy the school on September 24, 1874, along with the Deshler home, which was used as a boardinghouse for the school. It was thought to be a miracle that no one was killed. The school was torn down to build Deshler High School in 1922.

In 1887, the city of Tuscumbia started a public school system for both blacks and whites. The only property the city owned that could be used for a school for whites was the town square on East Seventh Street. The school became the Tuscumbia Public School with grades one through twelve.

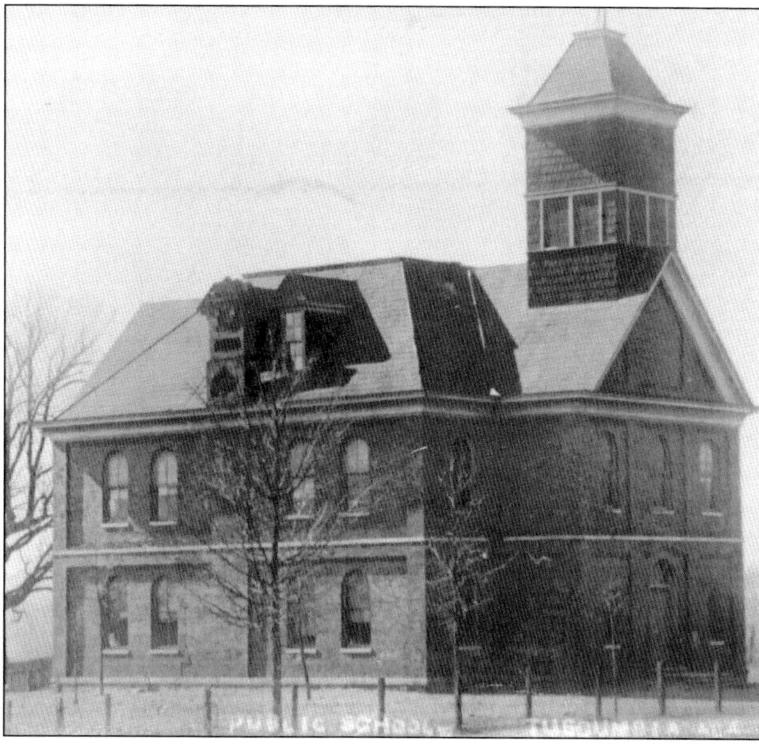

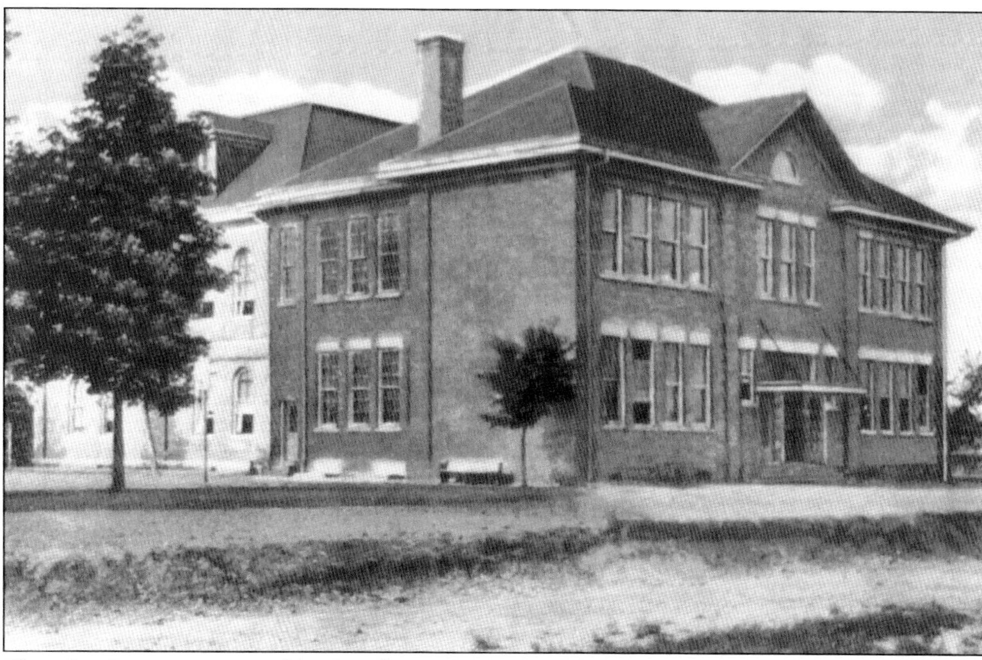

The school system grew quickly after the construction of the Southern Railway System roundhouse and shops north of town. The city decided to build an addition to the back of the school instead of building a new school; the growth continued. In 1922, the school system was in need of another addition or a new school.

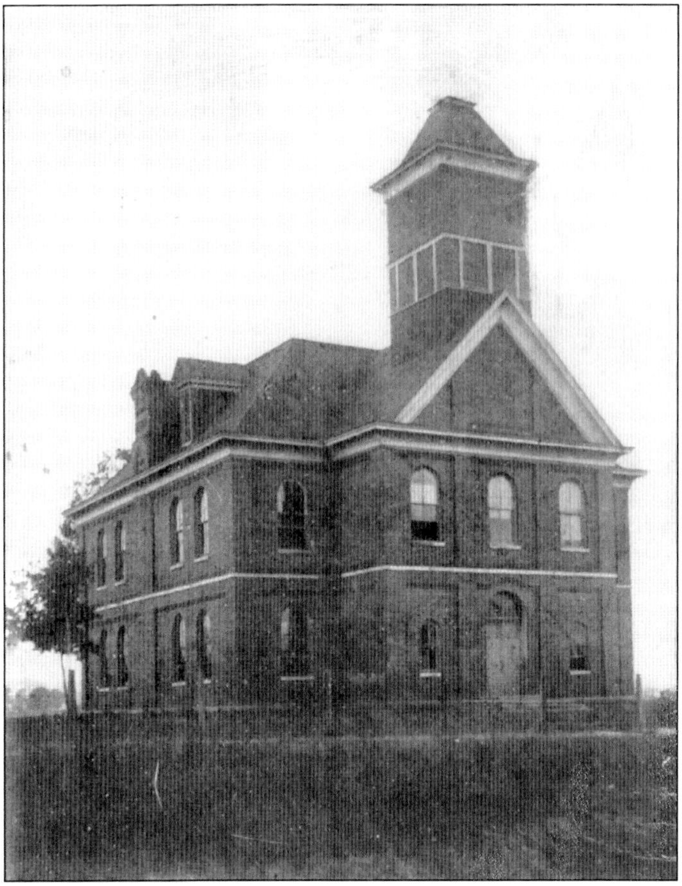

On December 18, 1928, the fire alarm was sounded at Tuscumbia High School. The maintenance man living on-site reported that he awoke to find a fire in the basement. He called the fire department, but the fire spread quickly. The building was a total loss.

The city decided to build a new grammar school, known as Cave Street School, on the same location as the old school. In later years, this building was used for Head Start. It was also used as the Tuscumbia School Board's offices until new offices were built near Deshler High School. The city sold the building to a private enterprise in 2010.

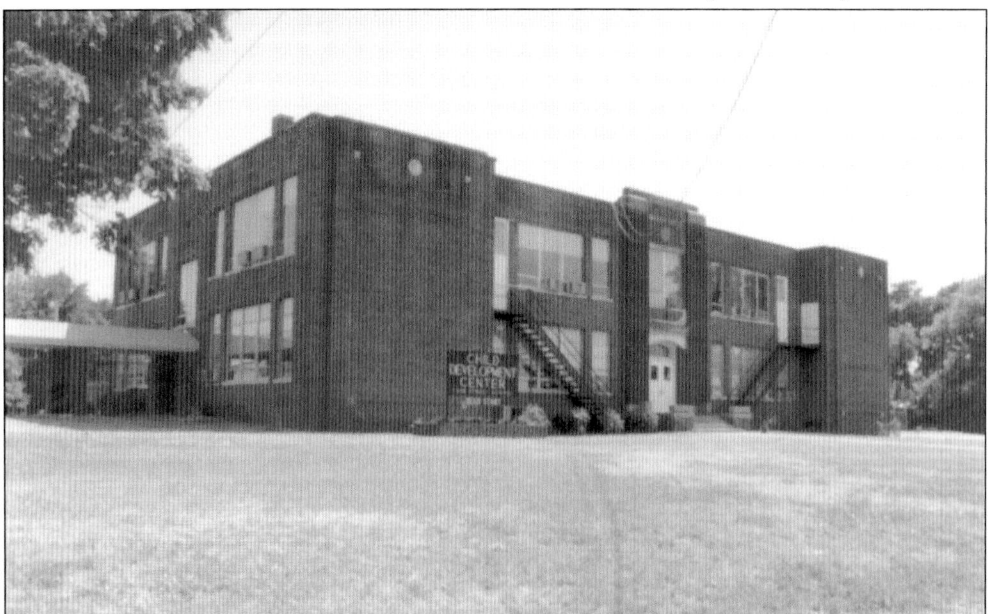

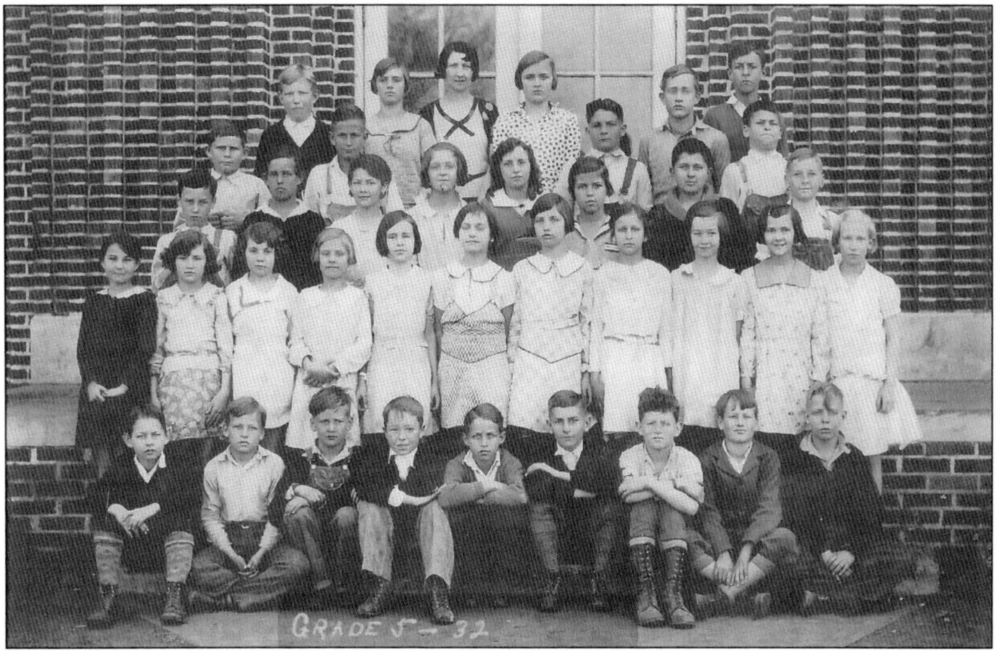

In addition to this school, the city went on to build other grammar schools. This school became known, not by the street it faces, but by the dominant feature in the area, a big cave. The school was known as Cave Street School. Pictured is Mrs. Casper's fifth-grade class in 1932 on the steps of the school.

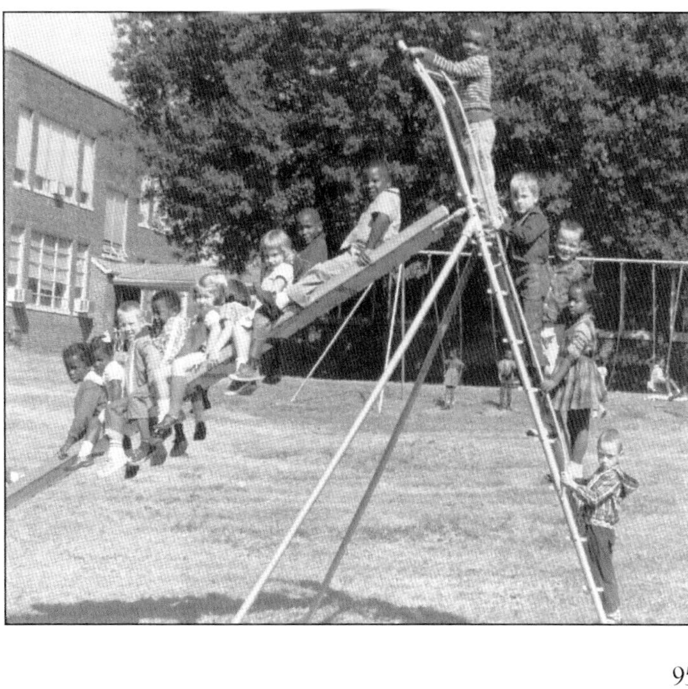

This is a picture of the rear of the old Cave Street School when it was being used as a building for the Head Start Program. It was taken during the 1967–1968 school year. Pictured are, from left to right, (on the slide) Lisa Jones, Vicki Crawford, Kenny Henson, Robert Martin, Anna Uhlman, Tina Thomason, Sherry Lindsey, Chester Byrd, and William Reed; (on the steps) Darryl Danley, Greg Malone, Timmy Reeves, Mattie Darby, and Timmy Patterson.

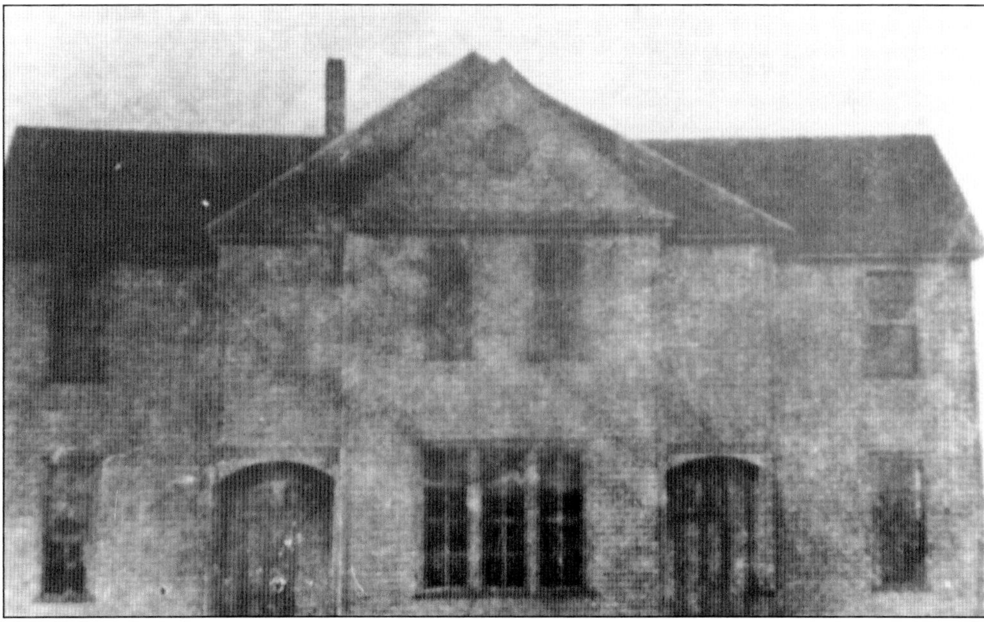

Formal education at African American schools in the area is thought to have begun around 1870. Osburne Colored Academy, pictured here, was built in 1877 and appears to have been renamed Tuscumbia Colored Public School. The name was changed to Trenholm High School in 1921 in honor of George Washington Trenholm, who was principal from 1896 to 1916.

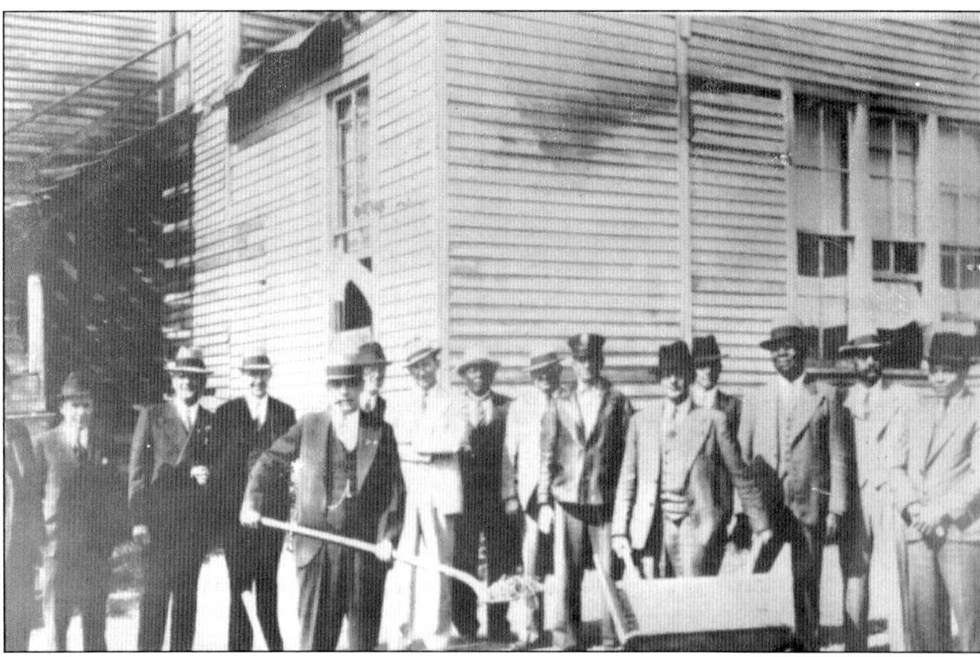

After over 50 years of education of African American children, the wooden Osburne Colored Academy School building began to deteriorate and needed to be replaced. This picture is of the groundbreaking ceremony for the new school. The old Osburne Academy building was torn down, and the new school was built on the same location.

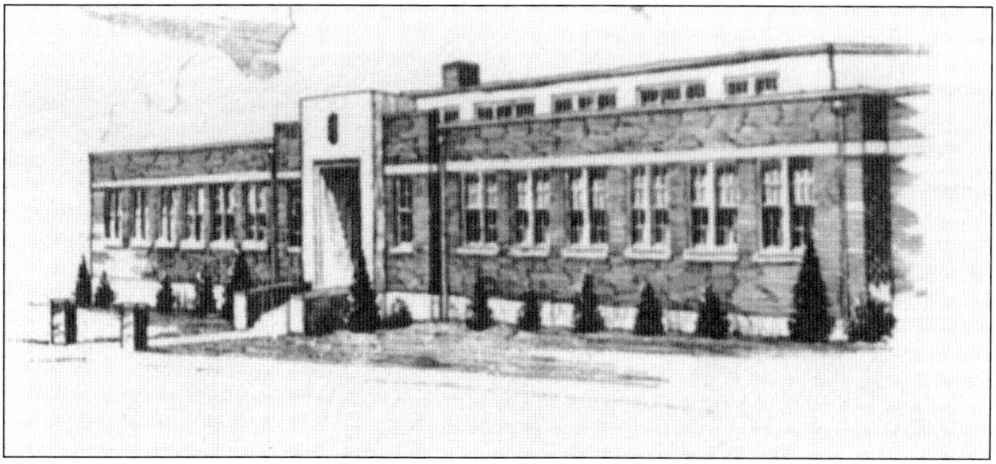

Trenholm High School became the center for culture, leadership, and recreation for the African American community and offered movies, concerts, lectures by well-known speakers, and sporting events. To meet a variety of needs for educational programs, community support was given to the school by parents and other community members by fundraising.

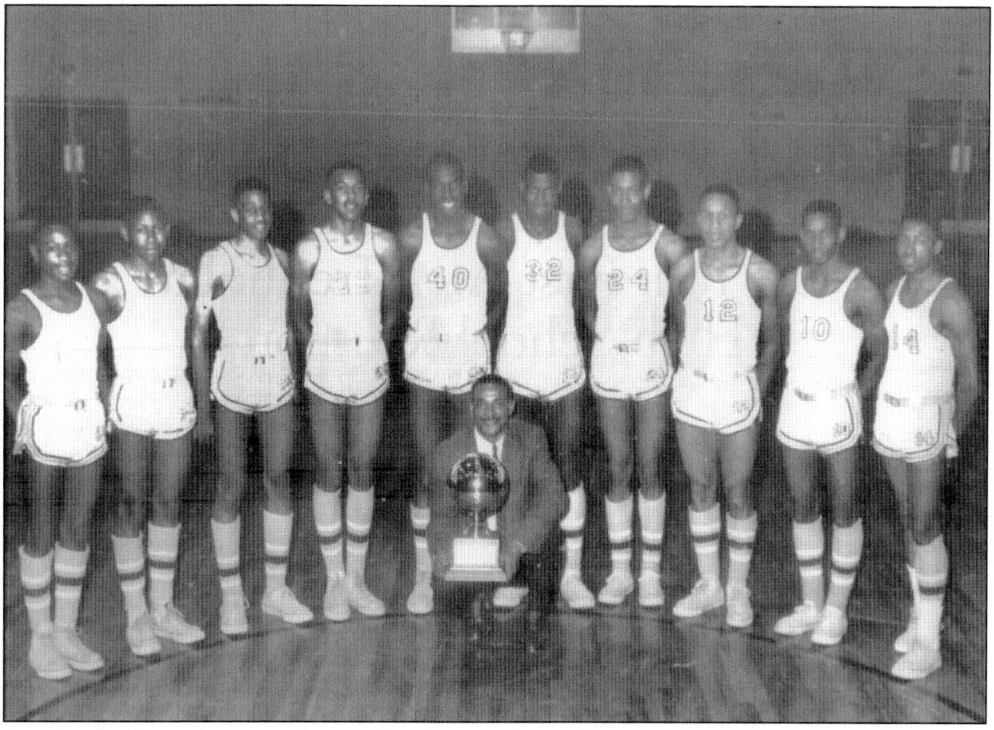

Coach Charles Mahorney, who was head coach for both football and basketball, led Trenholm High School to a state championship in basketball in 1965. Members of the team are, from left to right, Ed Thompson, Bernard Bailey, Clark Grimes, Leroy Marshall, William Robinson Jr., Walter Abernathy, Jake Pillar, Willie Lee Byrd, Leon Ricks, and Charles Moore.

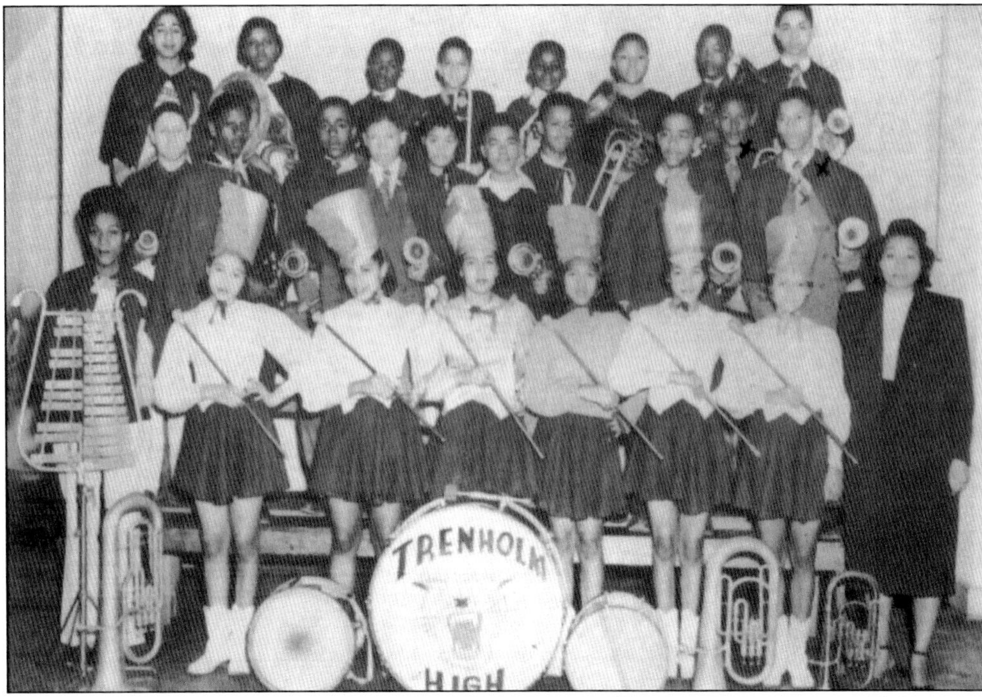

John Duncan was paid to travel from Alabama State College in Montgomery, Alabama, to Tuscumbia on Saturdays to develop and instruct students on band instruments. Mattie L. Gilchrist and Adlena Thomas worked very hard to start the band program. Pictured above is Trenholm High School's first marching band with director Mrs. A.L. Thomas.

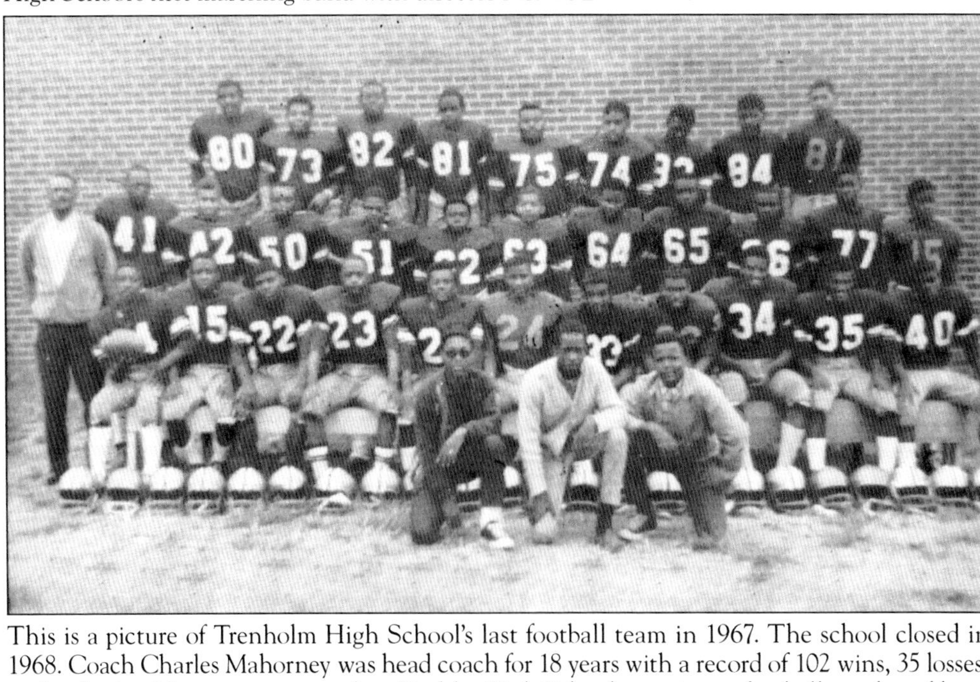

This is a picture of Trenholm High School's last football team in 1967. The school closed in 1968. Coach Charles Mahorney was head coach for 18 years with a record of 102 wins, 35 losses, and eight ties. He went on to coach at Deshler High School as assistant football coach and head basketball coach until he retired in 1982.

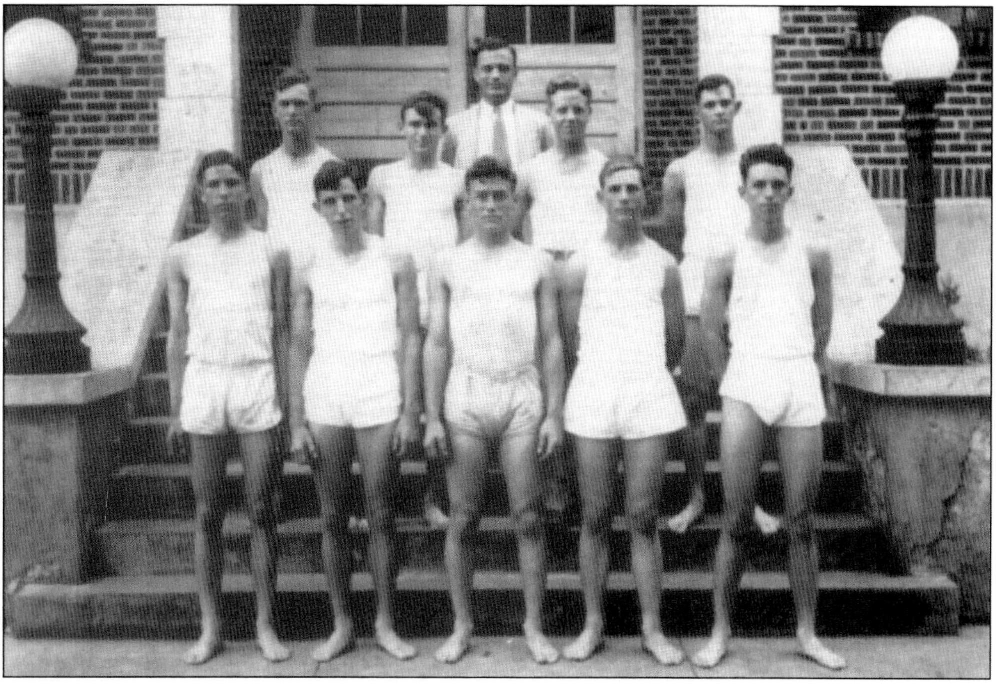

Sports have always been important in Tuscumbia. This is a picture of the first track team in 1929. The team was formed by coach L.C. Perry and used Gilbert Field as its home grounds. Pictured from left to right are (first row) Laurie Battle, Harvey Creech, George Williams, Carey Corbell, and Fred Brower; (second row) Bill Cloud, Robert Coleman, Coach Perry, Arthur Howard, and George Cloud.

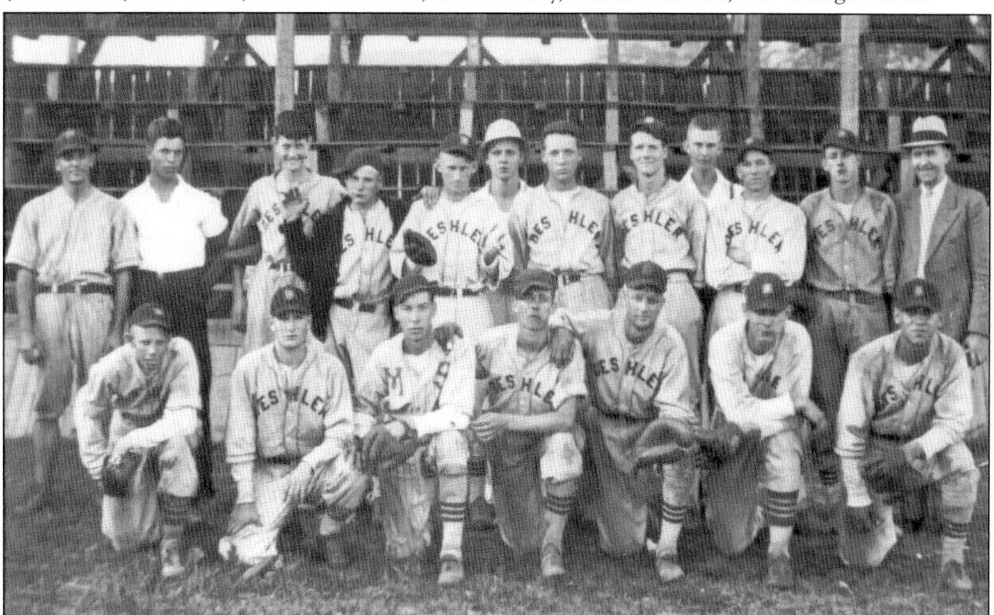

This is the 1934 Deshler High School baseball team. The picture was taken behind the grandstands at Legion Field in Spring Park. During the Great Depression, Deshler sports had to be cut for financial reasons. Baseball and football were the only sports that survived all the cuts during the 1930s, but even they had to have help from the community.

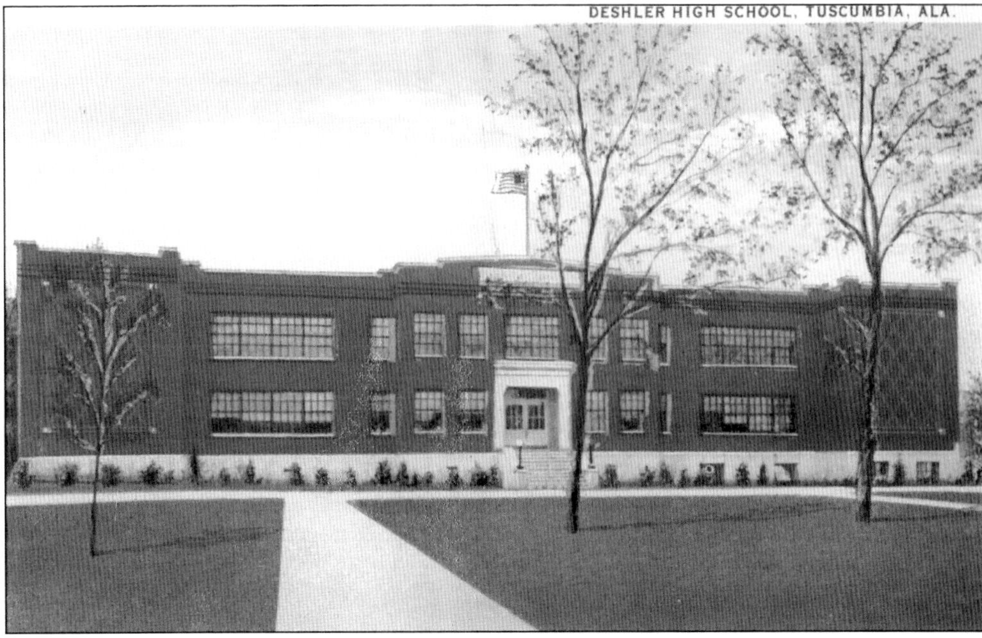

Tuscumbia thought it would be a good idea to approach Sheffield concerning the building of a joint school for both cities. It was to be located where the Helen Keller Hospital is today. Sheffield was not interested. A land search began, and the land occupied by the Deshler Female Institute was the only available land for a new school. The institute was torn down, and a new high school was built in its place.

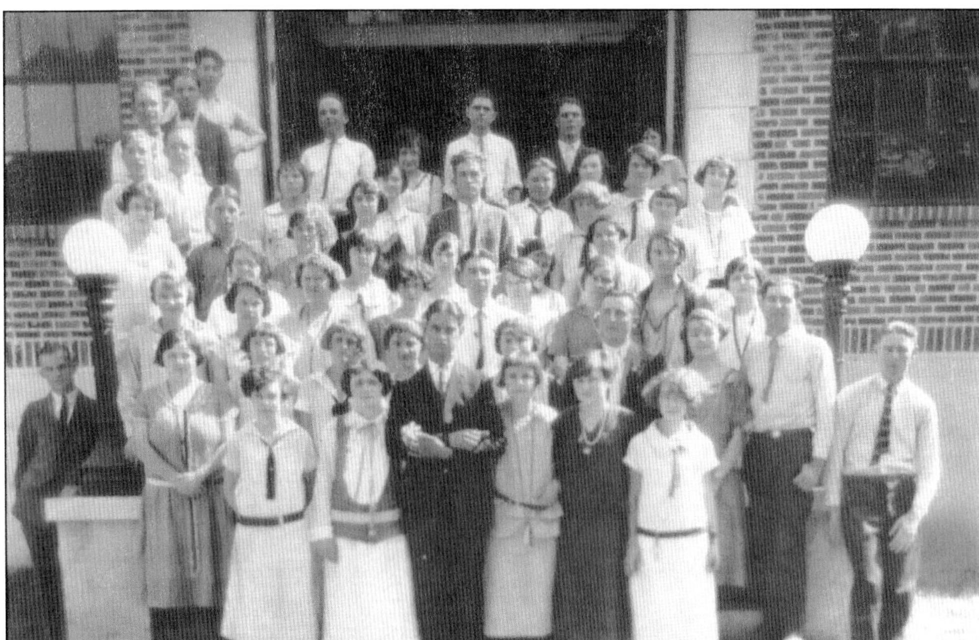

Since the land given to the city by David Deshler required that the school on the property be named in honor of Brig. Gen. James Deshler, the new school became Deshler High School. The first graduating class was in 1924, pictured here standing on the front steps.

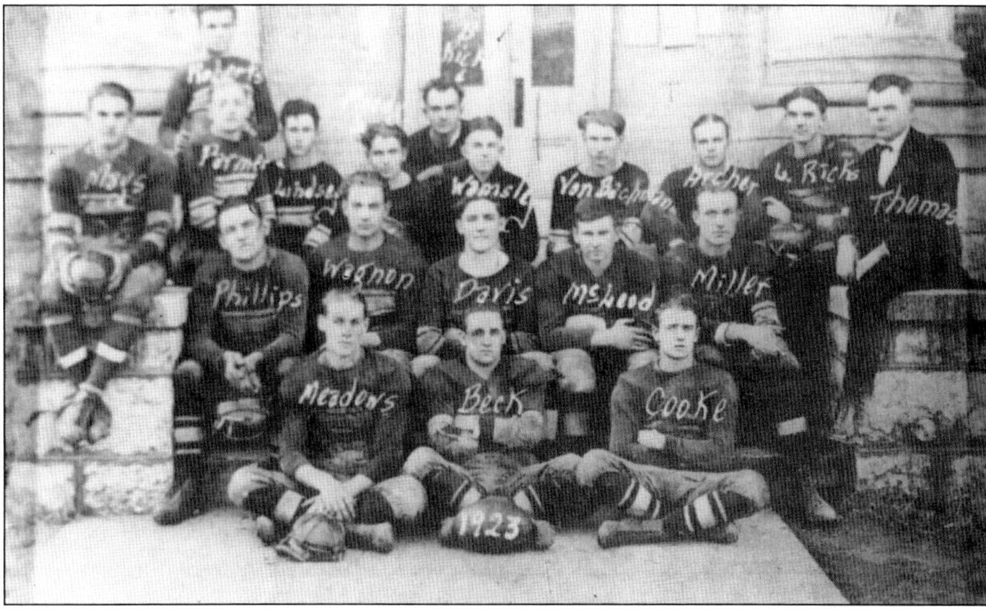

Tuscumbia High School's mascot had been the Bengal tiger. Deshler High School decided to keep the mascot, but gradually the Bengal was dropped. Today, they are known as the Deshler Tigers. When the decision was made to build a new high school and rename it Deshler High School, the students wanted to be known as the Deshler Tigers. In fact, prior to the school being constructed, the 1923 team wanted to be known as the Deshler Bengal Tigers. This is the football team of 1923.

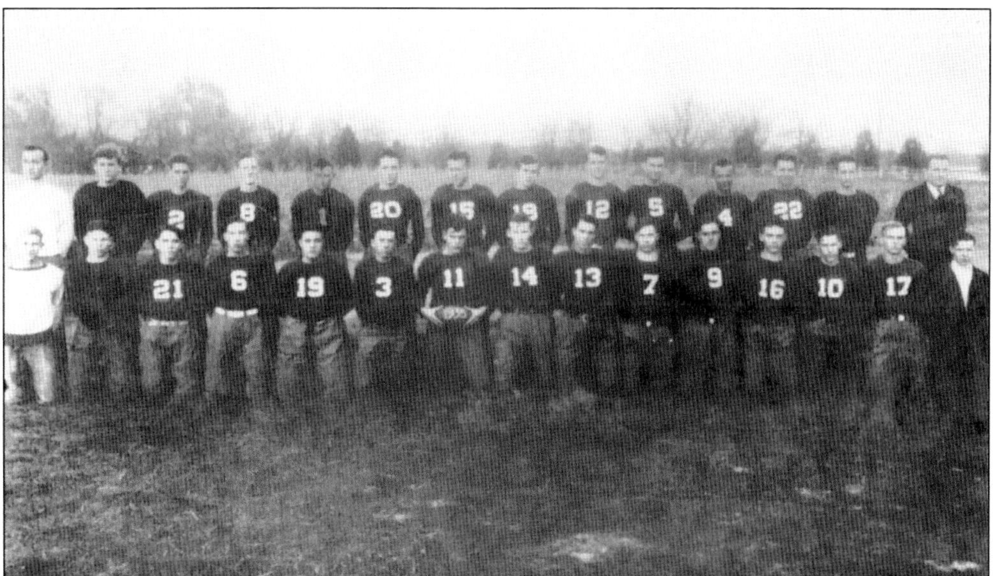

The Deshler High School football program grew to be one of the best in the state of Alabama. This 1935 team was the first to claim a state championship. Coach Howard Chappell said this was his best team. Coach Chappell loved to tell stories. One of his favorite stories was about a teammate of his from the University of Alabama, a very young Paul "Bear" Bryant, who helped to coach the defense at Deshler.

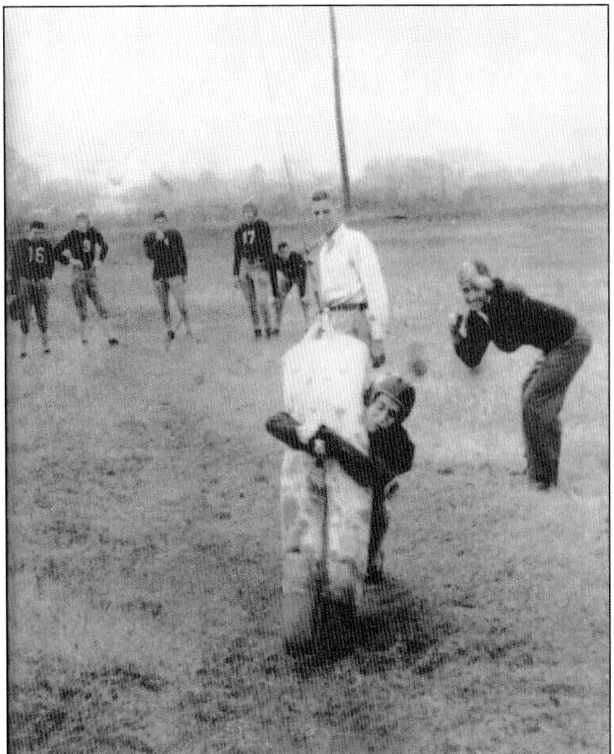

Coach Howard Chappell believed in the use of a practice dummy. He built a wooden frame with a dummy dangling down on a rope. The players would make a run for the dummy as it was swinging on the rope. This practice took place at Deshler's first football field, Gilbert Field.

Athletics . . .

In 1938, four underclassmen aroused the interest of the Deshler fans. They became known as "The Pony Backfield," a younger and smaller version of "The Four Horsemen" of Notre Dame. Donald McMahan, Jimmy Beck, Sam Ridley, and Ernest Garrett are seen here practicing on Legion Field in Spring Park. McMahan became ill and died before his senior year. In 1936, Legion Field was the first football field in the Shoals to have lights.

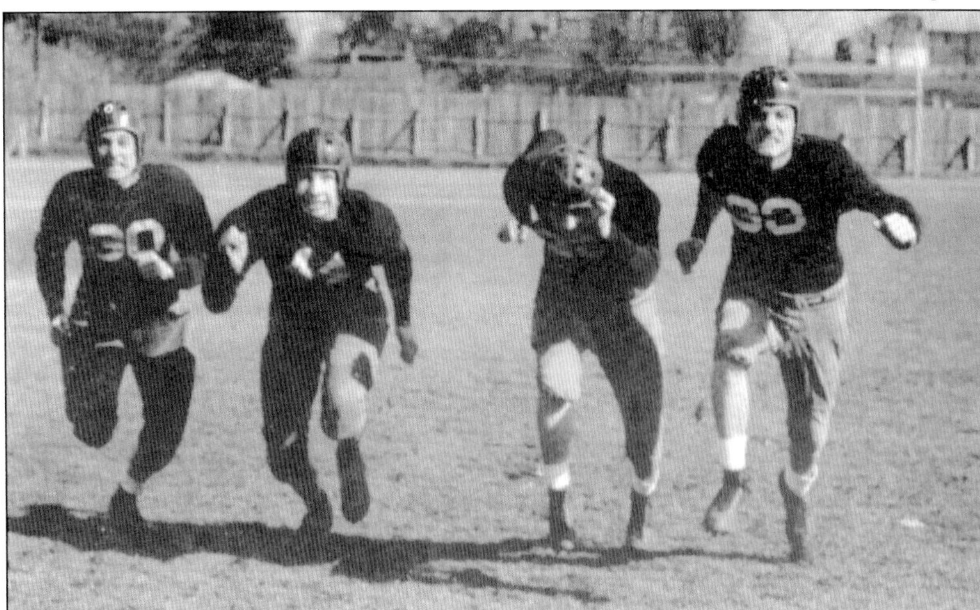

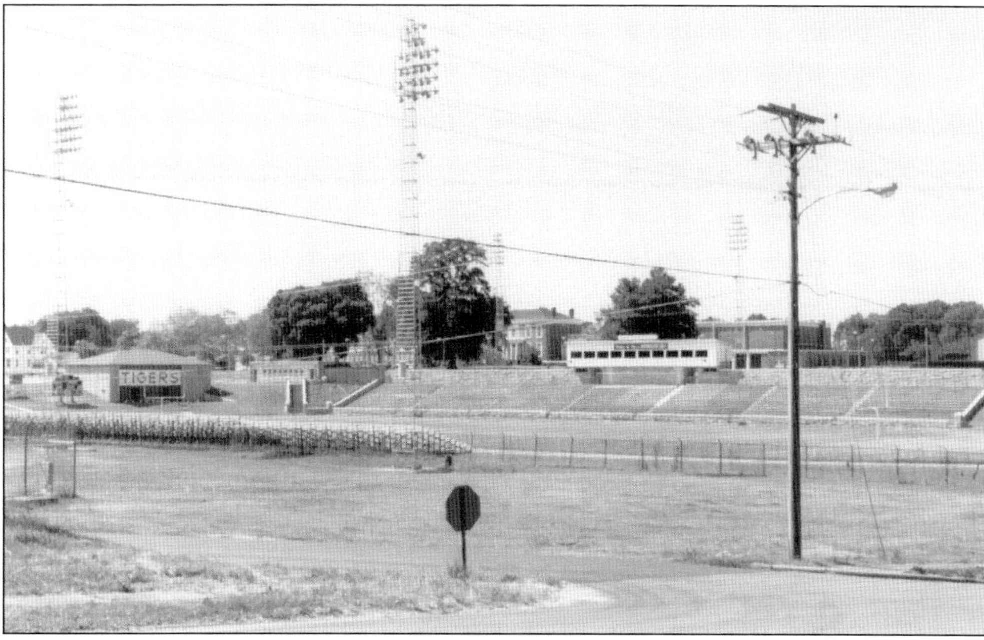

In 1941, Tuscumbia was able to acquire funds from the federal government to build the first football stadium in the Shoals. Deshler High School and Trenholm High School played their home games in Tuscumbia Municipal Stadium.

30 *LE MIROIR* 1930

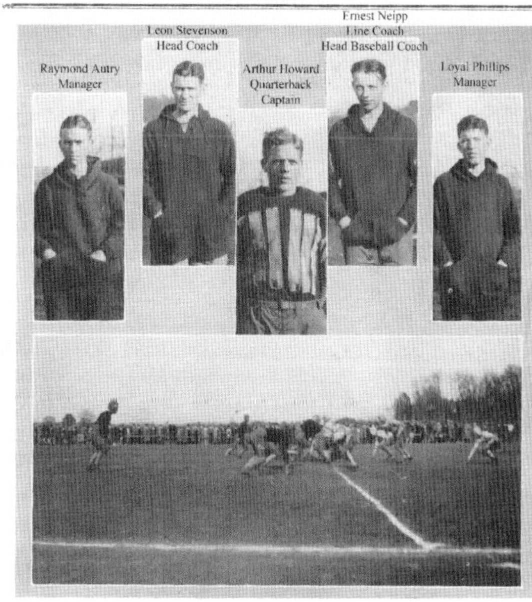

Thanksgiving Game 1929

Deshler, 25; Russellville, 0.

Deshler ended her wonderful football campaign of '29 with a neat victory over the strong eleven from Franklin County High—Russellville. The fans saw eight men in action in this game that will be lost to next year's team. A group of stella athletes like these come once in a great while and they have done much to make a name for Deshler that will be long remembered.

Deshler High School began playing football around 1922. In the early years, Deshler did not have a home field on which to play. Deshler's first home football field was Gilbert Field on North Commons near Tuscumbia's multipurpose center. This is an account of the Thanksgiving game with Russellville in 1929.

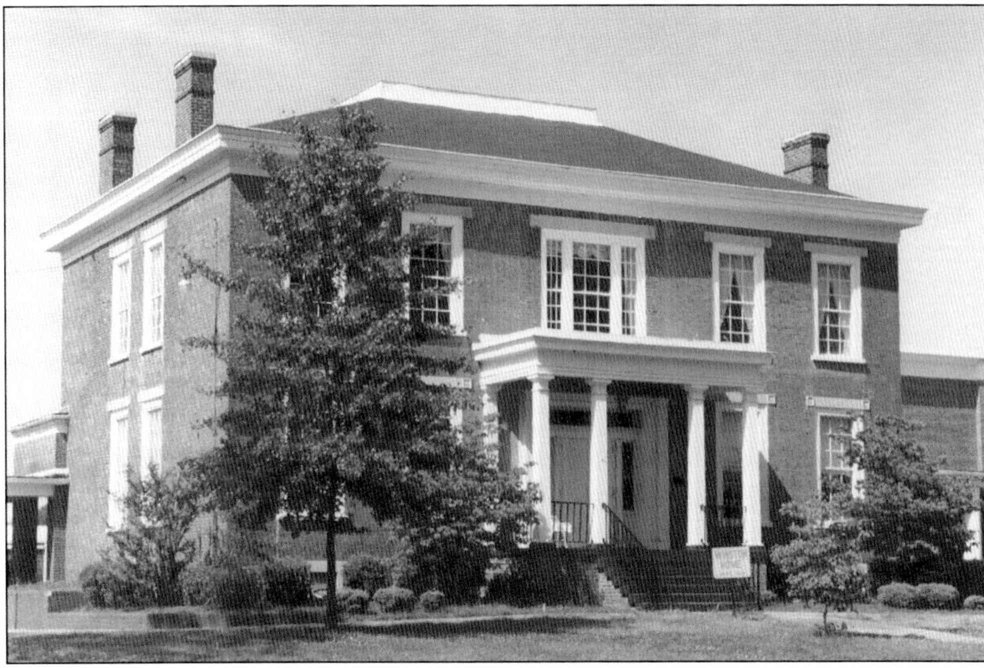

In the 1940s, Tuscumbia was outgrowing the high school on Main Street. A search commenced to find property around town with an area large enough for the school. The Winston family members decided to sell their ancestral home and land on North Commons to the city for the school. The Winston Home has been restored and is part of the Deshler High School campus today.

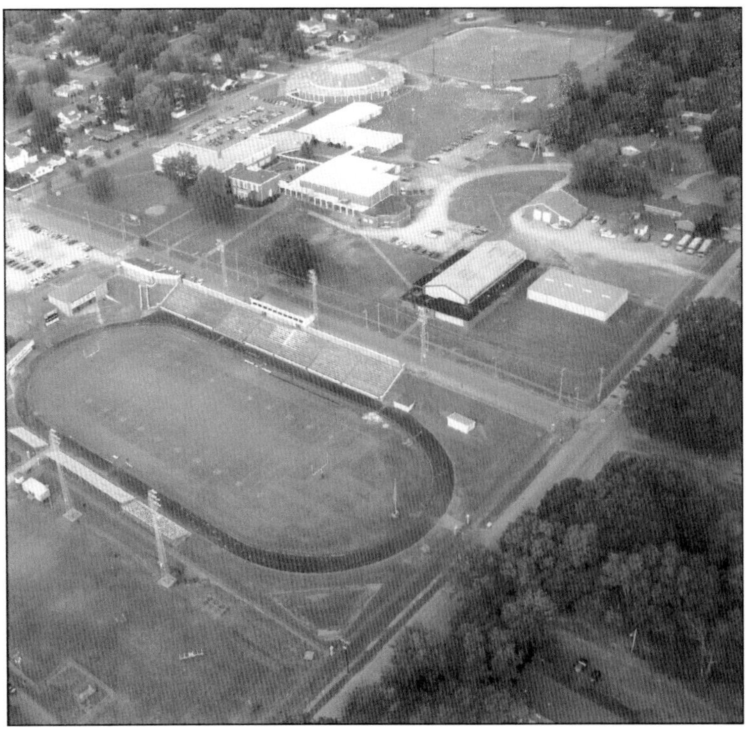

This is an aerial photograph of Deshler High School taken in 2006. The Tuscumbia School Board has built its new office between the auditorium and the old National Guard Building since this picture was taken. The National Guard Building, which was used as the Deshler High School gym for several years before the construction of the Deshler Dome, is now used by the athletic department.

Five

Religion

The combination of businessmen with visions for the future and the rapid growth of the young town meant that the population was in need of formal religion. Young traveling preachers began to make their rounds through the area introducing different faiths to Tuscumbia. Many Tuscumbians received them openly.

Within 20 years, the Methodists, Presbyterians, Baptists, and the Christian Church had constructed places of worship. Today, only the Presbyterian church building remains and is considered to be the oldest church building in continuous operation in Alabama.

The African American population began to form its own churches after the Civil War. Some of the churches met and were organized in downtown buildings, such as the cotton gin on Main Street. Today, there are many active churches in Tuscumbia.

These religions still play a strong role in the lives of many Tuscumbians. This chapter covers the importance of religion through the eye of a camera.

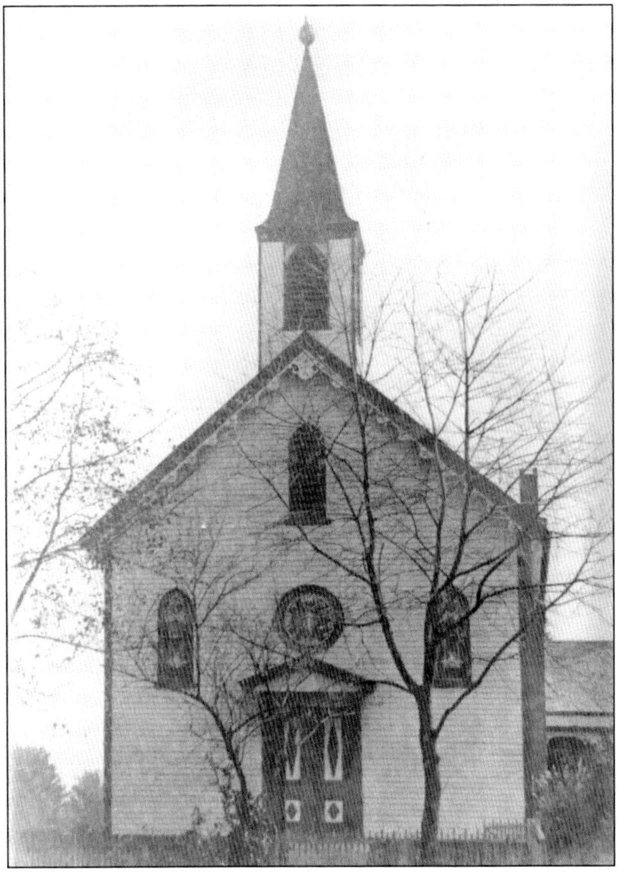

The Catholic faith may have been introduced to the Shoals Area by Spanish Conquistador Hernando DeSoto, but it would be 1861 before a priest, Father Baasen, would be assigned to the area. He held Mass in various houses before the church acquired land for a building from John Baxter. The first building was destroyed by a tornado in 1874. The church rebuilt this structure.

The second building, Heart of Mary, served well until it burned on October 3, 1924, forcing the church to rebuild. This new church, Our Lady of the Sacred Heart, was built in 1932. This church building served until the consolidation of the Sheffield congregation and the Tuscumbia congregation in 1959. The new Our Lady of the Shoals Church was dedicated in November 1974.

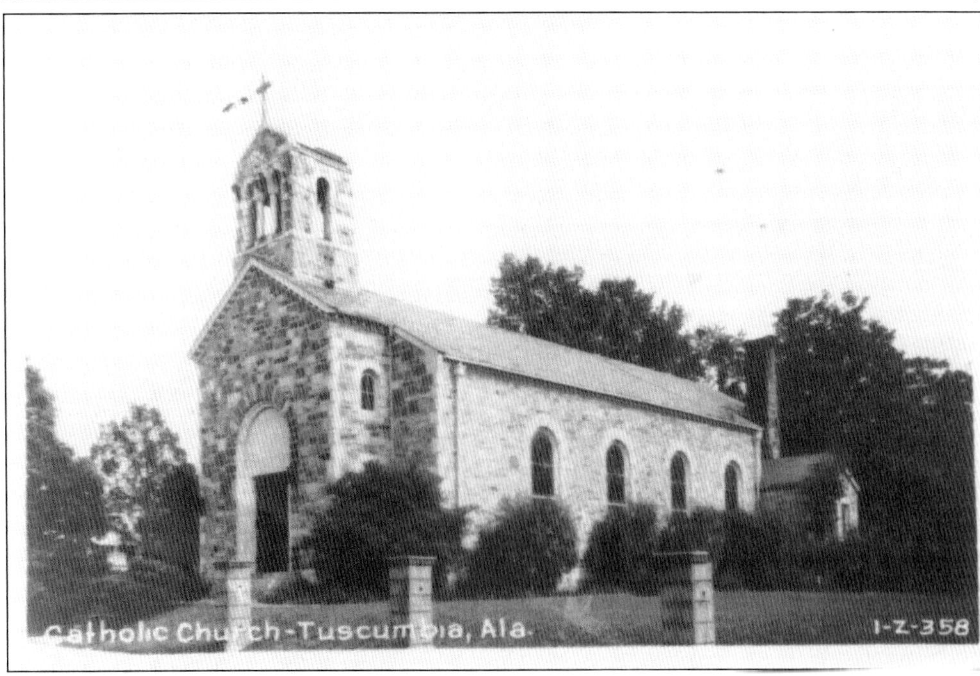

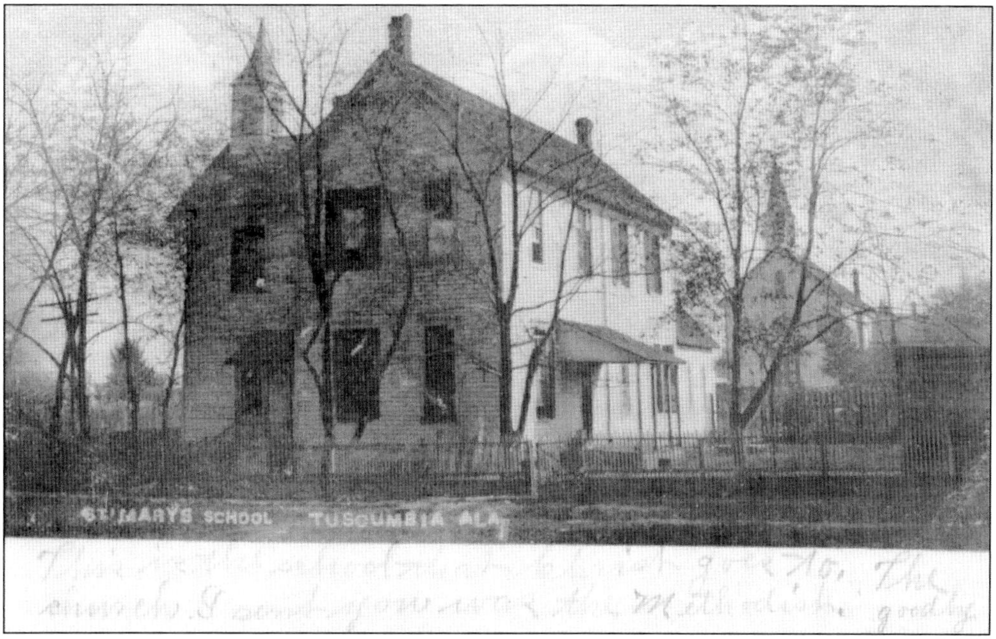

In 1881, Benedictine nuns arrived to start a Catholic school in the two-story house used by Father Baasen next to his barn, which had been used to hold services after the tornado. This grammar school closed in 1924. The 1932 church building was used until the consolidation of the Tuscumbia and Sheffield parishes. The church and school properties were sold, and the proceeds were used to build Our Lady of the Shoals Church in 1974.

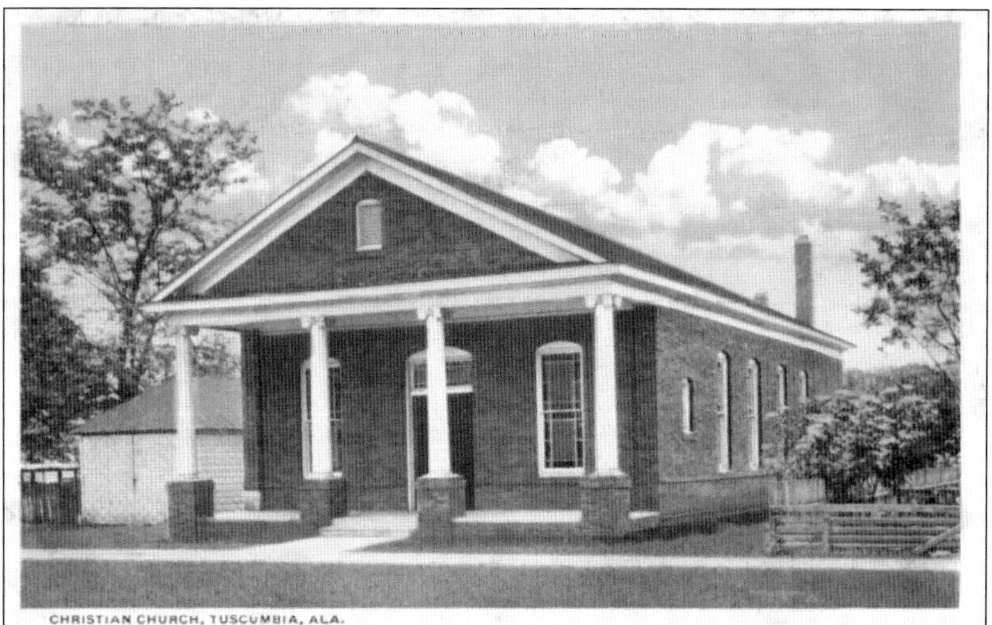

The Church of Christ had its beginnings with Dr. William H. Wharton in the 1830s. The congregation built its first building where First Baptist Church is today but lost it for financial reasons. The church built a new building in 1911. This building, pictured above, burned on October 27, 1924.

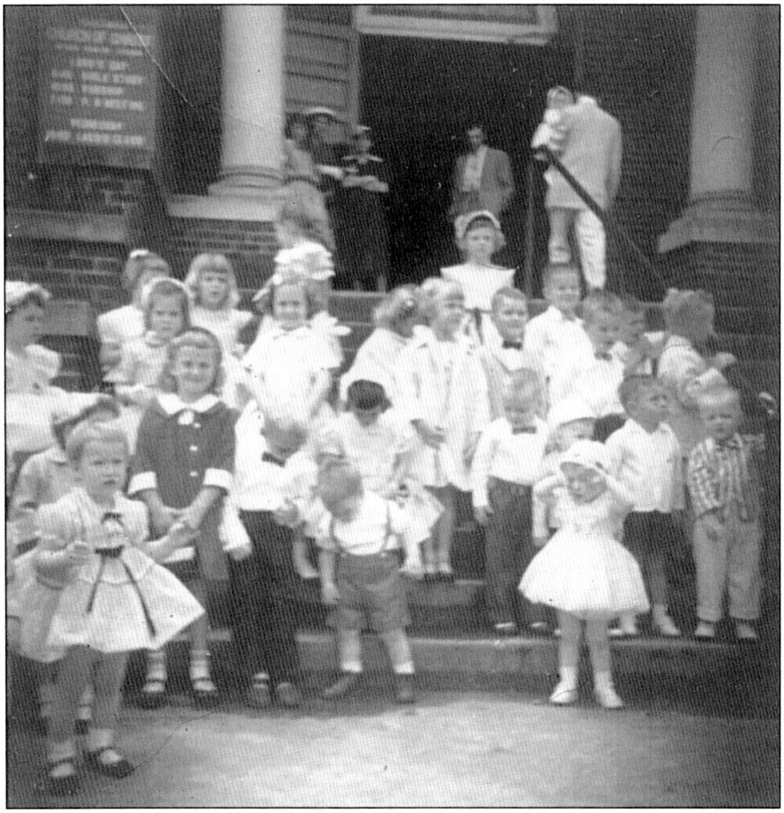

The 1911 Church of Christ building was insured for $3,000. The church used this money plus donations for the down payment on a new $30,000 building. This new building was constructed in 1925 and was designed to seat 350 people with nine classrooms. Today, it is used for classrooms and offices. This is a Sunday School class on the front steps of the 1925 building.

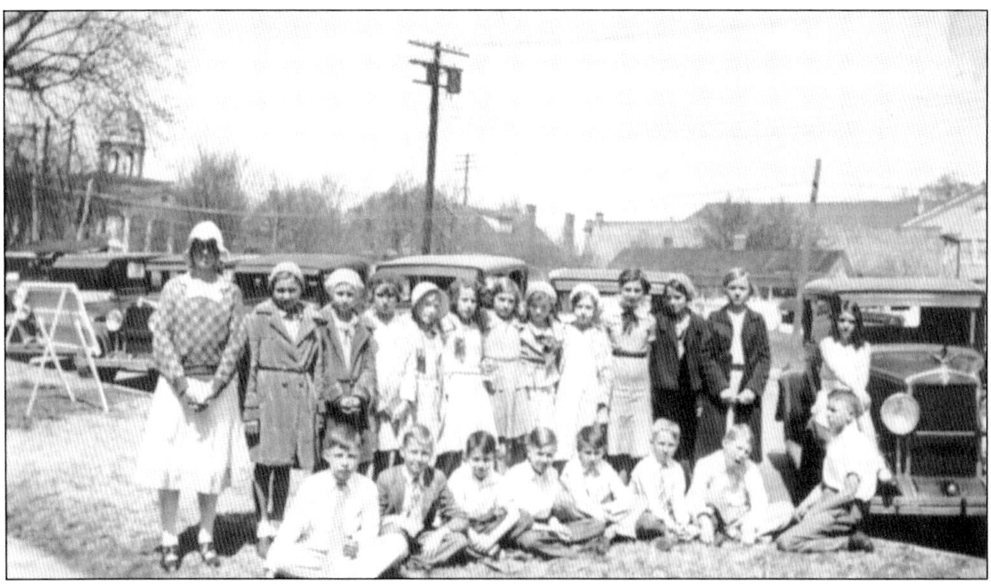

The Church of Christ was successful and growing. In April 1932, one of the church's classes went outside to the front of the building and had its picture taken with the Colbert County Courthouse in the background.

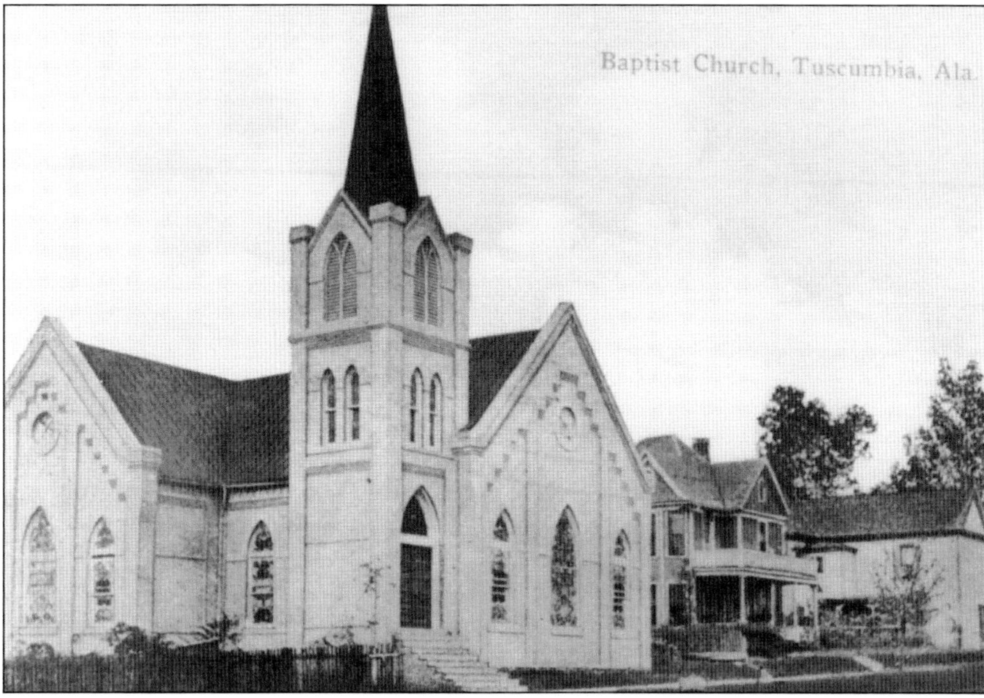

The Baptist church in Tuscumbia was established as the Concord Church of Franklin County in July 1823. Jeremiah Burns was the first pastor. The church first met in a partially finished building known as the Baptist Church House. After the Civil War, the Baptists were able to acquire property from the Christian Church; this is the location of the present-day First Baptist Church.

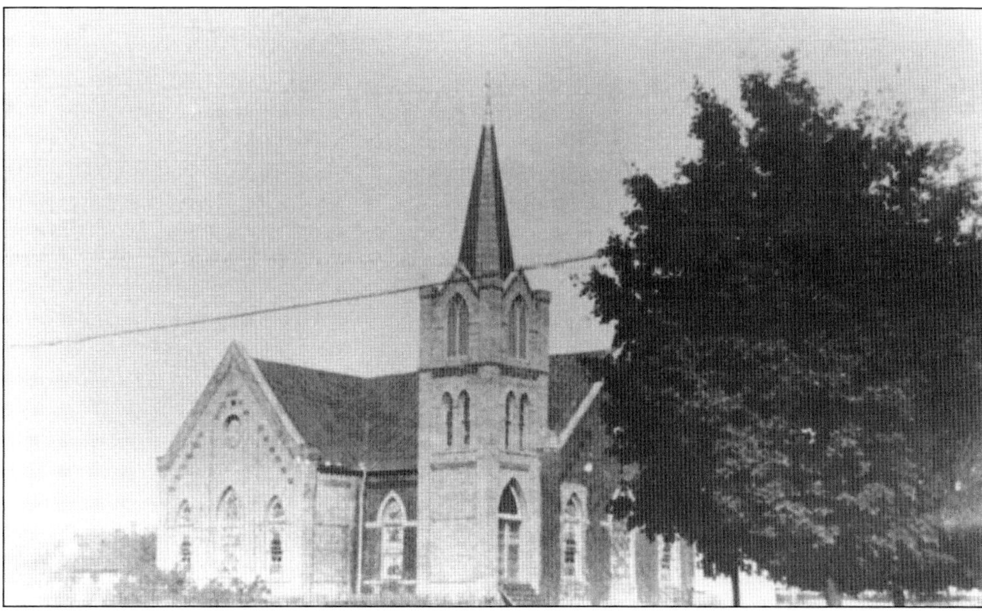

In 1903, the original New England structure of the First Baptist Church was enlarged. The magnificent Czechoslovakian stained glass windows were installed in the early 1900s, five on the north side and five on the south side. The bricks were painted at this time. Forty-five pastors have served the church since it started.

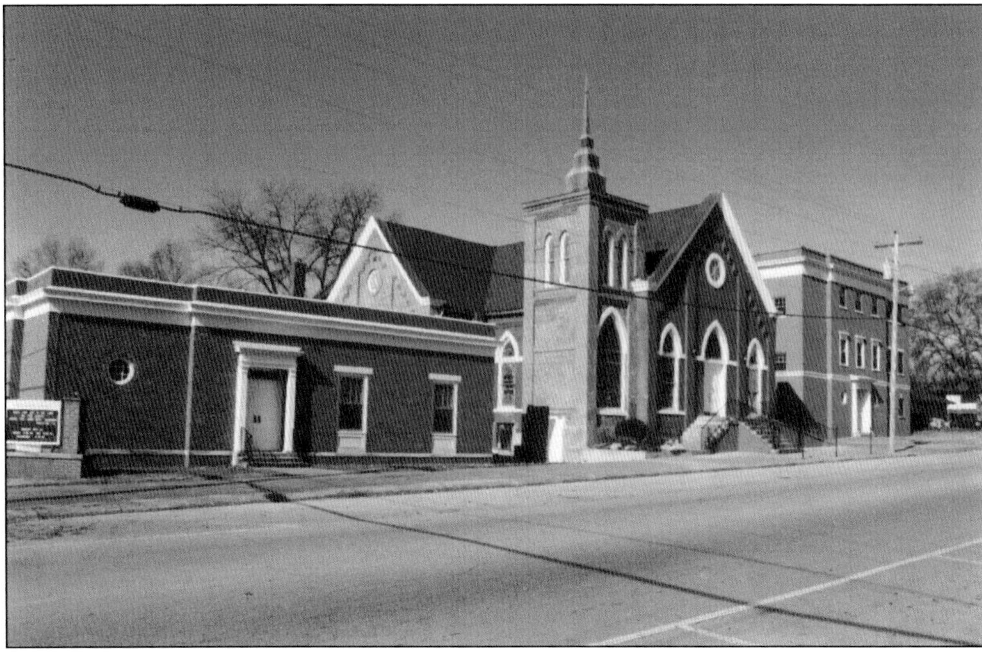

In 1954, the sanctuary was changed by moving the entrance door from the bell tower to the center of the building. The steeple was also altered, and a new balcony was built over the entrance. The side balconies were reworked to seat 170 people. The exterior brickwork has been restored to its original look.

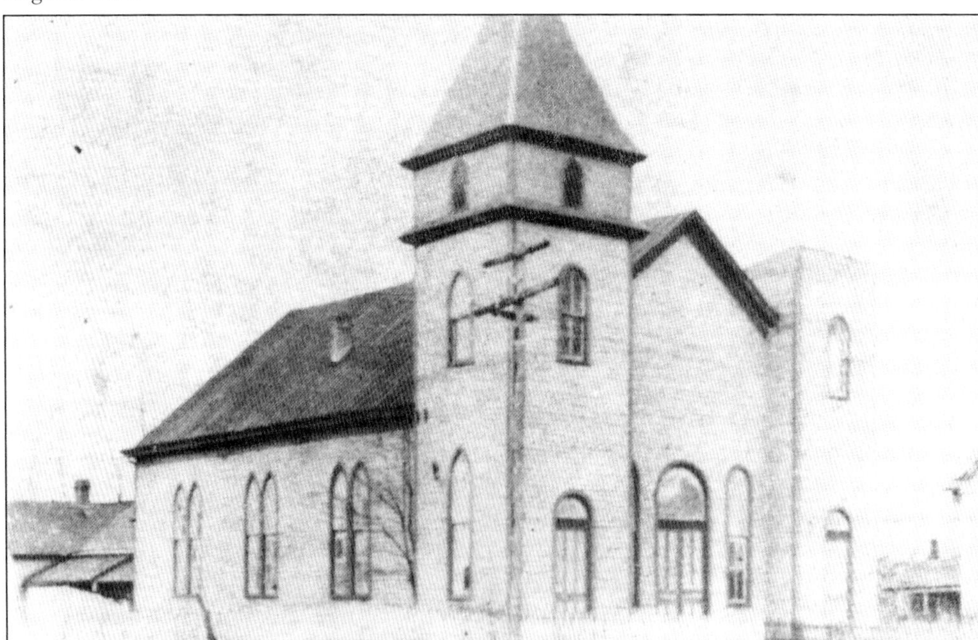

Early in 1866, a group of African Americans organized the Tuscumbia Missionary Baptist Church under the leadership of Elder W.E. Northcross. They met in various places, including a cotton gin. In 1892, the church was able to build this new brick structure. The church became the largest black congregation in Colbert County, with more than 900 members.

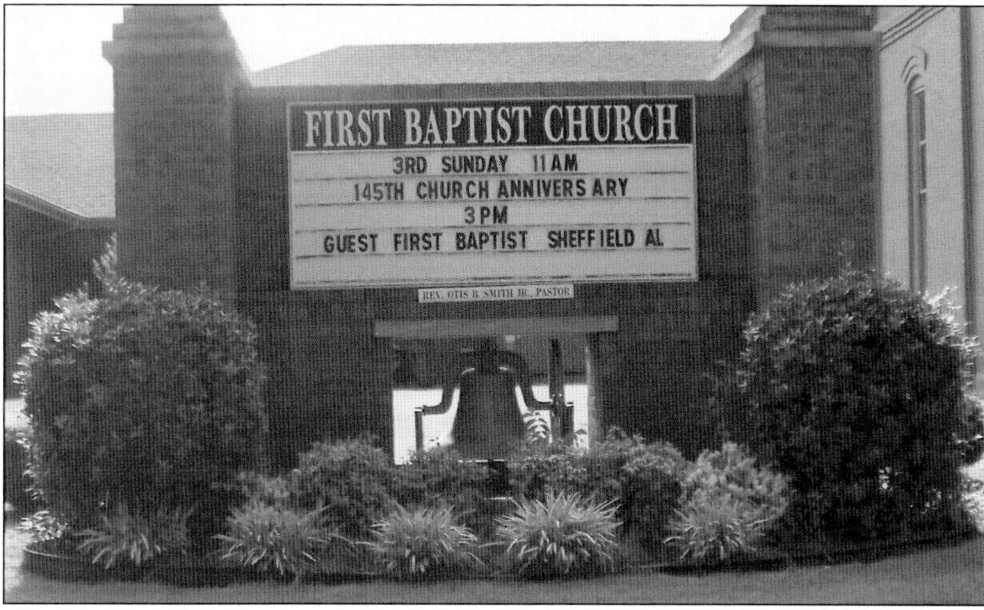

The church found that with the construction of the new building, a bell was needed. When the city had purchased the old Methodist church building and property as a location for the city hall, the bell was not needed, so the Baptists purchased it. Thinking the Methodist bell on a Baptist church might not be proper, the Baptists baptized the bell.

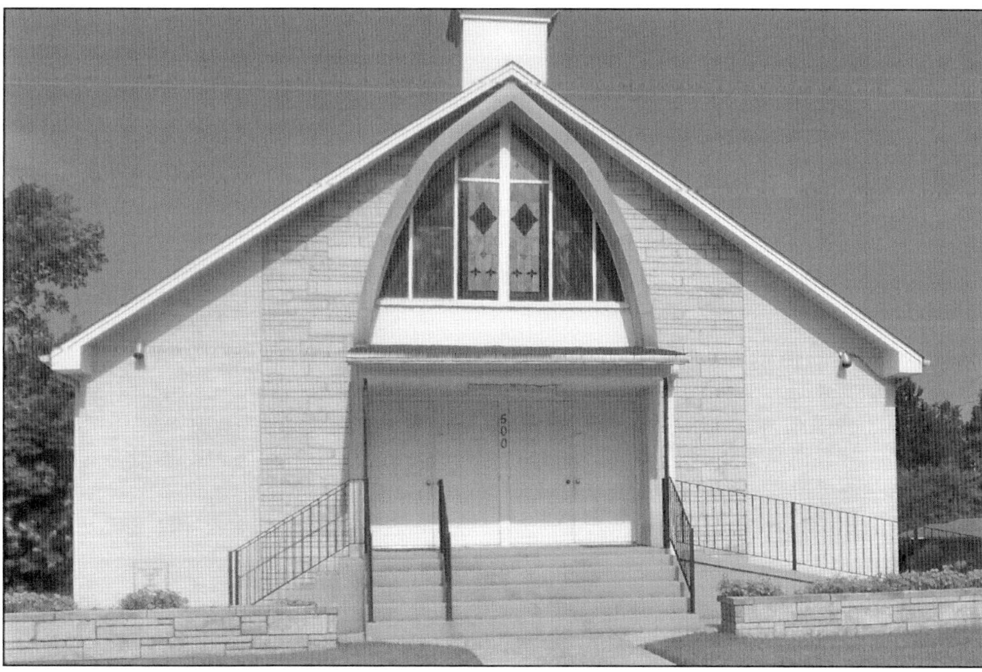

The High Street Church of Christ had its beginning with the "Christian Home" congregation in the Rick's Community. The Christian Home congregation was the first African American congregation in North Alabama. In 1918, the Tuscumbia congregation met in Trenholm High School. During 1921–1922, plans were made for a building to be erected on the corner of Ninth and High Streets, where it stands today.

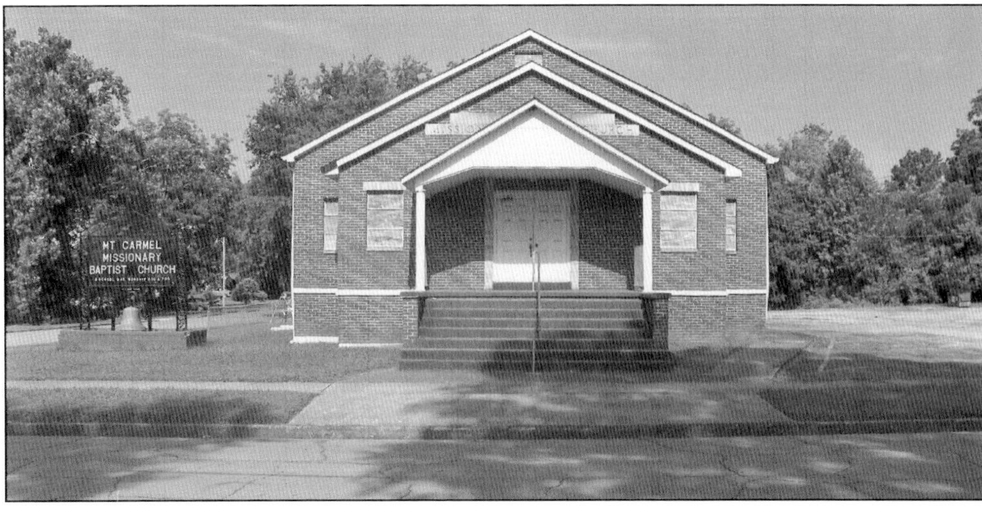

Mount Carmel Baptist Church was organized in 1929 in the home of Mingo White Sr. The church began with a piano, coal stove, and 200 cane bottom chairs. During a spring storm around 1959, the walls of the building were blown down. They were restored, and dedication services were conducted on February 14, 1960.

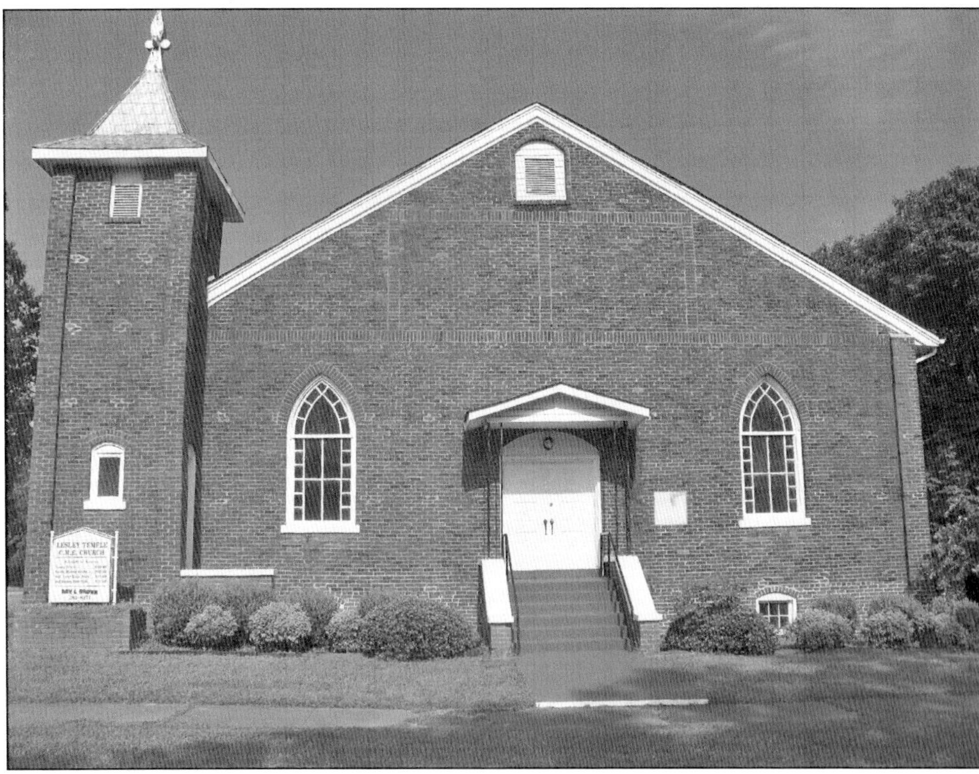

Lesley Temple Christian Methodist Church (CME) was founded in 1880. It met on Gin Hill near Woodmont Drive in Tuscumbia. The present building was begun in 1922 and completed in 1928. When the First Methodist Church was built on Main Street in 1926, the pews, alter rail, light fixtures, and a small bell from the old church were given to Lesley Temple. The pews are still in use today.

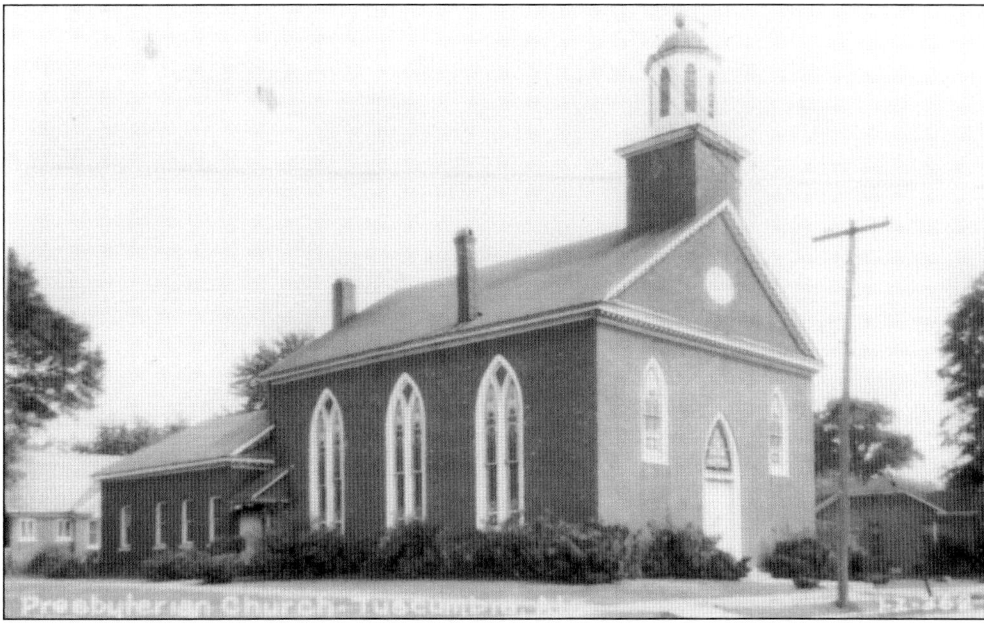

The Presbyterian Church was organized in 1824 in the Challen House Hotel, located off Main Street on Spring Hill. Land was acquired when Pres. James Monroe signed a land grant for the church on the corner of Fourth and Broad Streets.

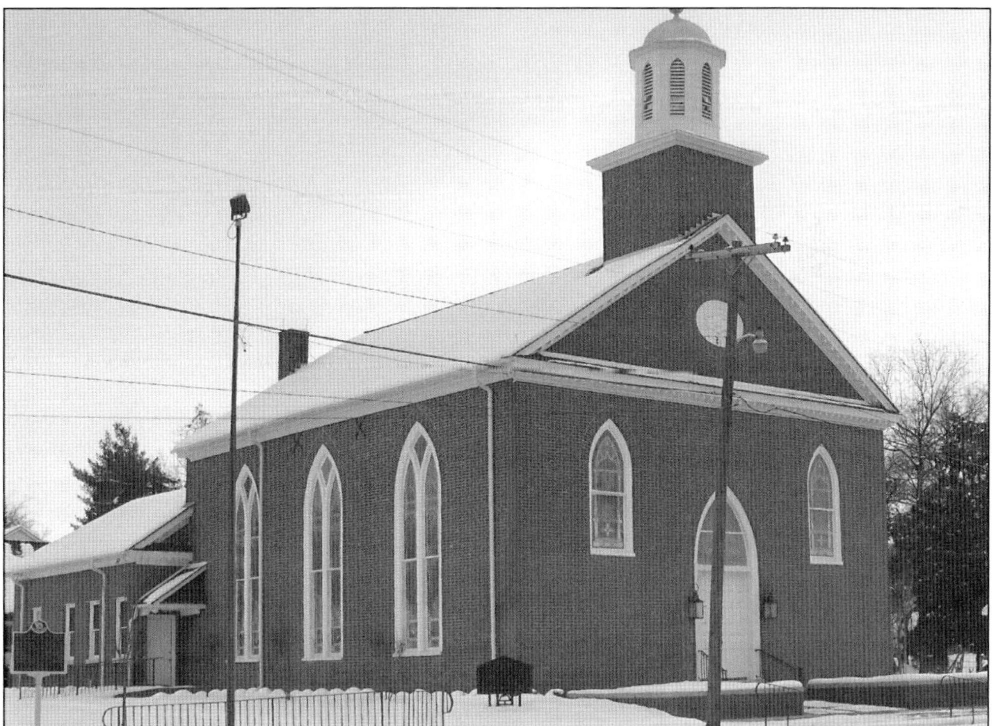

The Presbyterian Church building was built with sun-dried bricks in 1827. It is still used as a place of worship, making it the oldest church building in continuous use in Alabama. It still contains the elevated slave gallery and the sanctuary looks much as it did when it was built.

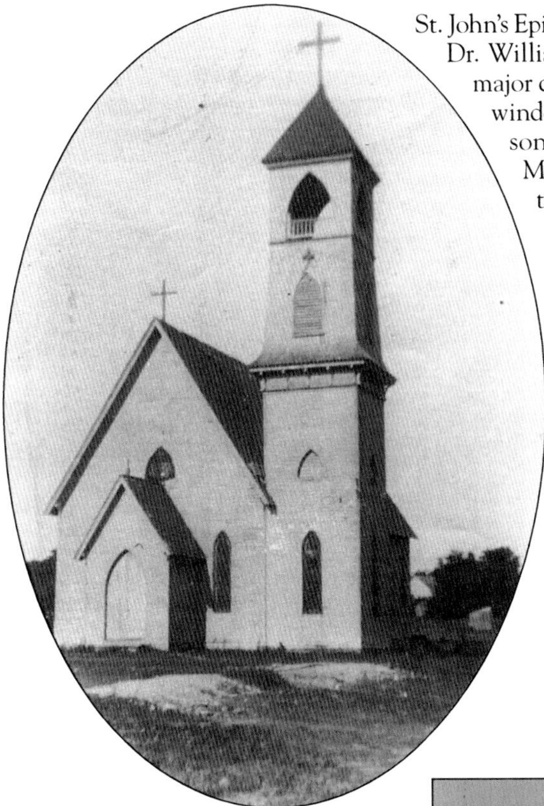

St. John's Episcopal Church was founded in 1839. In 1852, Dr. William Newsome donated a lot and became a major contributor to the building fund. A chancel window memorializes Dr. Newsome and his two sons, William O. Newsome and Alexander Moore Newsome, one of whom was killed in the Battle of the Wilderness and the other in the yellow fever epidemic of 1878.

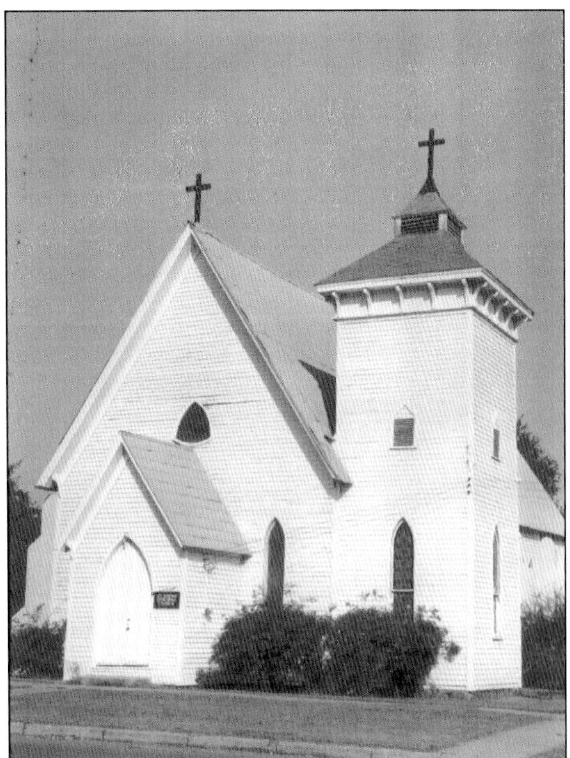

The church building was damaged by the tornado of 1874. Metal rods were placed in the ceiling to help support the structure. Concrete buttresses were added later because of the damage. St. John's has been closed for regular service since 1955.

The First Methodist Church, pictured here, was built fronting old Andrew Jackson's Military Road. It was built around 1826–1828. The Presbyterians also met in this building until they were able to build their own church on Broad Street. The Methodists moved to their present building on Main Street around 1926–1927.

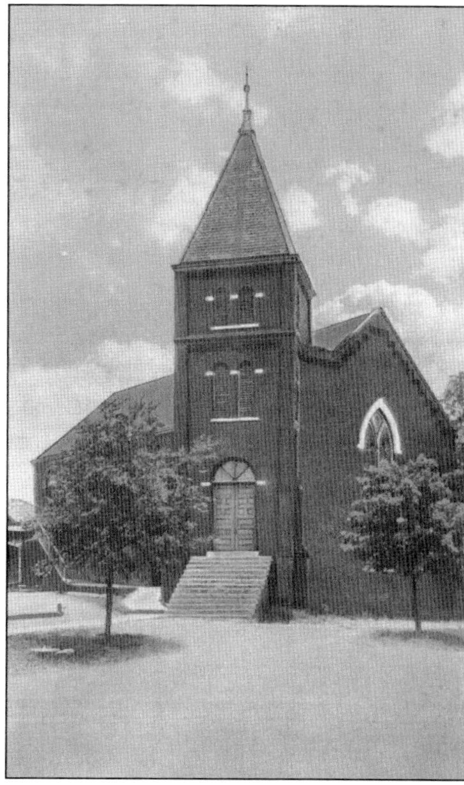

This is a picture of Class No. 14 of the First Methodist Church. This picture was taken on Easter Sunday in 1920. This building was sold to the city after the construction of the new church on Main Street. The city used the lower stories for the police and fire departments for years.

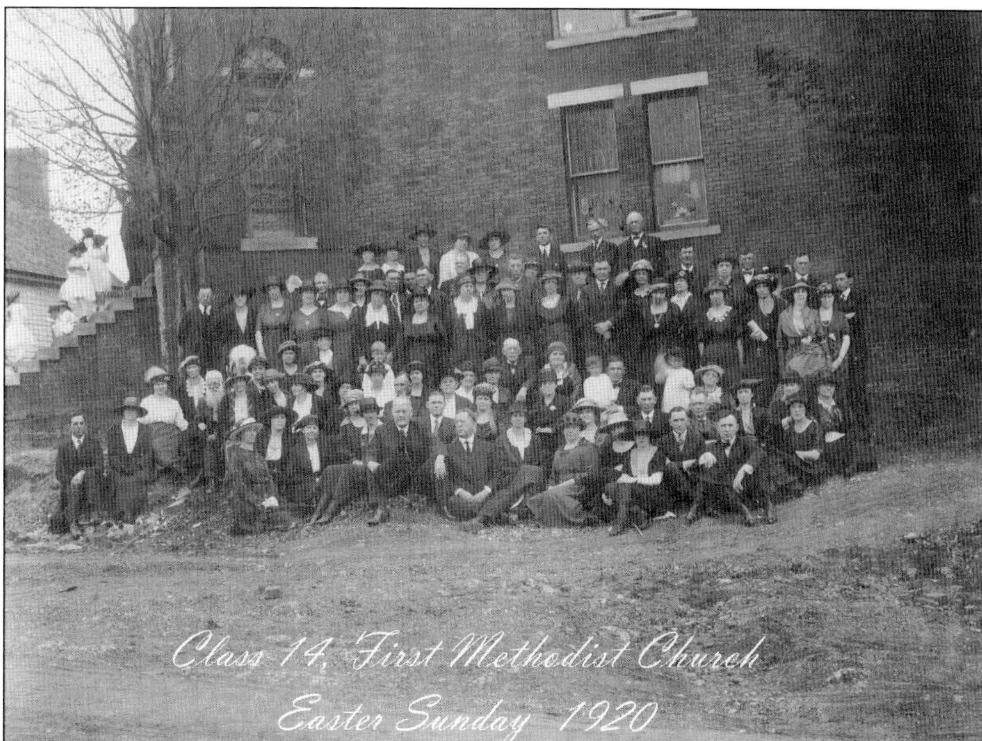

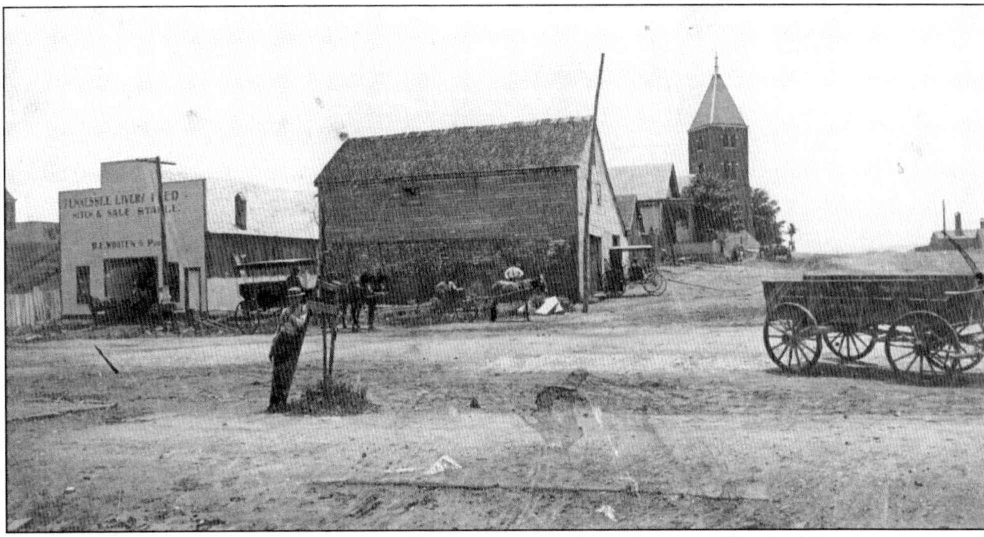

This is a view of the southeast corner of Sixth and Dickson Streets. The building in the center is the Tuscumbia Wagon Works with one of its wagons. The Methodist church can be seen in the background on the hill. Today, the Tuscumbia Police Department is located where the church was.

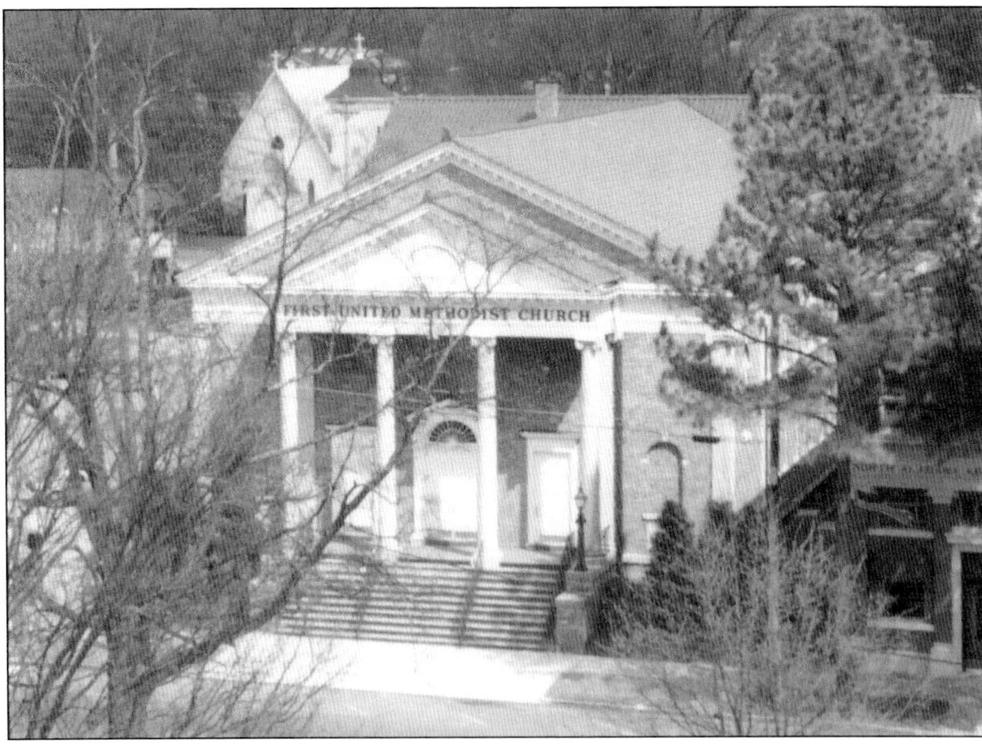

When members of the Methodist church built their new building on North Main Street, they no longer needed the old building on South Dickson Street. They sold the building to the city. The city remodeled by doing several things, including removing the auditorium and cutting down the bell tower. The building became the city's administration building. This is the new Methodist church building on Main Street.

Six

Tuscumbians

Tuscumbians came from many backgrounds. Men and women had visions of the future not only impacting the history of the Shoals Area but also the state, nation, and world. Tuscumbia became America's first frontier railroad town. Many advancements in railroading were established here, including the use of sand for traction. Trains all over the world use sand for traction today. The explosion of the Tuscumbia & New Orleans Steamboat Company's steamboat *Ben Sherrod* while in a race on the Mississippi River caused the rules for steamboats to change for the safety of passengers.

Helen Keller, "America's First Lady of Courage," was born in Tuscumbia. Her home is a popular attraction in Tuscumbia today. Baseball great Henry "Heinie" Manush grew up in Tuscumbia. The only foreign-born governor of Alabama, Robert Burns Lindsay, lived in Tuscumbia.

This chapter covers some of these people who had an influence on the town, state, nation, and the world.

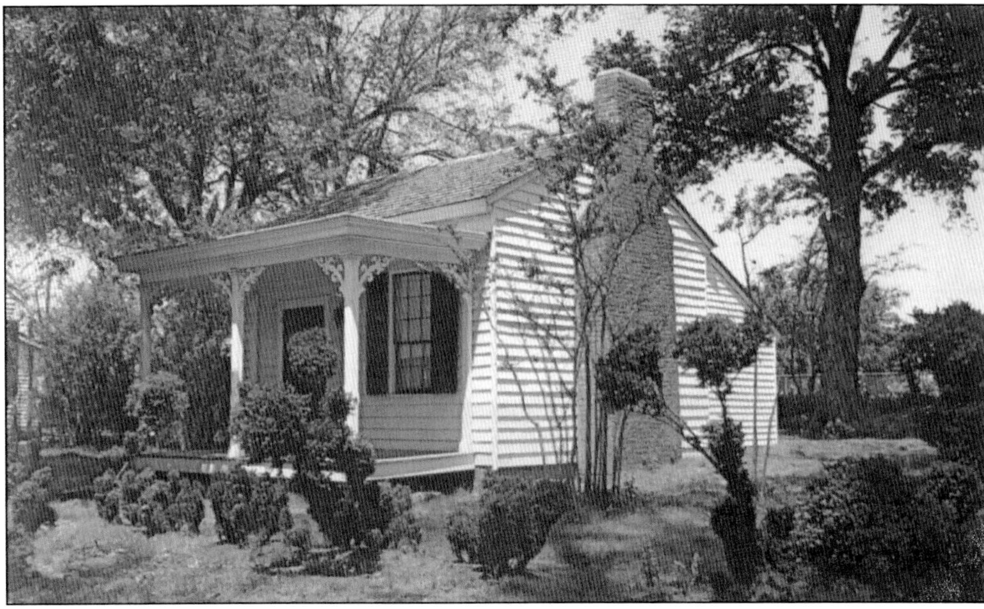

Helen Adams Keller was born in Tuscumbia on June 27, 1880. She contracted an illness when she was 19 months old that left her deaf and blind. The family made contact with Alexander Graham Bell, who advised them to contact the Perkins Institute for the Blind for assistance. The school's director asked a former student, Anne Sullivan, to become Keller's teacher. Sullivan and Keller lived in this small house together.

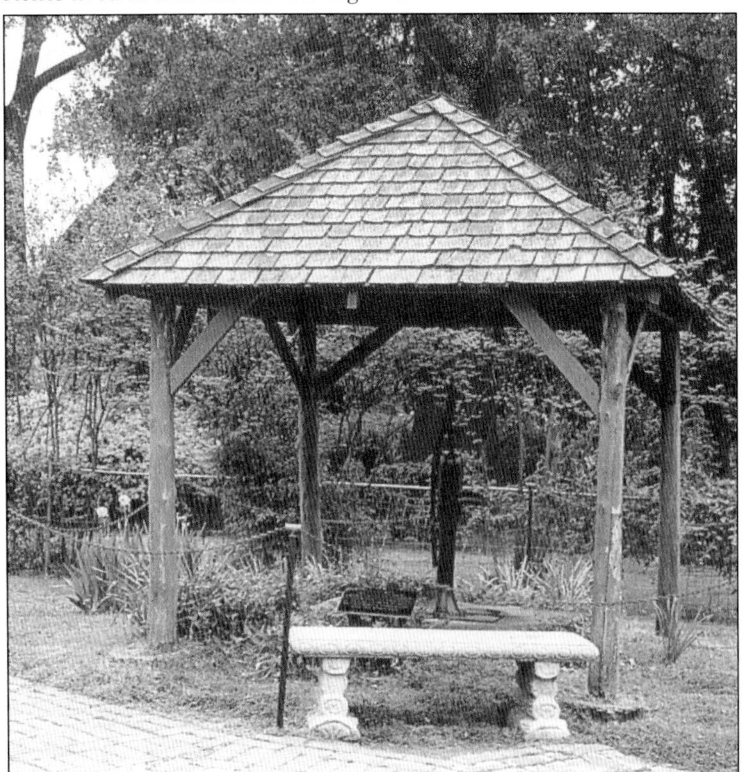

Anne Sullivan arrived at Ivy Green, the Keller home, in March 1887. She tried to communicate with Helen by spelling words into her hand. Helen did not understand that every item had a word identifying it. The big breakthrough came as Anne spelled "water" into Helen's hand as she ran water from this pump over the other hand.

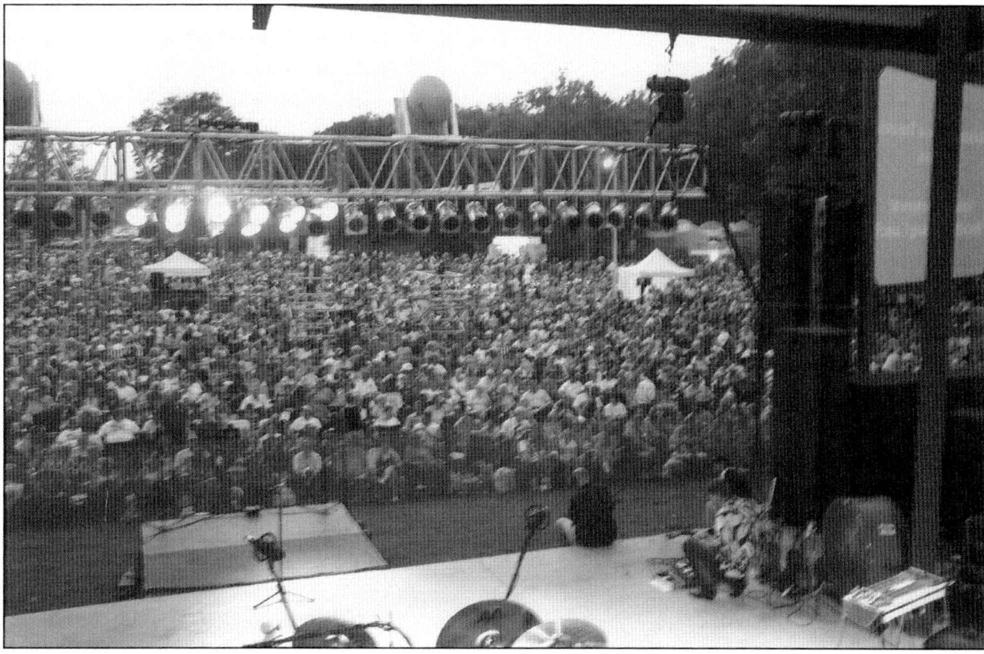

Helen Keller became a world-renowned speaker and an advocate for people with disabilities. She became known as America's First Lady of Courage. In 1954, Helen Keller's birthplace was made a shrine to the miracle that took place there. Every year, the Helen Keller Festival celebrates the "Miracle Worker." This is a view of a crowd on Saturday at one of the festivals.

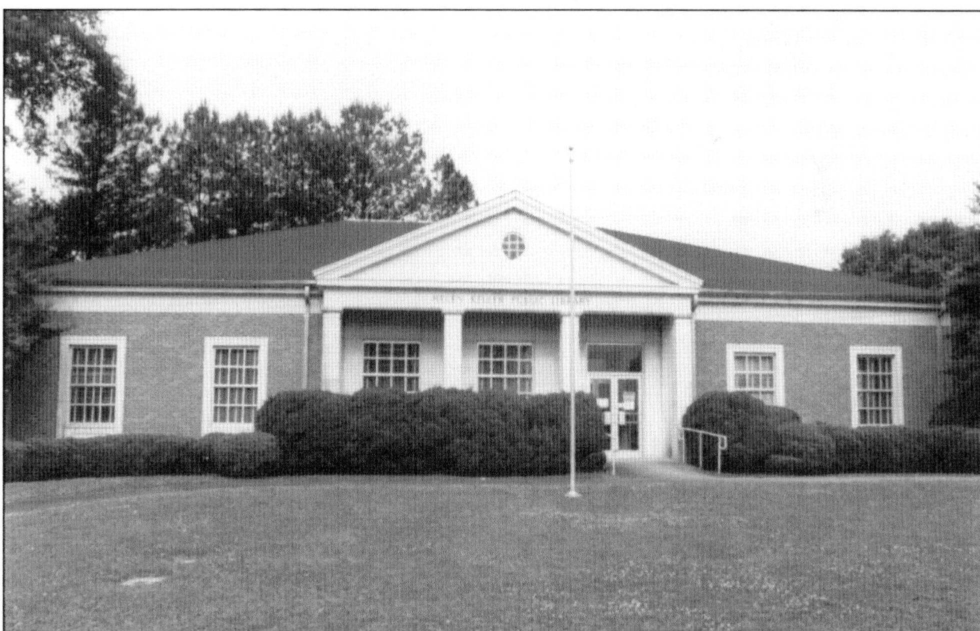

The Helen Keller Library is the state's oldest library in continuous service. Former governor Robert Burns Lindsay and Judge Fox Deloney secured the state charter on October 13, 1893. The association purchased the old carriage house on Main Street in 1893. This was the home of the library until the present structure, pictured above, was dedicated in June 1967.

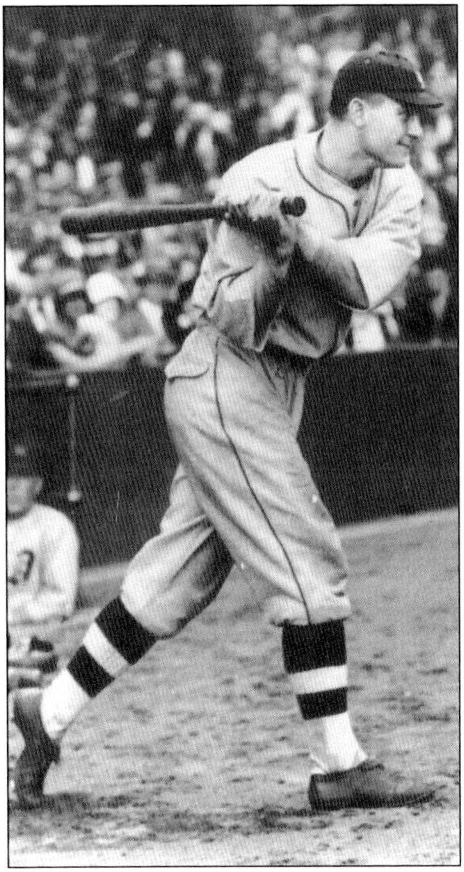

Henry Emmett "Heinie" Manush was born in Tuscumbia on July 20, 1901. He began his professional baseball career in 1920 and had a big season in the Western League in 1922. He was called to the major leagues with the Detroit Tigers in 1923. In 1926, he led the major leagues with a batting average of .378 and finished just behind Babe Ruth in slugging percentage (.564) and on base plus slugging percentage (.985). (Courtesy of Norma Manush.)

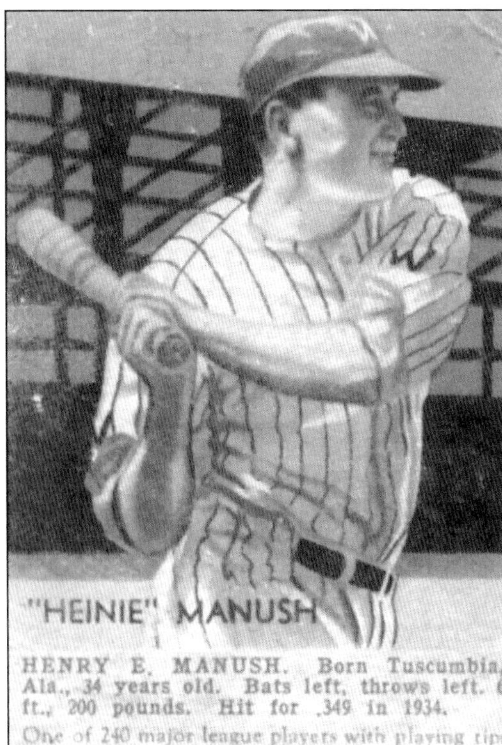

Heinie Manush was traded to the Browns in 1928, where he led the league in hits (241), doubles (47), and singles (161). He finished second to Mickey Cochrane as the American League Most Valuable Player. He was traded to the Senators in 1930 and played for them for six years. He finished his career with a lifetime batting average of .330, 2,524 hits, 110 home runs, and 1,183 RBIs. He has been elected to the Baseball Hall of Fame and the Alabama Sports Hall of Fame.

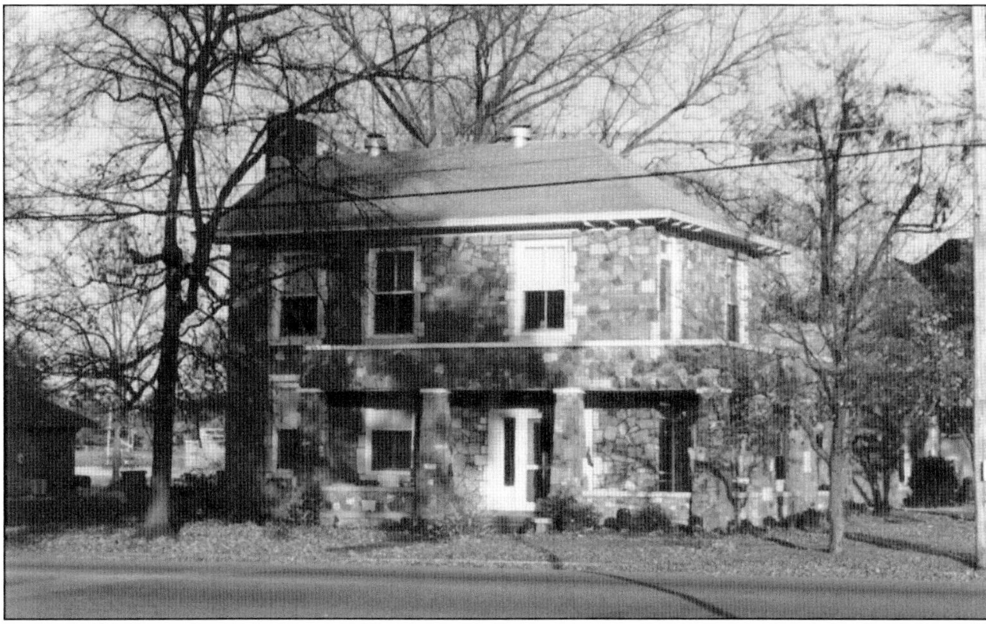

This is the home of Robert Burns Lindsay, Alabama's only foreign-born governor. Lindsay was born in Scotland in 1824. He moved to the United States in 1844 and to Tuscumbia in 1849. Lindsay opposed secession from the Union but served in the Confederate army when the Civil War began. In 1865, he was elected to the Alabama Senate and in 1870 was elected governor. He refused to run for a second term.

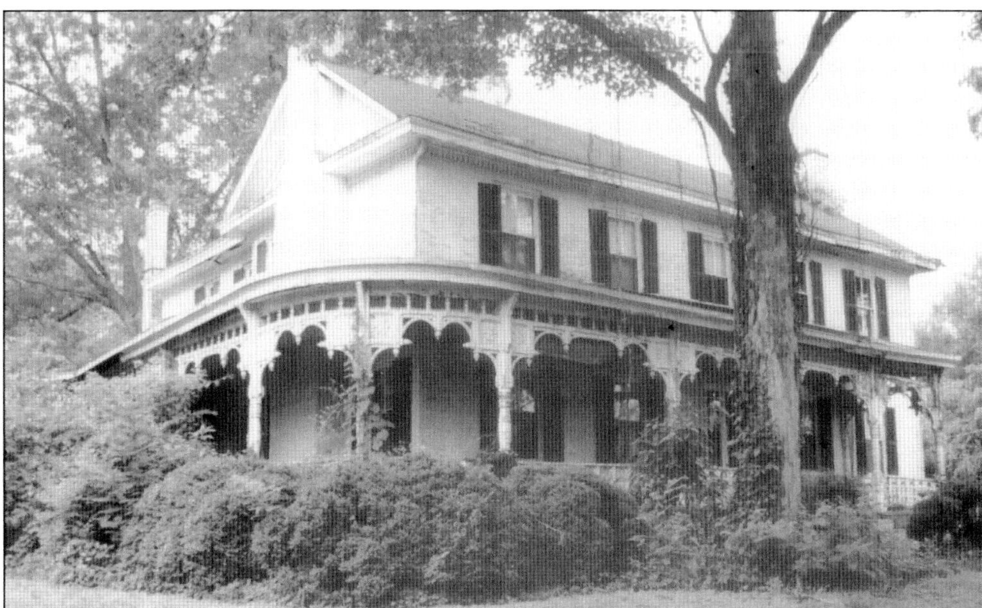

This house, known as Locust Hill, was built by Col. William Winter in 1823. During the Civil War, Union colonel Cornyn used the house as his headquarters. When Union soldiers left, it was reported they had done $3,000 worth of damage to the house. Capt. John Taylor Rather moved into the house after the Civil War. Captain Rather's granddaughter, Ella Rather, inherited the home and married James T. Kirk.

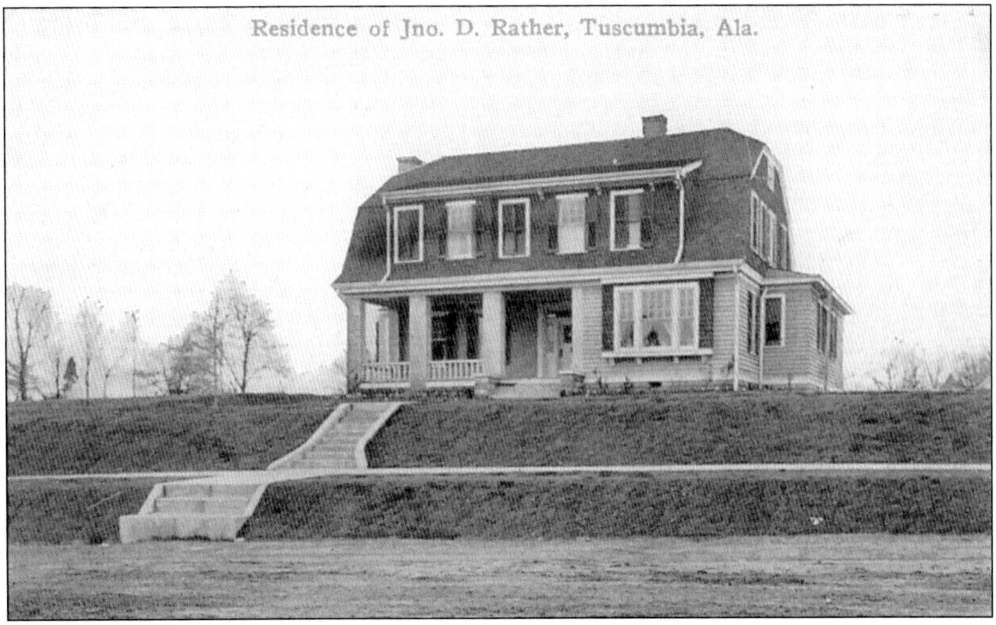

John D. Rather was the son of Gen. John Rather. He read law under J.T. Kirk and Judge E.B. Almon and was admitted to the bar in 1898. Howell and Elizabeth Ann Heflin purchased the house. Mr. Heflin became chief justice of the Alabama Supreme Court in 1971. Representing Alabama, Howell Heflin became a US senator in 1978 and retired from the senate in 1996.

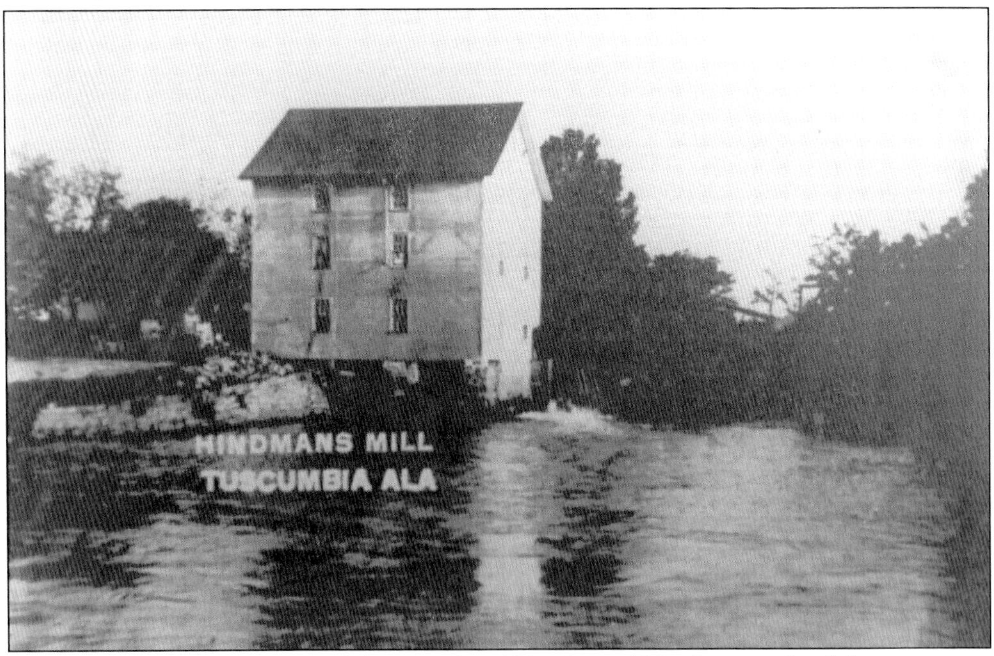

The first mill was reportedly built here in the 1830s. Samuel Hindman, a Confederate veteran from Virginia, moved to Tuscumbia in 1871 and bought this mill from Reuben Geise. The mill was destroyed by a tornado in 1874. Hindman rebuilt the mill for $5,000 in 1875. Joseph Hindman, Samuel's son, sold the mill to Thomas Newman around 1822. When Pickwick Lake was formed in 1933, the mill could no longer operate.

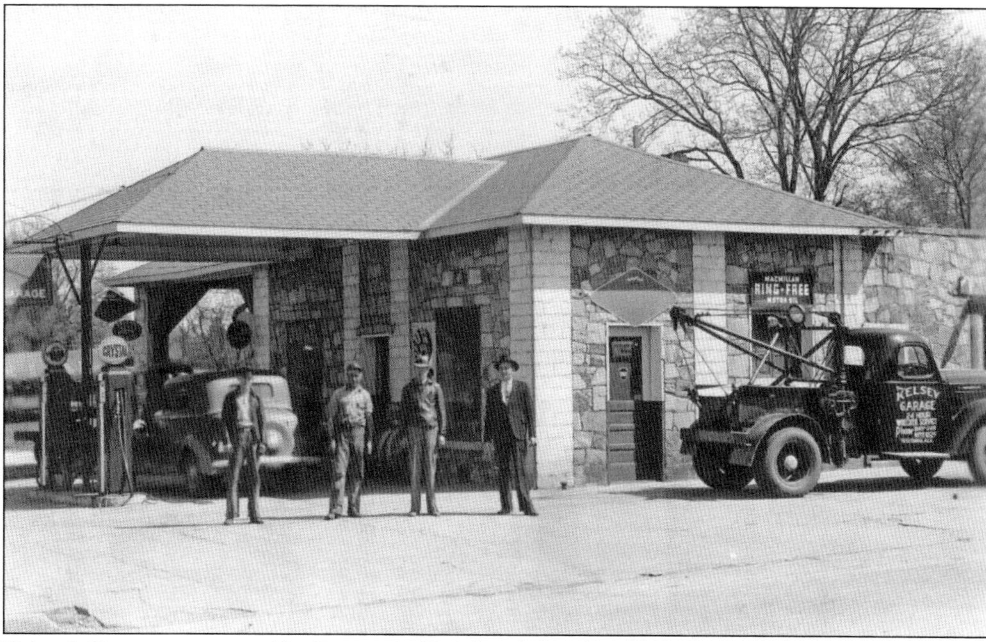

Kelsey's Garage was owned by Dewey C. (D.C.) Kelsey, who is remembered for his story of how he only had 40¢ in his pocket when he started his first garage. Kelsey went on to build Kelsey Motors on North Main Street, where he sold Studebaker and Packard cars. (Courtesy of Eugene Kelsey.)

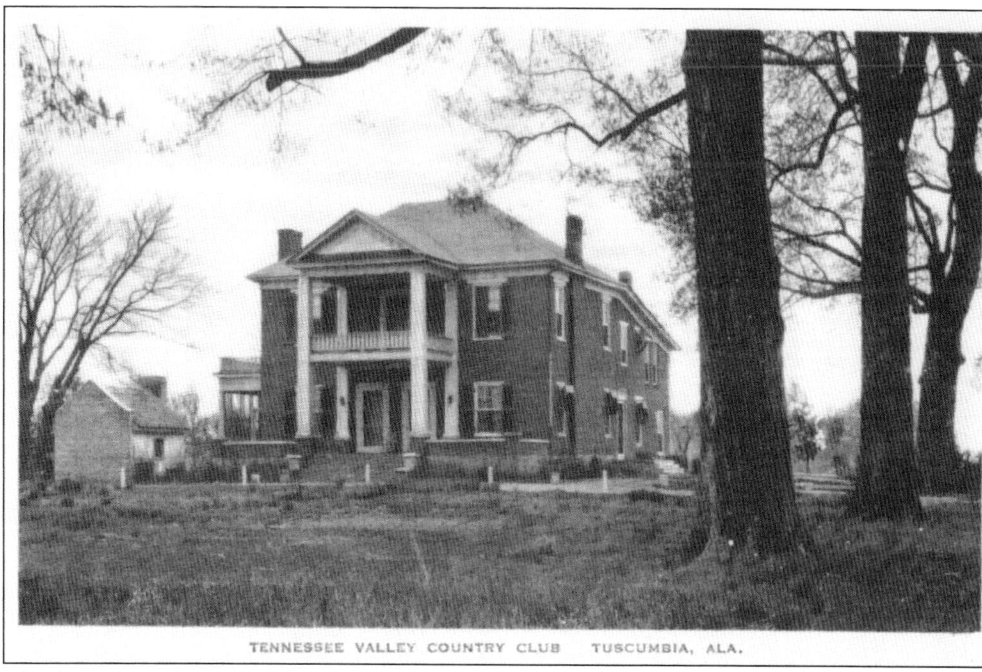

This home was built by Archibald Scott Christian around 1826. Christian owned a carriage shop, grocery store, and commission business. He was part owner in the steamboats *Mohawk*, *Ben Sherrod*, and *Pennsylvania*. This house has been the home of the Christian, Winston, Merrill, McWilliams, and Whitlock families. It is part of the Tennessee Valley Country Club today.

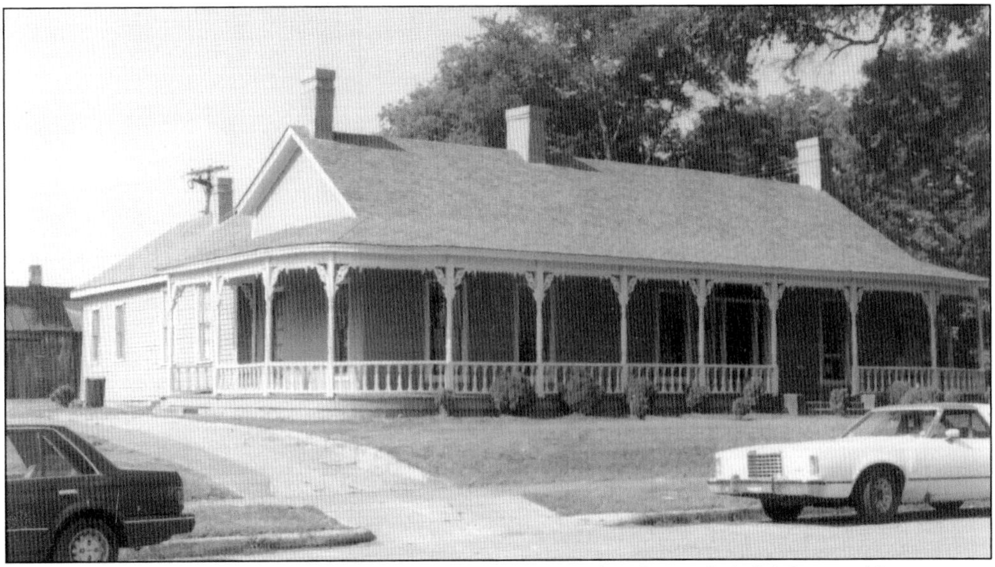

This is the home of Philip Godley, who came to Tuscumbia from Philadelphia and became an alderman of Ococoposa in 1820. He had a business downtown and was part owner in steamboats. He was elected as the first president (mayor) of the city named Tuscumbia. He was believed to have never said an angry word to anyone.

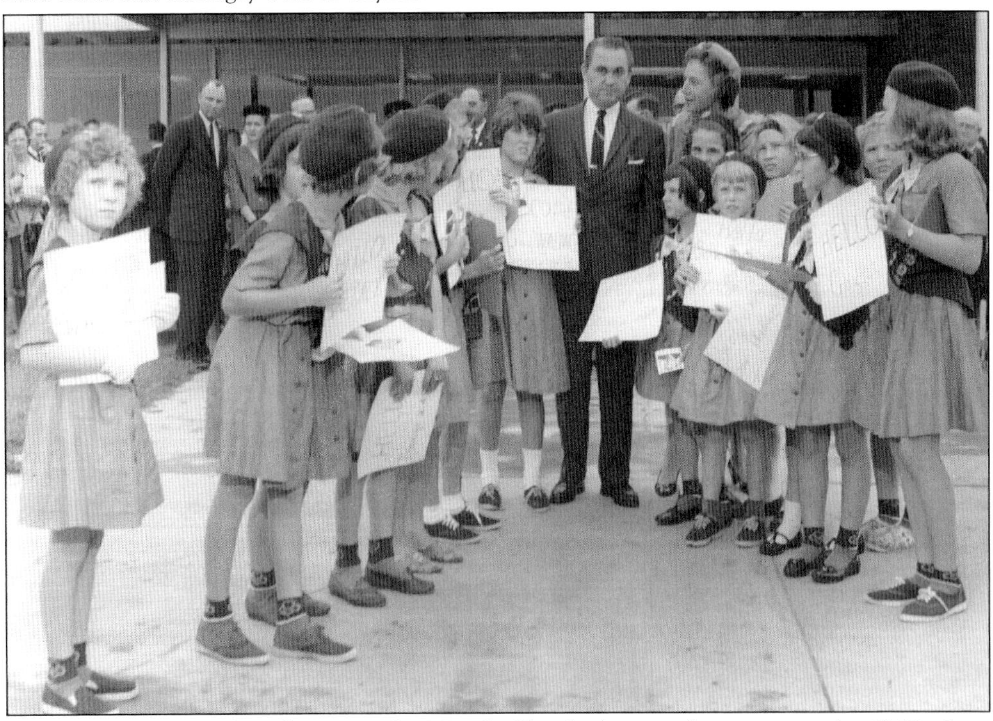

Gov. George C. Wallace flew into the Muscle Shoals Airport for a visit in the 1960s. Inez McWilliams asked permission to take her Girl Scout Troop to meet him during school hours. Howard Chappell, who was principal of R.E. Thompson Primary School at the time, agreed for her to take her Scouts since she was a substitute teacher. Governor Wallace was pleased to see them and had his photographer take this picture.

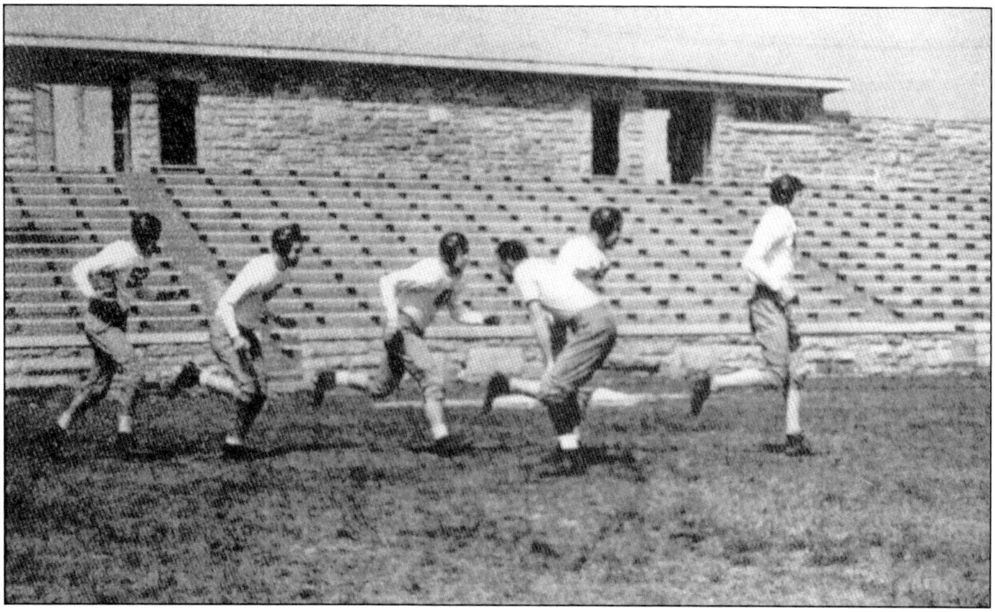

Deshler High School developed a strong football program in the 1930s under Coach Howard Chappell. There grew a need for a football stadium for both Deshler High School and Trenholm High school. The city was able to secure a grant to build a new stadium. Tuscumbia Municipal Stadium was completed in 1941, making it the first football stadium in the Shoals. The stadium became known as Deshler Stadium and was later renamed Howard Chappell Stadium in honor of coach Howard Chappell.

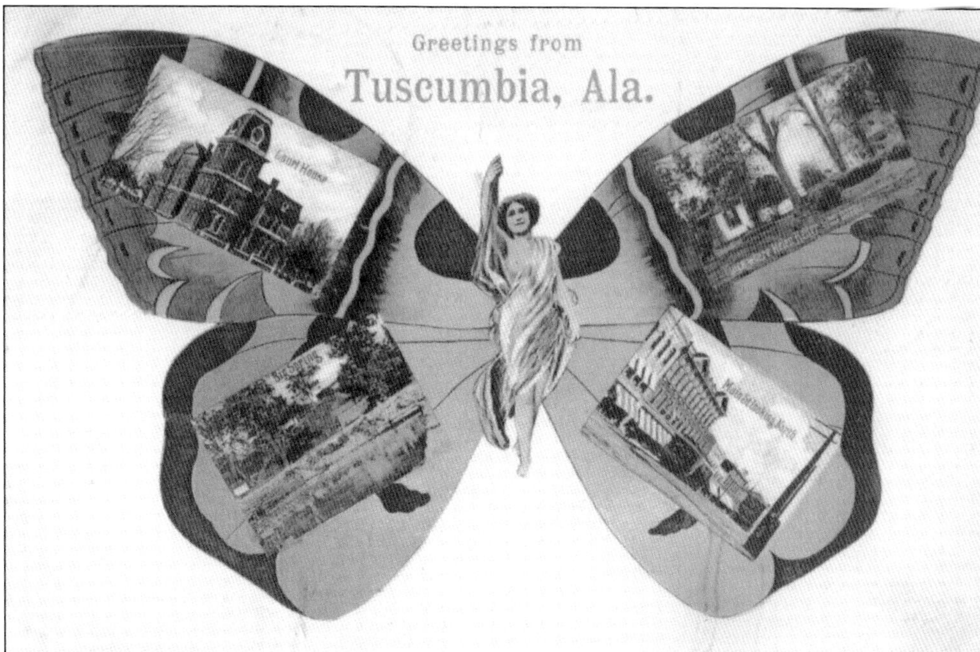

In the upper left-hand corner of this c. 1905 postcard is a picture of the original courthouse. Ivy Green, the birthplace of Helen Keller, is in the upper right; a picture of the big spring is in the lower left, and a picture of a streetcar on Main Street is in the lower right.

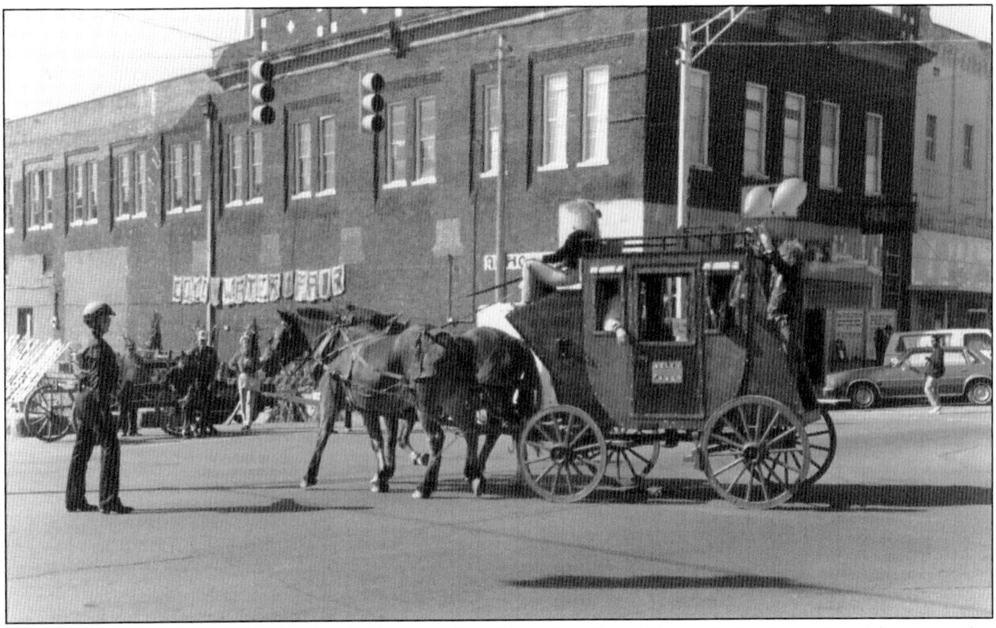

The Cold Water Fair was an annual event held in October. One of the favorite rides was the stagecoach. Riders would catch the stagecoach at the log cabin stagecoach stop and ride around town. The coach seen here is riding down Main Street at Sixth Street. The building in the background housed Craig's Appliance Store. Today it is the Coldwater Bookstore.

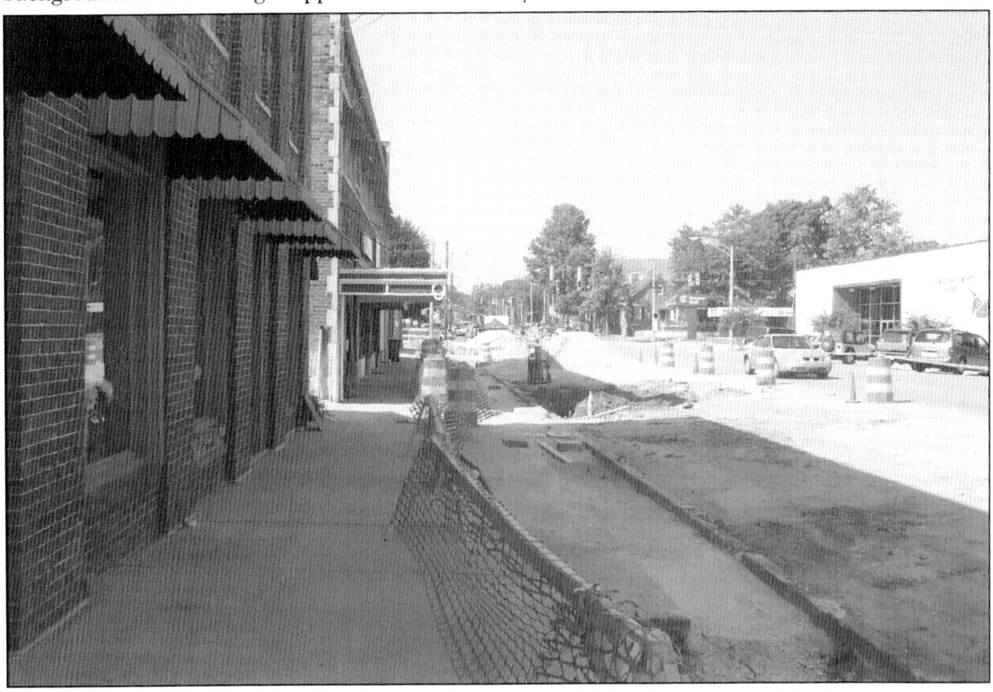

Tuscumbia had been a town where progress had stopped. The beginning of the 21st century saw a change take place. Many of the old businesses were remodeled or restored. This picture shows the beautification of downtown taking place. This contributes to the growth of Tuscumbia's downtown area.

This is a picture of Nellie Thompson (left) and Inez Walker taken in 1938. They were best of friends and graduated from Deshler High School in 1939. The picture was taken on the Tennessee Valley Authority Reservation. Thompson married and moved to New Mexico, while Walker continued her life in Tuscumbia.

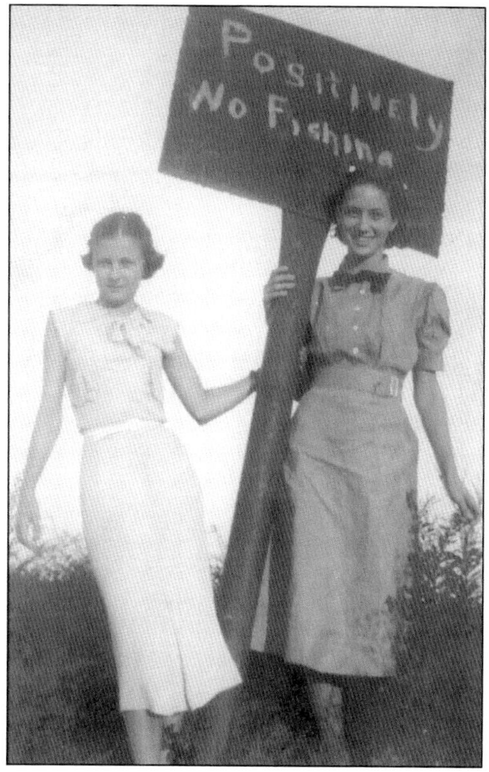

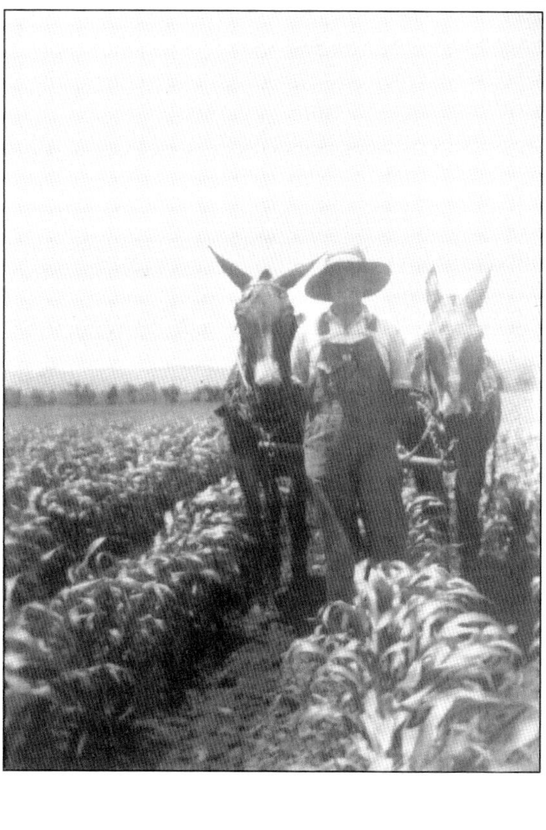

This is a picture of John Hubert McWilliams with the family mules. His class project was to repair this plow, which he proudly completed. He became an engineer for the Southern Railway and operated trains for Gen. George Patton's private railroad, the 718th Railroad Operating Battalion in World War II. On the Southern Railway, he became known as Buttermilk.